CHRIST THE LORD

CHRIST THE LORD

*A Study in the Purpose and Theology
of Luke–Acts*

ERIC FRANKLIN

THE WESTMINSTER PRESS
PHILADELPHIA

© ERIC FRANKLIN, 1975

PRINTED IN GREAT BRITAIN

PUBLISHED BY THE WESTMINSTER PRESS

®

PHILADELPHIA, PENNSYLVANIA

Library of Congress Cataloging in Publication Data

Franklin, Eric, 1929–
    Christ the Lord: a study in the purpose and
theology of Luke–Acts.

    Bibliography: p.
    Includes indexes.
    1. Bible. N.T. Luke and Acts—Theology.
2. Eschatology—Biblical teaching. 3. Luke, Saint.
I. Title.
BS2589.F7   236   75-28162
ISBN 0-664-20809-6

To
David and Kathleen
Stewart-Smith
and
Brasted
with affection
and respect

Contents

Acknowledgements

Thanks are due to the following for permission to quote from copyright sources:

Abingdon Press: *Studies in Luke–Acts* ed. L. E. Keck and J. L. Martyn.

Faber & Faber Ltd and Harper & Row Inc.: *The Theology of St Luke* by H. Conzelmann.

SCM Press and John Knox Press: *Jesus* by Eduard Schweizer.

Preface

These pages are offered as a small contribution to the current search after the meaning and significance of Luke's writings. That an unknown student of Luke–Acts should present ideas which run counter to many received opinions, and should in the process appear to be critical of the conclusions of some of the most authoritative and informative scholars on the subject, could appear to be little less than presumptuous. And, indeed, it would be so were it not that the giants in the field have, by their insights, opened up a whole new range of possibilities in the study of Luke's work and, by the very originality of their conclusions, presented a stimulus to others to take up the challenge offered by them. Every individual contribution to the debate must be viewed in their light and will, inevitably, be judged by their standards. An unknown writer, therefore, though he may escape the charge of presumption, is only too aware that he remains open rather to one of folly!

I wish to acknowledge the great debt I owe to Professor Geoffrey Lampe for setting me off on the pursuit of Luke and for bearing with my early efforts in comprehension. To the Rev. J. K. Byrom, formerly Warden of Brasted Place College, I give my gratitude for his constant interest and concern, and to the Rev. John Fenton I extend my thanks for encouraging me to proceed, and for his criticism and advice. Without the help of these three friends, these pages could not have appeared.

I am most grateful to Mr R. J. Brookes and his colleagues at S.P.C.K. for their willing help and their friendly dealings.

E. F.

Margate
July 1975

Abbreviations

BZNW	Beiheft, Zeitschrift für neutestamentliche Wissenschaft
BJRL	Bulletin of the John Rylands Library
ET	Expository Times
HTR	Harvard Theological Review
JBL	Journal of Biblical Literature
JEH	Journal of Ecclesiastical History
JTS	Journal of Theological Studies
NT	Novum Testamentum
NTS	New Testament Studies
SG	Studies in the Gospels, ed. D. E. Nineham, Oxford, 1955
SJT	Scottish Journal of Theology
SLA	Studies in Luke–Acts, ed. L. E. Keck and J. L. Martyn, London, 1968
TDNT	Theological Dictionary of the New Testament, ed. G. Kittel and G. Friedrich, London, 1964ff
ZNW	Zeitschrift für die neutestamentliche Wissenschaft

Works cited by abbreviated titles are detailed in the Select Bibliography

Introduction

In his survey of recent work on Luke-Acts, Professor C. K. Barrett writes: 'It is not for nothing that the Third Gospel has always been the stronghold of the liberal humanitarian interpretations of Jesus.'[1] Luke's Jesus was easily assimilated to the thought of a later age. His Gospel was seen as the expression of wide sympathies and his life of Jesus was accepted as a gradual, ordered, rational progress to Jerusalem, to a suffering which was at the same time a vindication and a triumph over the powers of darkness. To this the Evangelist was seen to have added a second volume which showed the universal appeal of Christianity as the fulfilment of what was best in man's natural aspirations. By recounting the inclusion of the Gentiles with a minimum of fuss and of doctrinal difficulties, he both avoided the scandal of particularity and also exhibited a favourable attitude to the world and its institutions.

Given such an understanding, Harnack could write of the Third Evangelist in sympathetic, uncomplicated terms:

> His medical profession seems to have led him to Christianity, for he embraced that religion in the conviction that by its means and by quite new methods he would be enabled to heal diseases and to drive out evil spirits, and above all to become an effective physician of the soul. Directed by his very calling to the weak and wretched, his philanthropic sympathy with the miserable was deepened in that he accepted the religion of Christ and as a physician and evangelist proved and proclaimed the power and efficacy of the word of Jesus and of the Gospel.[2]

Not all could rest content, however, with such a view, for though this picture of Luke's work maintained its appeal for many, it was nevertheless accepted with some unease arising from the fact that its alleged simplicity of outlook did not catch the real enigma that was Jesus and so failed to give a true understanding of the significance of what God had done through him. Though in his commentary on the Third Gospel William Manson writes, with a fervour coming close to Renan's ecstatic praise,[3] that 'Luke has cast his net wide and produced a gospel the most voluminous and varied, the most vibrant and sympathetic, the most beautiful and sweetly reasonable of all that we possess', he is, nevertheless, forced to concede that, judged by such a yard-stick, the Third Evangelist is both 'less intellectual and less theological than Matthew'—and presumably than most of the other New Testament writers also.[4]

Thus Luke tended to be dismissed as a theologian, largely one suspects because the use of him by the old liberals had caused everyone to acquiesce in the belief that he had no theology worth speaking of, and because his use by Baur and his followers, in their attempts to describe a tendency in his work, had discredited any approach which tried to determine the nature of the work as opposed to the significance of the events it described. Interest turned instead to Luke's use of sources and, through them, to the value of his work in determining the historical course both of the ministry of Jesus and of the early years of the life of the Church.

A breakaway from the confines set by such an approach came with the work of Dibelius, who looked at Acts as a book which—in the handling of the individual episodes at any rate—revealed the ideas and outlook of the author.[5] Luke was interested in the mean-ing behind the events and, even in his second volume, he remained primarily an evangelist.[6] Other work which reasserted the im-portance of the author was that of Cadbury in *The Making of Luke-Acts*[7] and of Creed in his commentary on Luke's Gospel.[8] Nevertheless, even these works were guarded in their approach to Luke as a theologian. For instance, though Dibelius asserted the kerygmatic aim of the speeches in Acts, he still limited the actual creative hand of Luke in them and maintained that they suggested a 'constantly recurring outline in written form', while their Christology, because it seemed near-Adoptionist, was thought to reflect the use of a primitive formula, and little consideration was given to the possibility that they might have been an expression of Luke's own christological ideas.[9] Again, Creed, though re-jecting a Proto-Luke, never seemed to allow for the full creativity of the Evangelist that such an approach called forth. Though he allowed that it 'is possible to discern in the book certain interests and tendencies of the evangelist's own age', he nevertheless maintained that 'there is no sufficient reason to suppose that the work was directly "tendentious" or that the writer wished to commend a particular theological attitude'.[10] In the same vein, Cadbury could write:

> In the main, however, it is safe to assume that Luke was carrying forward in his version of events the prevailing motives with which they had been handed down. His own purposes must have been minor and secondary. They are to be detected rarely, if at all, and only in the slight hints and details, or in some elusive tone or spirit that pervades his whole work.[11]

The theology of Luke himself was seen to remain rather peripheral to his work as a whole; it was to be found in various themes—in his ideas of the Spirit, of the universal mission, of the ongoing life of the Church and the postponement of the parousia—and was to be criticized in its lack of development of other themes—especially in its playing down of the significance of the cross, and of the union between Jesus and the Christian—rather than being seen as expressed in the total conspectus of the two volumes. His theology remained as an additional layer in his writing which was still primarily looked upon as historical, but it was not regarded as fundamental in shaping the whole work or as being of significance in determining the whole of his approach to such history as he recorded.

Nevertheless, these writers opened up a whole new era in Lucan studies and, though they themselves did not push their insights to their logical conclusions, the paths they pursued made it possible and inevitable for later writers to do so. As Wilckens puts it, 'Research thus hit upon the phenomenon of a characteristic Lucan theology'.[12] If the initial step in this was taken by Vielhauer,[13] developments occurred in Käsemann[14] and others, and perhaps the flower of this new line of thought was to be found in the theology of Conzelmann[15] and in Haenchen's commentary on Acts.[16] Now, for the first time, Luke's theology was seen to be the fundamental factor not only in determining the emphases and individual characteristics of the two volumes, but also in controlling the whole shape, outlook, method, and purpose of the total work. Luke chose to write history because this was the most serviceable vehicle for the expression of his theology, and his theology must be gathered from the overall way he handled his history.

This emphasis is wholly to be welcomed, for it puts Luke back firmly in the company of the other evangelists and no longer separates him from them because of his alleged historicism or humanism. Nevertheless, if current scholarship has reinstated Luke in this respect, it has, on the other hand, continued to separate him from the larger part of the New Testament theologians as a whole. The current view of the most informative and invigorating interpreters of Luke's work is to see it as breathing a very different atmosphere, not only from Paul, but also from John and Mark. As Flender sums it up: 'This makes Luke appear as an *epigone*, as one who has fallen from the heights of Pauline theology (maintained by Mark and recovered by John). With Luke theology becomes crystallized and salvation objectified. Luke stands on the fringes of the New Testament canon, or even outside of it, an example of "early Catholicism".'[17] Haenchen expresses it rather differently, since, for him, Luke's work represents a variant theology which grew up independently of Paul. 'This theology is no steep tumble from the Pauline heights—for on those heights Luke never stood.' In practice, however, this does not affect his estimate of Luke's theology, which he regards as inferior, so much so, indeed, that later in his introduction he expresses 'big surprise' that 'Lucan theology has found fervent supporters who maintain that it is precisely the Lucan doctrine of salvation history that permits a deeper understanding of revelation'.[18]

As this last quotation makes clear, the trouble is seen to centre upon salvation history which, with only few exceptions,[19] is generally thought to be at the heart of Luke's theological interpretation. Luke takes salvation history seriously. He sees it as the sphere of the continuing redemptive act of God. History becomes the means of incorporating men into God's saving activity in Christ, and the world is accepted as the place in which their salvation is worked out even if it cannot be fully realized in this life. Luke expects the world to go on into an indefinite future. Eschatology is therefore no longer at the heart of his message, but instead is reduced to a 'section on the last things'.[20]

In this, Luke is accepted as having undertaken a large-scale reinterpretation of the emphasis of the early Christian proclamation. For Bultmann and interpreters who think like him, this amounts to abandoning the essential stance of the early Christian kerygma, and Luke's use of salvation history is seen as something resembling a compromise issuing in the first essay in reductionism of the Christian Gospel.

> Whereas for the eschatological faith not only of the early Church but also of Paul the history of the world had reached its end, because in Christ the history of salvation had found its fulfilment and hence its end, according to the viewpoint of Acts the history of salvation now continues. While for Paul, Christ being the 'end of the Law' (Rom. 10.4), is also the end of history, in the thought of Acts he becomes the beginning of a new history of salvation, the history of Christianity.[21]

Others—notably Wilckens[22] and Cullmann[23]—have defended Luke's medium of salvation history on the grounds that it was already present in the outlook of his predecessors and, indeed, was inherent in the message of Jesus himself, so that what Luke undertook is seen to be a legitimate enterprise which developed what was present in the earlier proclamation in the light of continuing history and of the fading of the expectation of an early parousia. So Wilckens can say: 'The essential points of theological criticism levelled against Luke are gained not so much from early Christian tradition itself as from the motifs of a certain modern school of theology which disregards or misinterprets essential aspects of early Christian thought.'[24] Cullmann likewise maintains that 'it will not do to speak of an extended time being found for the first time in Luke. In the approaches of the other Gospels, and in Paul, and before that in the early Church, the interval is extended by comparison with its length in Jesus' message, even though it is still limited.'[25]

Nevertheless, even these writers accept that Luke's work reflects a considerable change of emphasis. Salvation history, which in his predecessors was still controlled by eschatology, now takes over and becomes the scheme in the light of which the whole Christian proclamation is to be understood. Cullmann writes that the Third Evangelist 'abandons any chronological limitation of the intermediate period. Luke deliberately attaches an indefinite duration to the period and consistently carries through a division of salvation history into periods on the basis of an interpretative reflection, as Conzelmann has shown.'[26]

On all sides, therefore, Luke is accepted as having a theology which is of necessity very different from that of his predecessors, and the reason for this is seen to be in his effective abandonment of the eschatological beliefs of the early Church. He might have still believed in the End, but its importance was largely academic, since it no longer exercised any real influence over him and he no longer expected it to impinge directly upon the faith and life of his readers. Salvation history was now paramount; to all intents and purposes eschatology, if not sunk without trace, was at least stripped of any effective part in fashioning the expectations and practice both of Luke and of those to whom he was writing.

The present work is written from the conviction that such an estimate of Luke gives a wrong picture of him and that, though the interpretations of him as an exponent of salvation history have done inestimable service in recovering his theology, nevertheless, they are still perhaps too influenced by the older Liberal understanding of Luke which took him out of his own times and viewed his use of history and of mission and his expression of wide sympathies too much in the service of the thought of an age which was alien to Luke himself. On the other hand, we would suggest that Luke stood within the main eschatological stream of the early Christian expectations, and that salvation history in his two volumes, though present, is used in the service of his eschatology rather than as a replacement of it. Such a view has repercussions which call for a new look at his attitude to the Jews and at his purpose in writing an account of the developing witness to Jesus. It also means taking a further glance at the reasons for his particular understanding of Jesus and for his distinctive presentation of the life of the Lord.

In Chapter 1, therefore, we take another look at Luke's eschatology and come to the conclusion that he does not remove the End as an integral part of his own expectations and from casting its shadow over the lives of his readers. His concern with history arises, not because he expected the Church to go on indefinitely, but was forced upon him by the delay that had already occurred.[27] This delay caused him to reinterpret eschatology rather than to reduce it. The End, though taken fully into his thinking, was no longer thought of as the event which guaranteed the claims made on behalf of Jesus. This for him was rather provided by the ascension. The aim of his work is therefore to gain a response to the message that the ascension proclaimed—that Jesus really is Lord and that the eschatological action of God was effective through him.

In the light of this, Chapter 2 re-examines Luke's understanding of Jesus. It sees this as determined by his belief that Jesus was the climax of God's activity in Israel. As the prologue to the eschatological event of the ascension, the life is shown to be of one piece with prophetic and scriptural expectations which therefore determine Luke's portrait. His readers, however, are not called to join themselves to the past life of Jesus but to an acceptance of his present sovereignty.

But if Luke links Jesus so firmly to Jewish hopes and proclaims him as the Messiah of Old Testament expectations, the problem of the Jewish rejection of him becomes even more critical, and could of itself entirely overthrow Luke's claims. Chapter 3 therefore re-examines Luke's attitude to the Jews. It presents him as favourably disposed to the Jewish nation, whose history comes to a climax in the Lord. Nevertheless, he takes Jewish rebellion seriously and accepts the remnant idea of the Old Testament. Their rejection of Jesus arises out of a perversity which has characterized their history. But Jews and Christians remain close, and Luke's work does not represent a Christianity which has turned aside from its Jewish source.

In the light of this, Chapter 4 returns to the theme of Luke's history in Acts and to the reason for his second volume. It maintains that the overall presentation is controlled by the belief in these happenings as the fulfilment of the eschatological expectations of the prophets. This especially includes the incorporation of the Gentiles, and Luke recounts this as proof that Jesus really was God's final act. The second half of Acts centres upon Paul because his arrival at Rome witnesses in a unique way to the power of the exalted Christ and so becomes powerful evidence for the truth of Luke's claims.

Chapter 5 discusses the nature of the response that Luke hopes to win from his readers. It is the response of men who know that they are living in the last days and who are ready to meet their Lord when he appears.

The final chapter applies our understanding of Luke's work to the Evangelist himself. It sees him as a firm God-fearer before he embraced Christianity, and thinks it possible that he was a companion of Paul. These last points, however, are only tentative; they do not affect the main argument of the earlier chapters, and they are not necessarily to be concluded from that argument.

1

Luke's Eschatology

The basic problem of Luke's theology is, quite simply, the fact that he wrote the Acts of the Apostles. Once it is admitted that he is more than just a recorder of things as they actually happened and his writing is viewed as a tract for the times, as soon as he is accepted as an evangelist, preacher, or pastor,[1] then his work is seen to be an expression of certain presuppositions and the question of his theology comes to the fore. It is then that the existence of the Acts of the Apostles is decisive, for it means that Luke's theology embraces the beginnings of the universal mission and includes also that part of its extension which he has chosen to describe and which leads Paul to Rome. The risen Lord's words to the disciples, 'that repentance and forgiveness of sins should be preached in his name to all nations, beginning from Jerusalem' (Luke 24.47), mean that for Luke theology must embrace history, not in the way simply that history can be used to illustrate theology, but in the sense that theology must provide an adequate explanation of history. It must indeed account for the situation in which his readers find themselves. The Gospel has spread from Jerusalem to Rome, but the Roman powers remain largely unconverted, the Jewish people have remained predominantly hostile, and the lives of Christians have by and large been subject to persecutions and disappointments which have resulted in a failure of nerve (18.8). It is this situation that Luke's history must embrace and his theology justify if his desires to be an evangelist and pastor are to be achieved. From this situation and the Evangelist's approach to it, his theology must be ascertained.

In recent years the fundamental attempt to do this has, of course, been made by Conzelmann and it is witness to his achievement that any further efforts to unravel Luke's ideas must almost of necessity start from his results, and that their success or failure will inevitably be measured in the light of his standards. Conzelmann himself believes that the clue to Luke's work is to be found in his eschatology. He assumes that early Christians lived with the hopes of an imminent parousia of Jesus, that the failure of these expectations caused something like a crisis, that Luke's work arose out of this situation, and that he faced it by making a thorough-going reinterpretation of the early beliefs.

In general, this thesis may be criticized on the grounds that the expectation of an immediate return of Christ was less all-pervading than upholders of such a view maintain, and that the result when it did not happen was less traumatic for Christianity than is often supposed.[2] Nevertheless, such a general criticism does not undermine Conzelmann's estimate of the purpose and immediate background of Luke's work. The non-appearance of the parousia is of central concern for Luke, as both the amount of eschatological material that his work contains and also his reinterpretation of Mark on this point, make clear. Luke has three long eschatological discourses (12.35–59; 17.20—18.8; 21.5–36); the events in Jerusalem are recounted against the background of those who expected them to usher in the kingdom of God (19.11); and the history of the early Church in Acts is represented as the fulfilment of the Lord's promises to those who had asked about the restoration of the kingdom to Israel and had expected it to happen soon (Acts 1.6). Eschatological interest is not lacking, but his use of Mark shows a thorough reinterpretation of the beliefs that he found there. As we shall see, the consistency in this reinterpretation is provided by the need and desire to account for an interval between the time of Jesus and that of his return, and Mark is constantly altered with this end in view.

Conzelmann is therefore right to start with Luke's eschatology, for in the reinterpretation that emerges the basic clue to Luke's theology is most likely to be found. Conzelmann himself believes that Luke replaces eschatology with salvation history (p. 167).[3] On this, he makes three points which are of particular importance for our immediate concern and which can form the basis for further discussion. In the first place, he notes that Luke postpones the End. The early expectation is eliminated (p. 96) by a deliberate recasting of his sources in such a way that belief in an early return of Christ is abandoned (p. 135) and replaced by his scheme of salvation history which is both comprehensive and quite different. The 'last days' are now expanded into a longer epoch and the Spirit is no longer regarded as the eschatological gift (p. 95). This last statement brings us to the second point for our concern, that Conzelmann understands Luke to separate history from eschatology, which is limited to the End itself. History, removed from the End, to which it is but a previous act, ceases to be viewed in its light and therefore is no longer eschatologically determined or controlled. 'The historical events are not interpreted as eschatological signs but in a non-eschatological sense' (pp. 132–3). The Spirit is now thought of as the 'substitute' both for knowledge of the last things and for the possession of ultimate salvation (pp. 95, 136). The fate of the Temple and the fall of Jerusalem are denuded of any eschatological relevance (pp. 127, 130), while as history proceeds, the Christian life is to be determined, not by any such orientation, but by the Church's long period of suffering, which does not lead into the End but is over before its arrival (pp. 232–3). Eschatology is not allowed in any way to impinge upon redemption history. In keeping with this, Conzelmann enumerates his third point to concern us here, namely that, since eschatology is banished firmly to the future, any form of realized eschatology can have no place in Luke. This determines his understanding of Luke's view of the kingdom of God. Jesus does not proclaim the message that the kingdom is near, but rather the message of the kingdom itself, which is primarily, not the good news of its coming, but of its nature (p. 114). 'The Kingdom, far from being made into an historical entity, is removed into the metaphysical realm' (p. 113). Luke thinks in terms of its 'timeless nature', its transcendent character (p. 103).

These three considerations—that the End is postponed, that history is separated from eschatology, and that the kingdom is a transcendent reality—are of vital importance in the study of Luke's eschatology, and certainly all contain a large measure of truth. Nevertheless, all three are in need of qualifications. As Conzelmann presents them, they are too rigorously pursued in the interests of a theory of salvation history. But in actual fact, eschatology in Luke cannot so easily be relegated to an appendix. The End, though postponed, is not dismissed; history is not unaffected by eschatology; and the kingdom, though transcendent, already exerts its influence over history. In truth, Luke's escha-

tology is more complicated than Conzelmann allows, and his
action is more in the nature of a radical reinterpretation than of the
reduction with which, in Conzelmann's view, he ends up.[4] With
Conzelmann's conclusions and these approaches to them, we take
a further look at Luke's ideas.

LUKE 21

We turn first to consider that version of the Apocalyptic Discourse which appears in Luke 21, and especially to see it as a
revised version of Mark 13. Here, of course, the issue has been
complicated by the suggestion that the primary source of this
chapter is to be found, not in Mark, but in some other material
which Luke took over and into which he added those sections
from Mark which appealed to him.[5] However, such a position
remains unconvincing for, in its pursuit of primary sources, it
fails to take into consideration both the theological content of the
original and the theological outlook of the reviser. The counting
of words is an adequate basis for determining sources only if
Luke is accepted as an exponent of the 'scissors and paste' method,
and this, quite manifestly, he was not.[6] Moreover, such a treatment fails to account for specific and important alterations in
passages which are obviously taken over from Mark (e.g. 21.5,
8, 9, 11). These are alterations which are determined by the
theological considerations of the writer, and they must be recognized as such. What then emerges is a thorough but consistent
reinterpretation.

Luke's revision of the Marcan introduction (21.5–7; cf. Mark
13.1–4) reduces the atmosphere of apocalyptic speculation and
decreases the mystery and awesomeness of the original.[7] The
teaching is now for all and is not the prerogative of the initiated
few; it is given in the temple rather than *katenanti autou*; he omits
the Marcan *eipon hemin* and does not use Mark's *sunteleisthai*.
Now the question is about *tauta*—that is, it is as much concerned
with the earthly events as it is with the End which provides the
culmination of Mark's *panta*. The End does not have that exclusive domination which it is given in Mark 13.

This means that the End is no longer thought of as the decisive
factor which casts its shadow over the historical events and by

which they in turn are justified. By his introduction of *pro de toutōn pantōn* Luke separates the persecutions from the apocalyptic signs and considers them in their own right. Disciples who can no longer necessarily see their sufferings as productive of the End are now to find their hope in the expectation of individual life and salvation. Death rather than the End will bring their sufferings to a conclusion (21.19). Steadfastness is given them, not by the thought that these are the beginnings of apocalyptic travail, but by the presence of the risen Christ. The universal witness, which in Mark 13 is seen as an integral part of the End by being its necessary prelude, is not mentioned, for Luke relates this in Acts, and it is justified, not by the return of Jesus, but by his exaltation. Again, the destruction of Jerusalem is treated in historical rather than apocalyptic terms. It is not presented as an act of God but is seen as the fulfilment of prophecy, 'For these are days of vengeance, to fulfil all that is written' (Luke 21.22). Nevertheless, this reference to the fulfilment of prophecy means that it is not entirely divorced from eschatological expectations. Its fall, if not caused by God, is caught up in his plans, and this is further emphasized by Luke's expectation of its distress only 'until the times of the Gentiles are fulfilled' (21.24). There is here a hint of a future restoration, and this again suggests that even its fall is not to be divorced from Luke's eschatological beliefs.

Luke then has not entirely separated events in history from eschatology. Equally, Luke's reconstruction is made with the expectation of the End very definitely in view. Explicit thought about the parousia remains. To the description of the actual appearing of the Son of man he has added in verse 28 an explicit statement of hope and expectancy: 'Now when these things begin to take place, look up and raise your heads, because your redemption is drawing near.' Since in verses 25 and 26 he has added to Mark's account of the heavenly omens a reference to earthly distresses which reflect something of the events of his own day, the parousia is drawn into the orbit of contemporary expectations. Though *en nephelē* in place of Mark's plural is written with the ascension in mind, Luke is not here referring to that event but is describing the return in its terms. By pin-pointing the parousia as the specific time for redemption, and putting it forward to his readers as a hope that is relevant to their lives, he accepts it as a reality for them. Unless he was a fraud, he is to be seen as accepting it into the orbit of his own expectations and as expecting it to be a matter of experience to some of those for whom he was writing.

The Lucan ending to the discourse (21.34–6) follows the same line of thought. In verse 19, the deaths of some Christians have been anticipated; others, however, are presented with the possibility of escaping 'all these things that will take place and to stand before the Son of man'. This can only refer to the parousia, for verse 34 has spoken of 'that day' which will have a universal significance and verse 36 uses *panta* which embraces heavenly signs as well as earthly disorders.[8] Again, then, Luke presents the parousia as having a real bearing upon the lives of his readers. It is an event that will be experienced by at least some of them. Far from being pushed back into the remote future, its coming is anticipated by Luke and he expects it to impinge upon the lives of his contemporaries to give them the ultimate inducement to that urgency which the Christian life demands. It is not suggested that they were to live as though this would happen, even though they knew in their hearts that it would not. Luke has not yet embraced such a compromise. He still believes in the return and he does not expect it to be long delayed.

In the light of this, verse 32, which takes over from Mark the mention of the time of the parousia, is seen to be of one piece with the rest of Luke's discourse. His omission of *tauta* is probably merely stylistic, for *tauta panta* appears in verse 36, and it therefore has no special significance. *Panta* clearly includes reference to the parousia. *Hē genea hautē* means 'this generation' but is made to include the contemporaries of Luke as well as those of Jesus. As we shall see, the historical Jesus is for Luke also the exalted Lord, and the evangelist and his readers are therefore included within his *genea*.[9] A near return is therefore expected. The Marcan reference to the ignorance of Jesus regarding the actual time is omitted, not because Luke thinks that the verse is not about the parousia, but because it introduces a note of uncertainty. It was this that Luke wanted to avoid and, for the same reason, the Marcan ending to the discourse is replaced by his own, more positive conclusion.

But though verse 32 maintains its reference to the parousia, it is appended to the parable of the fig tree, which in Luke is not directed to that event but to the presence of the kingdom of God

(21.31). In Luke's thought, this does not necessarily mean the same thing. In place of Mark's *engus estin epi thurais* (13.29) he has *engus estin hē basileia tou theou*. He is turning attention away from the parousia, so that the earthly distresses and even the heavenly signs are not viewed primarily in relation to that, but are seen rather as witnesses to the reality of the kingdom of God. In view of Luke's general thought about the kingdom, this does not refer to its parousia manifestation but, as in the charge to the Seventy at 10.9, 11, concerns its present, local existence. The kingdom is a present reality, and it is in the light of this that the disciples are to face their trials. They are to find their orientation not from a future event, but from the certainty that the kingdom exists in the present. This agrees with other thought in the chapter. The trials will enable them to gain their souls rather than be the means of ushering in the parousia. When they stand before kings, Jesus himself will give them a 'mouth and wisdom'. Witness is to the present authority of Jesus rather than to be seen against the background of the return. The basis of their hope and confidence is in the present.[10]

In Luke's handling of the discourse the End is delayed but is far from eliminated, nor does it cease to appear in the expectations of his readers. For the disciples, it remains the final object of hope and warning so that Conzelmann is seen to be too sweeping when he gives as his verdict that 'the imminence of the End has ceased to play any vital part in Luke'. Indeed, too much should not be made of Luke's separating the fall of Jerusalem from the Last Things, for this is most likely already an event in history. It has not ushered in the End, and therefore his treatment accords with facts. Nevertheless, the End is not divorced from Luke's own generation. Some will see it as their moment of redemption; others will meet in it their time of judgement. It is not pushed to a remote future. On the contrary, Luke would seem to be encouraging a lively belief in its coming.

But the End is not the determining factor in his thought. It is important not for what it achieves, but for its witness to the Son of man. It does not give the ultimate term of reference to the chapter or provide the focal point in the light of which the other events are to be viewed. That is given rather by the presence of the kingdom. The nearness of the kingdom—and this is not necessarily to be taken in a temporal sense—gives the hope against which the sufferings and achievements are to be viewed, historical events to be assessed, and the future hope to be expected. This is why Luke does away with Mark's scheme which makes his chapter into a plan of the Last Things. As Kümmel says of Mark: 'It is his intention here in the first place to impart a revelation about the eschatological events, their sequence, their meaning, their dangers.'[11] Luke however carefully avoids this by leaving out Mark's references to time—'the end is not yet' (Mark 13.7); 'this is but the beginning of the sufferings' (13.8); 'he who endures to the end will be saved' (13.13). For Luke, the chapter does not have a plan that finds its climax in the End which gives significance and value to the other happenings. The parousia, rather, becomes one event among many which, though still a certainty and an object of real hope, is, nevertheless just one further witness to the fact of the kingdom.

LUKE 17

The eschatological material of chapter 17 is to be seen, not merely as a single unit in which a theme is developed in three inter-related sections (17.20–1; 17.22–37; 18.1–8), but also as one part of a larger discourse which is concerned with teaching about faith. This more extended discourse begins at 17.5 where the apostles say to the Lord, 'Increase our faith', and finds its climax at 18.8 where the same Lord says, 'Nevertheless, when the Son of man comes, will he find faith on earth?' It includes an exhortation to do what it is one's duty to do (17.7–10), and the story which praises the faith of the Samaritan in contrast to the puzzle presented by the lack of faith on the part of the nine Jews (17.11–19). Clearly, the whole section is about the continuing duty of having faith in a situation where it is being severely tested both by the failure of the Jews to respond and, above all, by the failure of the parousia to appear (17.20–1, 18.8). That this is the emphasis of this section is brought out by the fact that, apart from 22.32, Luke nowhere else adds further references to faith to those which he finds in his sources.

By framing the first part of the eschatological teaching proper in the form of an answer to a question put by the Pharisees, Luke is able to make Jesus refute a form of expectation which was no doubt current in the evangelist's own day and then, in the light of this, to give some positive teaching about the nature of the kingdom. This is to be seen primarily as a corrective of false views, but it is nevertheless a definitive statement in the light of which the rest of the discourse is to be understood. The answer that is given suggests that underlying the question, 'When is the kingdom of God coming?' is the belief that signs and wonders are both a necessary mark of the presence of the kingdom and also an indispensable pre-condition of its coming.[12] In his reply, Jesus says two things. He first asserts that the kingdom does not come *meta paratēreseōs*. The kingdom is not some future event which manifests preliminary signs which can be seen and on the basis of which the time of the kingdom's coming can be calculated. And secondly, men will not be able to say of the kingdom: 'Lo, here!' 'Lo, there!' It is not something which can be localized, something which can be perceived and identified by the senses. The kingdom is not something which can be externalized, its coming into being the object of the physical senses or of mental calculations. It cannot be guaranteed by identifiable, visible signs. It is rather *entos humōn*. For Luke this asserts that the kingdom is a present reality. He uses the present tense, whatever may have been the meaning of any supposed Aramaic original. Though the second part of the discourse uses the future tense, this first part does not provide parallel information but is rather the basis for the teaching of the second part.[13] Luke therefore means verse 21 to have a present reference. The kingdom is a present fact, a present reality. It is unlikely that *entos humōn* conveys for Luke the meaning of 'within you'.[14] That it is said to Pharisees is no argument against this, for Luke is contemporizing the saying which he is addressing to his readers, but though Luke comes close to a spiritualizing of the kingdom, he never stops there. This verse is followed by teaching on the parousia, and this would not be possible if he thought of the kingdom only as an inward reality. For the same reason we must reject Perrin's interpretation of Luke's meaning as 'the Kingdom is a matter of human experience' and his observation that 'it is to be found wherever God is active decisively within the experience of an individual and men have faith to recognize this for what it is'.[15]

It is therefore likely that *entos humōn* means 'in your midst', 'amongst you'.[16] The kingdom is a present reality. Jesus alone is the sign of its presence. Nevertheless, as Kümmel points out, the verse leaves the actual mode of its presence obscure. It is unlikely however that it sees the events of the life of Jesus as enshrining the kingdom, for that would be to point to just those external marks which the previous verse has denied. There is no objective, visible manifestation which can be identified as the kingdom. Again, the verse does not talk about the 'coming' of the kingdom. It is not something which is brought into existence either by the ministry of Jesus or by his return. For Luke the kingdom is a reality the existence of which is guaranteed and described by Jesus rather than something which is inaugurated by him. The verse points to the transcendence of the kingdom. It exists now, and its effects are felt and seen in the ministry of Jesus. But that ministry witnesses to it rather than embraces it, and 17.20–1 point to the hidden nature of the kingdom.[17]

In the second section the audience changes and it is now disciples who are addressed. Having set out the true nature of the kingdom, Luke gives the disciples encouragement to accept this and to decry false expectations. The kingdom is a fact but its transcendence means that of necessity it is hidden. A hard time lies ahead for the disciples when they will long to see 'one of the days of the Son of man' but this will be denied them (17.22). At this point, Luke is still not thinking primarily of the parousia, which is not yet the main concern. 'The days' are those times when the disciples are allowed to see beyond the limitations of the present to the certainty of Jesus in glory. They refer to the post-ascension period and, in the light of the transfiguration and the ascension, to such occasions as the vision of Stephen (Acts 7.56), the conversion of Saul (Acts 9.3) or the appearance of Jesus through a dream (Acts 23.11).[18] The parousia itself is of course to be included. The disciples will long for the assurances provided by such events, but Luke's realism knows that they will be few indeed. When these do not come and when the parousia is delayed, they will pin their hopes on substitute manifestations of the End which are content with less than the full revelation of the glory of the Son of man. Verse 24 is therefore a statement of the full significance of the parousia. When it comes, it will not be mistaken and all substitutes will stand condemned. The rest of the chapter is then taken up with describing the suddenness of his appearing, so enhancing both the certainty and magnitude of the event, and with exhortations to vigilance, for his appearing is the occasion of the final judgement.

The final section (18.1–8) concludes the discourse by drawing together its themes of obligation and hope and infusing both with a note of stark realism.[19] In the light of the delay of the parousia and of the troubles that have been oppressing the disciples, Luke rounds off his section with the parable of the Unjust Judge, of which the introduction (18.1) and the application (18.6–8) are likely to show his own hand.[20] The introduction is an exhortation to faith and an expression of confidence in its vindication. The first half of the concluding verse says that such vindication will be soon, while the final half-verse makes it take place at the appearing of the Son of man. In the light of the discourse as a whole, this can only mean the parousia for, unlike 17.22 but like 17.30, it refers to a single happening. Luke then has himself probably transformed a parable to make it give very definite teaching about the parousia hope. Addressed to his readers, and in the light of the discourse as a whole, it means that they can have certainty in the reality of the kingdom. But they stand at some distance from the death and resurrection of Jesus. They are still oppressed and hopes are beginning to fail. In the face of this, Luke maintains that the parousia, though delayed, is nevertheless a certainty and one that will come about soon. Yet even now, some further delay, in itself short but, as far as the disciples are concerned, one which offers them a severe test, is a possibility. This will be hard for them to bear, so much so that 'when the Son of man comes, will he find faith on earth?' This points to a widespread crisis of confidence in Luke's own day. Of itself 18.8b could have suggested a substantial delay in the coming of the End, but Luke leaves it to be interpreted in the light of 18.8a which, since *en tachei* must bear a temporal significance, speaks of its happening soon.[21] The main part of the delay must therefore be transferred to Luke's own time; it has been worked out in the period which intervened between the life of Jesus and the situation of his own day. The parousia—soon—is not the ground of hope—that is the existence of the kingdom and the fatherhood of God—but it is the final witness to it.

Three main conclusions emerge as a result of our examination of these two discourses. In the first place, it suggests that the expectation of a near End is not eliminated by Luke, that he does not substitute for the *Naherwartung* the belief that history will continue into an indefinite future. He retains a firm conviction that the parousia will not be long delayed. It is not sufficient to say with Conzelmann that it is pushed back into the remote future, neither is it possible to take its nearness out of the sphere of strict temporal calculations. Luke retains a time-sequence, though, unlike Mark in his chapter 13, he does not determine historical events by reference to it. He believes that it will occur soon, even when he allows that it may not occur immediately. Many of his readers will live to experience it.

Much of the emphasis upon the postponement of the parousia in Luke is to be accounted for by the fact that he and his readers stand at some distance from the life of Jesus, by the fact, quite simply, that the parousia has not happened. He has therefore undertaken a reinterpretation of earlier expectations, but this finds its direction, not in looking forward to some indefinite extension of time, but in looking back at what has happened between the event of Jesus and the time at which he is writing. If anything, the effect of his work is to encourage the expectation of the early return of Jesus rather than the reverse.

But—and this is the second point—Luke is also a realist. He is writing primarily to sustain the faith of his contemporaries, a faith which would appear to have been shaken by the non-occurrence of the End. He does this by removing from the parousia the significance which Mark at any rate assigned to it. He changes the pivotal point of the early expectation, the point of reference, the event in the light of which the others are to be determined. Luke does not make the events of Christ depend upon the parousia for their climax, for it does not bring in the kingdom, neither does it effect the glorification of the Son of man. It remains a subsidiary event, one of hope it is true, one which, if it ceased to be expected, would make the rest of Luke's assertions barely credible, but its character in Luke is that of witnessing to something that already is. It sets the seal on something rather than providing the occasion on which it is achieved.

That to which it witnesses is, of course, the kingdom of God and the glorification of Jesus. The third point, then, from these chapters is that Luke sees the kingdom as a present reality, and that it is its existence as a present, though hidden, fact that is to provide the background against which his readers are to work out the situation in which they find themselves. These chapters say nothing about the glorification of Jesus, for that is fully worked out elsewhere, but they do present something of the distinctive outlook of Luke on the nature of the kingdom, the assurance of which is guaranteed by the glorification of Jesus.

These points must now be looked at in the light of Luke's work as a whole.

THE KINGDOM OF GOD

In Luke, Jesus preaches the good news of the kingdom of God (4.43; 8.1; 9.11) but, unlike the definitive statement of Mark 1.15, the content of that preaching is nowhere given as 'The kingdom of God is at hand'. Whereas in Mark 4.11 the 'secret' of the kingdom is the certainty of its future coming and the nearness of this because of the presence of Jesus, Luke unfolds the 'secrets' of its nature and of those who are to receive it (8.9–10). The joy of Palm Sunday is found, not as in Mark in the expectation of the coming kingdom, but in the announcement of Jesus as king (19.38 cf. Mark 11.10). The nearness of the kingdom is a fact but, as the preaching of the Seventy makes plain (10.9, 11), this is centred, not in a future act, but in its present existence. The future may reveal it, but it will not make it any more a reality than it is now.

But does this mean that Luke has no place at all for the future establishment of the kingdom in time? Even though he retains belief in the parousia and still regards it as a near event, does he really allow for this in his thinking about the kingdom? To a large extent the answer to these questions will depend upon the interpretation of the version of Mark 9.1 which is found at Luke 9.27: 'But I tell you truly, there are some standing here who will not taste of death before they see the kingdom of God.'

Mark's version is concerned with the parousia. This, at any rate, is how Matthew and Luke understand it, Matthew by making the parousia reference explicit (Matt. 16.28), Luke by his omission of Mark's 'coming with power'. What Luke meant by his alteration is, however, less easy to decide. It is usually taken as a reference away from the parousia. So Conzelmann suggests[22] that Mark's future pointer is replaced by a 'timeless conception' of the kingdom but, although it remains possible that *idōsin* here

may imply a spiritual apprehension,[23] Luke's use of the same
verb at 21.27 points rather to the literal witness of an actual event.
But is the witness given at the time of the parousia? Ellis maintains
that the use of *heōs an* means that those who are to see the kingdom
will, nevertheless, die later and that it therefore refers to some
spiritual experience before the Christian's death.[24] However,
since Luke's use of the same construction at 21.32 describes a
situation that is not brought to an end by the events of the subordinate clause, this suggests rather that here death is thought of
as being totally removed by the presence of the kingdom and that
those to whom 9.27 refers will never die. But in any case, Luke is
taking over the construction from Mark where it does refer to the
parousia and, since Luke accepted it in this way, his retention of
it suggests that he too was pointing to that event rather than to
something concerned with the deaths of individual Christians.
The real problem is the relation of verse 27 to verse 26 which
talks about those of whom the Son of man will be ashamed at his
appearing. Usually, they are thought to stand in some form of
contrast, referring either to different groups at the time of the
parousia or to different occasions also. So Ellis contrasts the unbelievers who will see the kingdom 'only in the glory of the
parousia' with those who 'will experience the Kingdom in the
context of losing their lives for Christ'. However, since we have
seen that reference to the parousia cannot be excluded from verse
27, we can rule out the second of these possibilities. But is there
really a contrast at all? Do the two verses refer to different groups?
Luke's use of *de* in place of Mark's *kai* does not necessarily suggest
one, for this is a characteristic of his style.[25] Verse 27 comes at the
end of a section which, addressed 'to all' (23), is an exhortation to
constancy in discipleship and a statement of the perils of apostasy.
It finds its climax in the warning of a rejection by the Son of man
at his appearing and this is strengthened by verse 27, which
proclaims the imminence of this event. It continues the thought
of verse 26, is directed to the same people, and cements its warning.

Luke's version therefore refers to the revelation of the kingdom
of God at the time of the appearing of the Son of man, when both
his glory and the reality of the kingdom are made visible. It looks
to the final manifestation rather than to any partial, preliminary
appearance and is an event which all will see.

He omits Mark's 'come with power' not because he tones down

the parousia reference but because he is transforming the significance of the event. Verse 26 shows that, as far as Luke was concerned, it was not the parousia which brought about the glorification of the Son of man, for he adds that he comes in a glory that is already his. In the same way, verse 27 shows that it is not the parousia which causes the kingdom to be established in power. That is already happening for power is already present in the overthrowing of Satan and in the ascension of Jesus. The kingdom is always with power, for it represents victory over the powers of darkness, and what happens at the parousia is the revelation of something which is in fact already happening. The parousia does not bring about a new stage in the establishment of the kingdom, for it is already a reality. Nevertheless, in the future it will be revealed for all to see. This means that it is for Luke more concrete than Conzelmann's phrase 'a timeless conception' suggests. He does not remove the parousia from relation to it. Though it is already established, already effective, already 'with power', it is still hidden and awaits the parousia when it will be revealed for what it really is. But it does not need that new stage to bring it fully into being; it already is and will soon be fully manifest.

Luke 9.27 therefore does not remove the parousia reference. It does not envisage the 'on-going life and work of the Christian community as it settles down to face, so to speak, the long haul of history'.[26] The parousia, and a near one at that, enters fully into Luke's calculations and is taken into his thought about the kingdom. What he does is to change not its imminence but its significance, and his new shape does not reduce its importance.

In Luke the only two references to the future 'coming' of the kingdom are found in passages which are strongly influenced by the cultic life of the Christian community, and which therefore do not lend themselves to an easy adaptation. In the Lord's prayer (11.2), Luke could well have written the petition for the coming of the Holy Spirit, for it represents an expression of its eschatological activity which is close to his own understanding, but if he wrote the petition for the coming of the kingdom, this would no doubt have been out of the usage of the community rather than as an expression of his own theology.[27] Liturgical usage would also account for 22.18. The idea of the anticipation of the banquet in the kingdom of God would appeal to Luke, but the thought of the 'coming' of the kingdom remains somewhat alien.

But if Luke emphasizes that the kingdom exists in the present, it nevertheless does not mean that he regarded it as having already appeared on earth. Its present manifestation is witnessed to, rather than to be found in, the things of this earth, for Luke is consistent in thinking of the transcendence of the kingdom. He does not express a belief in its immanence. The *entos humōn* of 17.21 speaks of the kingdom's reality rather than of its earthly presence. In 10.9, 11 it is not embraced in the Mission of the Seventy, but their works are seen as bearing witness to it. It casts its shadow—or rather its glory—over this life, but only as this world reflects the victory that is being won in the transcendent. Acts 14.22 speaks of entering the kingdom through earthly distresses rather than of finding it in this life. The Lucan parables of the mustard seed and of the leaven (13.18–21) are parables of contrast rather than of growth.[28] They point forward to the final manifestation. The present workings of the kingdom, though they cannot be seen, are real and will be vindicated in the glory revealed at the End. They point to the complete hiddenness of the kingdom in the present.

Again, Luke's handling of the significance of the miracles directs attention away from the kingdom's immanence. They are seen not as marks of the embodiment of the kingdom but of its reality. In themselves they are not actual expressions of it; it does not embrace them, and they are not a part of it. They witness to Jesus who is the proclaimer of the kingdom (7.21) and to the fact that in him God is overthrowing Satan (11.17–23). His work is the visible pointer to the conflict between God and Satan in the realm of the transcendent (13.16). It is the tip of the iceberg. Jesus casts out demons 'by the finger of God' (11.20, cf. Matt. 12.28). God himself, rather than the Spirit, is their author, for Jesus is God's instrument, by which Satan is defeated and the reality of the kingdom assured.[29] Luke 16.16 points also to the battle that is taking place in the heavenly realm.[30] The time of Jesus is the time of conflict when on earth the reality of the kingdom is proclaimed while, in the transcendent, the battle is entered against the demonic powers—the 'rulers of this world' (1 Cor. 2.6–8)—who are engaged in their final struggle against it. So the success of the Seventy has its final significance in that it witnesses to the falling of Satan like lightning from heaven, while their own names will be written in heaven (10.17–20). What happens on earth is the visible manifestation of something greater, that in the heavenly sphere the kingdom of God is established and that it throws its presence over the lives of Christians here and now who will one day enter into it.

This accounts for the strong emphasis upon the transcendent in Luke–Acts. The birth of Jesus proclaims glory in the highest (2.14) and is accompanied by a new activity on the part of the angelic creation. Authority over the world has been given into the hands of the devil and must therefore be wrenched from him (4.6, Luke only). After the temptation he departs from Jesus only for a time (4.13). The healing of the bent woman is a further trial of strength (13.16). The mission of the Seventy secures his downfall (10.9–11, 17–20). The climax of the struggle comes with the passion of Jesus, when Satan has his most urgent fling. He takes possession of Judas (22.3) and he would, indeed, have taken all the Twelve, but Jesus' prayer for Simon ensures that they will not pass permanently into his power (22.31–2). The arrest is the hour of the power of darkness (22.53) but Christ's faithfulness enables him to be seated at the right hand of God (22.69). Psalm 110.1 will be fulfilled and the power of Satan, if not finally destroyed, will be vanquished as the kingdom of God is shared by the Son who rules until the enemies are subjugated. Because of this, men may now 'turn from darkness to light and from the power of Satan to God, that they may receive forgiveness of sins and a place among those who are sanctified by faith in me' (Acts 26.18). Because of the exaltation of Christ, the power of Satan has been broken, the supremacy of God has been made a reality and, in spite of the trials on earth, the disciples may pass through them to enter into the kingdom of God (Acts 14.22).

THE END

Though the situation brought about by the passing of time caused Luke to undertake this large-scale reinterpretation in the field of eschatology, we have seen that this does not mean that he abandoned belief in the coming of the End. If anything, rather than pushing it back into the remote future, his aim was to reinstate it as a relevant part of contemporary belief. His rethinking gives credibility to his warning of the need for urgency for, even though he sees this as partly accounted for by the fact that death is pressing in upon individuals (12.20),[31] for the group as a whole it is to be found in the expectation of the parousia. Statements about the delay in the coming of the parousia are to explain why this event has not yet happened and to counteract the problems that this has caused, rather than to persuade his readers of a further delay and to anticipate a history that projects into the future. His aim is to reawaken faith, and this inevitably includes a belief in the parousia which remains as the final witness to the Lordship of Jesus.

It is therefore his own readers who now stand in the second or third watch (12.38); the delay has already occurred (12.45). Now is the time for them to be ready, 'for the Son of man is coming at a time when you do not expect' (12.40). The Lucan introduction to the parable of the Pounds counteracts, not the expectation of an early return on the part of his contemporaries, but the belief in an immediate return as it was held by the earlier disciples. 'As they heard these things, he proceeded to tell a parable, because he was near to Jerusalem, and because they supposed that the kingdom of God was to appear immediately' (19.11). This introduction gives the parable a definite historical setting in the light of which it is intended to be understood and, in this, is in contrast to the parable of the Steward (12.42–8) which is addressed directly to Luke's contemporaries. 'Peter said, Lord are you telling this parable for us or for all?' (12.41). His readers are meant to accept this, not as the proclamation of a further postponement, but as the declaration of an imminence which is made all the more urgent by a delay that has already occurred (12.56). Bultmann's assertion[32] that in some parts of the New Testament the commands to watchfulness provide indirect evidence for the strength of eschatological expectations must be applied to Luke here, and on this point Bartsch[33] is correct in seeing them as evidence of Luke's concern to encourage a belief in the return of Jesus.

It is here, however, that we have to face the problem of Acts, for the very existence of this volume is usually taken as proof that Luke could not have expected an imminent parousia. Wide assent has been given to Käsemann's dictum that 'You do not write the history of the Church if you are expecting the end of the world to come any day'.[34] Such a statement, however, neatly by-passes the fact that Mark, who believed in an imminent parousia, still thought it worth while to write a gospel, and one which is not unconscious of the problem of continuing history.[35] More important, though, it closes, or at least severely restricts, discussion of the question of the purpose of Acts by asserting that Luke set out to write a church history. Whether it is felt to be a good or bad one, whether Luke is seen as an accurate historian or considered to have been led astray in the interests of edification or of salvation history, is ultimately beside the point. Nearly all voices start from the assumption that what Luke records in Acts is history written on the understanding that history will go on. They assume that Luke knew that this was the first chapter of a long tale, and even if he had no intention of writing further chapters, at least his first would be of use in developing later ideas. But this remains only an assumption and appears to limit the full insights of Redaction criticism and their application to Acts. It fails also to allow that a strong reason for Old Testament history writing was to be found in using the past history of Israel in order to evoke an appropriate response in the present. There is no guarantee that the Deuteronomic historian expected Israel to have a future.[36] The fact that Luke chose to write history does not make him primarily a historian or necessarily debar him from the existentialist court. His Gospel suggests that he believed in the return as a relevant part of the future of some at least of his contemporaries. Acts must be interpreted against this, rather than this strand of the Gospel be ignored because of hasty conclusions drawn simply from the fact of the existence of Acts.

But there is undeniably less interest in the parousia in Acts than there is in the Gospel. There is, above all, little reference to it in the speeches and, if it is true that we are here to see the clear outline of Luke's theology, this omission is puzzling. Does this suggest that Luke's thought developed between the writing of his two volumes, and that such belief in the early return as he had when he wrote the Gospel represents no more than undigested and uneasy acceptance of others' beliefs which he laid aside as time went on?[37] Against this, however, is the fact that references to the End just cannot be stripped so easily from the Gospel. They are a part of its very fabric and must be left. And the mere existence of Acts does not indeed require such surgery. References to the End, though few in number, are enough to show that Luke wrote against the background of such a belief (Acts 3.20; 10.42; 17.31). Since the speeches are Luke's comments upon the significance of the episodes to which they are attached, in most of them his thoughts are naturally directed to the past rather than to the future. But the real reason for their absence is that, in Acts, the change of emphasis from the parousia to the present exaltation which the Gospel reveals is followed through quite systematically, so that the book becomes a justification for faith in Jesus as the present Lord, which is the belief on which the whole volume is grounded and to which the whole story points. Nevertheless, the book also witnesses to the certainty that the parousia will take place. The ascension is its guarantee (Acts 1.11); the gift of the Spirit is the pledge of its coming rather than its substitute (Acts 1.8), and even the promise of universal witness which the same verse contains is not a mark of its delay, for that is probably seen by Luke to have been illustrated by Paul's arrival at Rome.[38] The fact of Acts is therefore an indirect but explicit guarantee of the coming of the End and, in the light of the gospel usage, this is how Luke most likely intended it to be understood.

Luke's interpretation was occasioned, not by the desire to alter the time of the End, but to change the significance that some of his predecessors had placed upon it.[39] Because of disappointments, he shifted the emphasis away from it so that it was no longer required as the necessary condition for the full existence of the kingdom or for the complete glorification of Jesus and the overthrow of his foes. Instead, the emphasis fell upon the present status of Jesus, upon the fact that he really could be accepted as Lord in the present in spite of the ambiguities of the situation in which his disciples found themselves.

This change of emphasis is seen most clearly in Luke's reporting of Jesus' reply to the high priest during the trial: 'But from now on the Son of man shall be seated at the right hand of the power of God' (22.69 cf.Mark 14.62). Mark's version finds its climax in the parousia, which becomes the final glorification of Jesus and the ultimate source, therefore, of the disciples' hope. To this the exaltation can only be regarded as a prelude. Luke, however, by his omission of Mark's use of Daniel 7.13, removes reference to the parousia and so places the whole emphasis upon the session at the right hand of God, which itself is now seen as the final and complete glorification of Jesus.[40] His alteration is controlled, not by a desire to express a delay in the coming of the End, but by the wish to replace a future hope with a present belief. Now is the time of Jesus' glory. He is the present Lord; the object of his work has been achieved; men can now have faith in his immediate status to which the parousia, when it comes, can add nothing. Luke adds *apo tou nun* in order to show that, as far as his readers are concerned, the glorification is a present fact based upon a past achievement connected intimately with the cross and passion. Luke's Gospel brings the resurrection and ascension into close proximity with each other so that the cross is seen to begin this movement to glory. But he omits Mark's *opsesthe* because the glorification remains hidden. Veiled from the high priest, it must be the object of faith on the part of Luke's readers.

It was this present status of Jesus which was the real object of Luke's concern. He and his readers lived at some time distant from the life he describes. The witness to it had, indeed, continued, but the response remained varied. The Jews by and large continued hostile; the state remained something of an enigma. Christians were persecuted, and many had died, and still the parousia did not come. In this second–generation situation it was small wonder that the early Christian belief that Jesus was Lord seemed almost impossible to substantiate. But this was Luke's aim—to justify belief in Jesus and to show that his sovereignty, though hidden, was nevertheless real. He retained a belief in the parousia, for it was impossible really to have faith in the lordship of Jesus, and to believe that this was a matter of urgency, without accepting it as the final act which provided the ultimate vindication of the Christian hope. But what he did was to reduce its status, so that it became, not the accomplishment of Jesus' glorification, but the witness to it. It did not add anything to Jesus, but would reveal for all to see what already was a fact, that Jesus was Lord, that he was at the right hand of God, that the kingdom of God was a reality, and that its enemies were subjugated and defeated. Luke removes Jesus' full glorification from a future hope and brings it into the present as an actual reality. It was this belief which caused him to put emphasis upon the ascension as the pivotal event of his narrative, so that it becomes for him both the means whereby Jesus achieved his full status and also the concrete expression of his proclamation of that fact.

THE ASCENSION

Practical considerations brought about by the passing of time caused Luke to shift the emphasis from the future to the present, but this soon resulted in a theological conviction which made the *sessio ad dextram* the central plank both of his own beliefs and of the faith he was trying to evoke from his readers. Through this, he hoped to fulfil his purpose that they might 'know the truth concerning the things of which (they) had been informed' (1.4). As the act which both enables the glorification and effects it, the ascension is the visible and concrete expression of Jesus' status. For Luke, its importance lies in its value as a theological statement of his significance. This does not mean that he did not accept it as history, nor does it necessarily follow that he was not taking over traditions from earlier sources, but it does suggest that his reasons for describing it as an actual, separate event in history were controlled in the first instance by theological rather than by straight historical considerations.[41] At this point, the historical description becomes in the first instance the vehicle for the theological convictions which are themselves the outcome of his pastoral, evangelistic concern. The overriding importance of his theological motives is furthered both by his handling of the scheme which his acceptance of the ascension as a separate episode makes necessary, and also by the actual way in which he describes the event itself.

Luke's careful scheme is distinctive in the New Testament.[42] He alone describes a limited number of resurrection appearances which are brought to a definite end by an ascension which itself then becomes a prelude in time to an initial, single outpouring of the Spirit. This is controlled by his thought of the ascension as an event which, separate from the resurrection, is understood as the actual moment of the glorification of Jesus.

This emphasis causes him to describe the resurrection appearances as preludes to the glorification rather than as expressions of it. As Evans says: 'What most distinguishes Luke's account from that of the other gospels is that the resurrection is not an end in itself or a symbol of exaltation or parousia, but a point of transition.'[43] The appearances do not yet express his glorification. Whereas in Mark, the empty tomb witnesses to the overwhelming nature of the event,[44] which in Matthew is enhanced by a number of details having the nature of apocalyptic wonders, in Luke it causes only perplexity and doubt (24.4, 11). In Matthew, when the risen Christ appears, he inspires worship (28.9, 17); in John,

he causes joy (20.20) and, later, a full confession of faith (20.28).
In Luke, this is not so. The hearts of the disciples at Emmaus
may have burned within them, but Luke associates this, not with a
response to the person of the risen Jesus, but with the insight
provided by his teaching (24.32). When he appears to the Eleven,
they are 'startled and frightened' supposing that they beheld a
spirit (24.37). It is not until the ascension that joy and understanding come to them (24.52–3).

In Luke's scheme the resurrection, though of vital importance,
has nevertheless a clearly-defined significance. This is detailed in
Acts 1 as, first, to give a proof that he really was alive, that the
judgement of man had been reversed and the actions of God
revealed, and, secondly, to speak of the kingdom of God (Acts
1.3). This latter could mean the disclosure of the kerygma which
the disciples were to preach, so that the witnesses were to become
the valid link between the period of Jesus and that of the Church.[45]
More likely, however, it refers to further teaching by Jesus of the
kind which he gave during his ministry, but which they then were
unable to understand and accept. In the light of the resurrection
this can now be put right. More especially, it points back to the
Emmaus story for, since Luke, in Acts 1.3, infers that he knew of
further appearances, those recorded in his Gospel must have been
recounted by him as typical and illustrative of the significance of
the resurrection appearances as a whole. Emmaus talks of the
means by which Jesus entered his glory, of the necessity of the
suffering and of the scriptural justification for it (24.25–7). The
resurrection removes the *skandalon* caused by the cross and leaves
open the way of faith to be expressed by the ascension.

The distinctiveness of Luke at this point has been denied by
Robinson who, taking over the argument of Benoit and accepting
only the shorter text of Luke 24, argues[46] that this position over-
burdens Acts 1. The event in Acts 1.9–11, though in the form of an
ascension narrative, is not the moment of Jesus' glorification, but
is rather simply his final departure to the Father. The real ascension, that is the event which accomplished the exaltation, occurred
on Easter Day and was the prelude to the resurrection appearances
rather than their climax.

This view, however, can only be rejected.[47] In the first place, it
ignores the fact that Luke's resurrection appearances are devoid of
any hint of glorification. Secondly, it underplays the significance

of the cloud in Acts 1. This, as the sign and means of Jesus' entry
into the heavenly place, is the witness to his glorification: indeed
it is the means of its attainment, and links the ascension to the
parousia in such a way that it determines the manner of that event.
Thirdly, Robinson's view links the ascension to the outpouring of
the Spirit simply as a series of events, rather than seeing it as
actually enabling the gift which is the witness to the exaltation.
Fourthly, the marks of a theophany are not stressed (though they
are not as limited as Robinson maintains), not because Luke does
not view it in these terms, but because he thinks of heaven alone
as the place of the glorification. The cloud carries him there, but
it also veils the heavenly from their sight. Luke conceives of the
glory in spatial terms and it is not revealed on earth until the
parousia. The only exceptions to this are the transfiguration,
which Luke explicitly links to the ascension, and the vision—
though perhaps 'view' or 'preview' would be better terms—of
Stephen. But Stephen is distinctive as the first martyr. Yet it is
the death rather than the martyrdom which is important here.[48]
At the point of death, Stephen sees into heaven and views the Son
of man in his glory. No one else on earth beholds Jesus glorified.
Luke does not say that Paul, at his conversion, saw Jesus. A light
comes from heaven (Acts 9.4; 22.6; 26.13), a voice is heard (9.7;
22.9), but no person is seen.[49] Visionary appearances to Paul at
Corinth (18.9) or at Jerusalem (23.11) are of an entirely different
order and certainly do not show Christ in glory. In them, the
emphasis is upon the significance of the message, and the vision
occurs only to authenticate that.[50]

However, Robinson's view does show that, if our understanding
of Luke is right, it means that he is not entirely consistent here.
Not only is his scheme distinctive in the New Testament, it also
runs counter to other statements in Luke–Acts which link the
glorification more closely to the resurrection. At Emmaus, the
risen but not yet ascended Christ justifies the passion in terms of
an entry to a glorification that has already been accomplished:
'Was it not necessary that the Christ should suffer these things
and enter into his glory?' (24.26). The answer to the high priest
could be used to suggest the same understanding (22.69), as could
the promise to the thief (23.42–3). In Acts, the majority of speeches
suggest no intermediate stage between resurrection and exaltation
(Acts 3.15–16; 4.10; 10.40–3). At Antioch, Paul declares that the

resurrection was the cause of the exaltation and so was the fulfilment of Psalm 2.7 (13.33). Even when, in 5.30–1, the exaltation
as well as resurrection is mentioned, it is not necessarily thought
of as a separate event. Only in 2.32–5 are the two treated separately
so that different functions are assigned to them.[51]

All this points to the conclusion that Luke's scheme is an artificial one and is most likely to have been of his own making. It is
the vehicle which he uses, when he spells out his beliefs, when he
is developing his argument, to emphasize and to justify his contention that Jesus is the present Lord.

The final stage in his scheme is provided by his account of the
gift of the Spirit at Pentecost which is linked to the ascension both
in the narrative itself and in the explanation of its significance that
is found in Peter's speech. In both accounts of the event Jesus
points the disciples forward to their return to Jerusalem to await
the gift of power which will enable their effective witness (24.49;
Acts 1.8). The ascension and Pentecost are separated only by the
account of the election of Matthias, which is itself a necessary
prelude to Luke's understanding of the gift of the Spirit as the
eschatological renewal of Israel. Though the time references seem
to separate the two events, this is not really so, for the 'forty days'
is indeterminate and 'towards Pentecost' has a symbolic rather
than a literal significance.

Peter's speech makes the link explicit and shows how the gift
of the Spirit, by being dependent upon the ascension alone,
witnesses to that event. Verses 33 and 34a differentiate between
the resurrection and ascension and the two are justified by different
proof-texts, the former by Psalm 16, and the latter by Psalm 110.
By omitting the last verse of Psalm 16, Luke limits its application to the resurrection alone and so is able to make the ascension
the fulfilment of Psalm 110, which is given a crucial significance
in this speech. By using it as the link with the Joel quotation, he
can make Joel's promise issue in an appeal to baptism in the name
of Jesus. The gift of the Spirit can therefore be connected directly
with the ascension, which thus becomes the eschatological event
enabling the last days to begin, and, by its presence, witnesses to
the truth of the assertions about Jesus of Nazareth.

Following on from this, Luke sees the inspiration of witness to
the lordship of Jesus as the Spirit's primary function. Because of
his use of the ideas of Joel 2 and of his belief that the exalted Jesus

possesses and bestows the Spirit as a gift (Acts 2.33), he thinks of it primarily in Old Testament terms. He does not develop a more personal understanding of the Spirit's activity because, though hints of a deeper appreciation are to be found (Acts 5.3; 9.31; 13.2; 15.28) his thought is directed to his understanding of it as the eschatological witness to Jesus. This is directly the result of his emphasis upon the ascension, of the significance he gives to that event, and of his concentration upon the Spirit's function in relation to that.

The second result of Luke's theological emphasis upon the ascension is found in the fact that he describes it as an independent event, not merely once, but twice, for this cannot be accounted for by the supposition that he had two accounts of the one event in different sources and felt constrained to include them both. His use of Mark shows that he was no slave to his sources. Moreover, similarities of thought and of expression, and even the differences, clearly reveal the hand of Luke himself.

It is true that Luke 24.50–3 has sometimes been seen as simply the description of a solemn parting which, though looking forward to the ascension, is nevertheless not that event, but is of the same kind as the other appearances which Luke records in that chapter.[52] In this case, any special sense of climax or finality is given it by its position in the book rather than by its place in the life of Jesus. However, even the shorter text of these verses is not so easily assimilated for, as Barrett points out, it contains an account of a 'parting so decisive that one cannot but be surprised to find them together again'.[53] The descriptions of the going of Jesus and of the attitude of the disciples to that departure mark off the event from the other resurrection appearances and suggest a new stage both in his career and in their understanding of its significance. The scene suggests the accomplishment of the *analēmpsis* to which 9.51 had pointed. *Meta charas* and *eulogountes ton theon* express the disciples' response in terms which are characteristic of the eschatological atmosphere of the Infancy narratives (1.14, 64; 2.10, 28). Parallels to Acts 1 are found in the commands and promises of Jesus, in the return to Jerusalem, and in the presence of the disciples in the Temple. As Davies writes: 'There is too close an identity of ideas and expressions to allow of any other explanation, than that the two passages are concerned with the same event, i.e. the ascension.'[54] The longer text of this part of Luke 24 is therefore to be accepted as making explicit what is suggested in the rest of the description. It was probably omitted in the interests of harmonizing Luke and Acts in such a way that the Gospel account was made into the prelude to the actual ascension which, by this means, was thought to be recorded in Acts alone. This, however, was to misunderstand Luke's intention and was a complete failure to perceive the significance he placed upon that event.

Luke described the event twice because he put such great weight upon it.[55] It is impossible to visualize his writing the first volume without including the ascension for, as we shall see, it alone makes sense of his understanding of the nature and course of the earthly life of Jesus. Without it, even with the resurrection—at least as Luke describes it—he would not have been other than one of the prophets. Only with the ascension could that Old Testament figure be really worshipped as Lord. He could indeed have written an easier first chapter of Acts if he had put less stress upon it, but the purpose of his second volume would then have been quite different. It could then have been described as church history and Luke could have been seen as a rather starry-eyed church historian. But the very difficulties of the first chapter arise out of his preoccupation with the ascension and with the significance he gave to it.

Theological differences, or rather the different theological points he was trying to make, explain the differences between his two accounts of the ascension, for it is viewed against either what has gone before or against what is to follow. Luke 24 sets the event in the context of the life of Jesus, Acts 1 in that of the life of the early Church. Yet Luke handles it as more than just the narrative of a climax or of a beginning. It is rather that he describes the ascension in each book in order that it should give meaning to the contents of the whole book, for it puts the whole volume into perspective and shows its significance. Each narrative of the ascension demands that the reader should pass a value judgement upon what is described in the book as a whole, and at the same time states its own answer in declaring its conviction that Jesus is Lord. In the Gospel, each episode has to be viewed in the light of the conviction expressed in the narrative of the ascension (and since Luke did not necessarily expect his readers to start at the end, he used the infancy narratives to make precisely the same proclamation, so that the beginning of the Gospel was already referring to its end); in Acts, each episode has to be viewed in the light of its witness to the ascended one and to the fulfilment of his promises.

In Luke 24 the ascension is not described as an event which is apart from what has preceded it, but is seen rather as the climax of the resurrection appearances and, through them, of the life as a whole. It is the event which gives unity to what has gone before. Many of the narratives in the gospel have looked forward to it. The birth of Jesus was greeted by that heavenly joy which now passes to the disciples (2.14); the baptism, which in Luke is described as an objective event rather than as the subjective experience of Jesus, pointed out the heavenly origins of the Spirit and so of the inspiration and direction of Jesus; the last temptation in Luke was that which rejected an apocalyptic visitation of the Temple, for the movement of Jesus from heaven to earth reverses the true direction of his life; the hill at Nazareth led not to his destruction but to his wider ministry. The transfiguration points to the *exodos* which is to be accomplished at Jerusalem, and the disciples behold his glory only from afar. They have a glimpse of his heavenly glory rather than a preview of his parousia. This leads into the journey to his *analēmpsis* (9.51). He is 'constrained' until his baptism is accomplished (12.50) and the journeyings of the first two days must lead to the climax of the third (13.32). Before the arrival at Jerusalem, Jesus talks of a nobleman who goes away to receive a kingdom (19.12) and at the Entry itself the crowds welcome, not as in Mark a future coming kingdom, but a king who is about to ascend his throne (19.38). The life leads into the ascension, being a continuous, purposeful movement towards that event.

The actual narrative of the ascension describes Jesus in priestly terms, blessing his disciples as he is parted from them. The blessing marks the close of the earthly life; it witnesses to the ending of a chapter, but it nevertheless means that the life still has significance for them. It signals the drawing to a close of the period of the Jesus of history, but it does so in such a way that that life, that episode in time, is taken up into the period that is now to begin. It is an end which is at the same time not the end. It marks a beginning of something which comes out of what is ending. The life is caught up in the next stage.

For it is not just a departure but a recognition of who Jesus really is. Early responses, though true, are incomplete. The cloud, the worship of the disciples, their joy, and their praise of God represent both the glorification of Jesus and the acknowledgement of his true significance. But the glorification of Jesus is told in very restrained terms, for his ascension is his departure to this rather than its actual accomplishment. The episode is concerned primarily with the life which it brings to an end. It is a justification of the course of that life and so of the one who lived it, so that the suffering and the cross as well as the vindication through the resurrection are seen to make sense. The disciples, and Luke hopes his readers, can now see that this was the life of the Lord.

But the gospel account of the ascension also puts the life into its proper perspective. The disciples worship the one whom they know and who has now become Lord. The life, the earthly Jesus is not the object of their worship, nor the ground of their faith. That is found in the living Lord in whose light the earthly Jesus can alone be understood. On the other hand, however, the earthly Jesus tells who it is who is now Lord. Because of him they know the one whom they worship, the call he gives, and the life he bestows.

The account in Acts 1 is more difficult to unravel. Problems are caused by the unusual structure of the Greek of the first two verses and the consequent suspicion of corruption, by what seems to be a reference back to the ascension in verse 2, and by the mention of the resurrection appearances over a period of forty days. Verse 6 begins the actual description of the ascension with but slight connection with what has gone before, and is itself complicated by the concrete mode of its description, by the fact of the cloud, and by the presence of the two men. Verse 12 brings the disciples back to Jerusalem, though there is nothing to suggest that they had left it, and in so doing marks the Mount of Olives as the place of the ascension.

It is unlikely that the problem is solved by making verses 1–5 a later addition,[56] for any interpolator would almost certainly have set out to reduce rather than increase the problems. In the context of a solemn declaration, *anelēmphthē* is to be seen as a reference to the ascension rather than as a less significant pointer to Jesus' withdrawal from the world, and should not be removed from the text.[57] The reference to the forty days is not to be taken as a parenthesis in the interests of harmonization, but refers to the timing of the ascension itself, which is thus separated by this period from the resurrection.[58]

What then was his purpose in the first five verses? The passage is best understood if it is divided into two parts, the break coming at the end of verse 2 so that *hois kai parestēsen* introduces a new stage in the argument. The first two verses which find their climax in *anelēmphthē* are a summary of Jesus' life as Luke has recorded it in the Gospel. *Poiein te kai didaskein* which as a phrase Menoud says 'ne serait pas indigne de Luke', presents just such a summary as is found in Acts 10.36–8. The climax comes in the *analēmpsis* which could occur only after *enteilamenos tois apostolois*. The Western text spells this out as a command to preach the gospel, but this is unlikely to reflect Luke's understanding, for his first volume contains no such command. The mission is much more the direct work of the Holy Spirit impelling the apostles. In Luke 24 it is controlled by scriptural expectations, and in Acts 1 by the power of the Holy Spirit. The disciples are merely agents, for the initiative is God's alone and the mission itself witnesses to the exaltation of Jesus. The only command that is reported in Luke 24 is that to remain in Jerusalem, and if a single command is referred to, then it is this. If, on the other hand, the verse looks at the whole life of Jesus in the light of the ascension, then it refers to the general teaching after the resurrection. In either case, what it emphasizes is the making of the Twelve into the nucleus of the restored Israel in preparation for the eschatological event which is to take place at Jerusalem. The two verses are therefore a summary of the life of Jesus up to and including the ascension. This acts as the inescapable presupposition of the second volume and that which alone makes the second volume possible. Both volumes are therefore hinged around the ascension, and this inescapable fact accounts for the clause existing alone and not being followed up by the expected *de*. The *men* clause is a summary of the gospel; the *de* clause is the whole book of Acts, less these two verses; for these are the two witnesses to Luke's belief that Jesus is Lord

If verses 1–2 set the ascension in the context of the life of Jesus as a whole and remind Luke's readers of the lessons of his first volume, verses 3–5 bring out the particular significance of the resurrection appearances. A new element is introduced by the mention of the forty days, but this suggests an indefinite period, much as the 'many days' of Acts 13.31.[59] Its significance is to point to the reality of the resurrection appearances and the importance of the teaching then given. The ascension becomes the confirmation and acceptance of the resurrection vindication of Jesus' Messiahship, and the Pentecostal gift of the Spirit is established as the fulfilment of Jesus' post-resurrection teaching and promises. In this way, Luke enhances the theological significance of both the ascension and Pentecost as proclamations of the reality of Jesus' supremacy, and endows his own interpretation with the authority of the risen Lord.

The actual account of the ascension follows in verses 6–11, though it should be noted that only verse nine contains a description of the event itself, for the rest is concerned rather with answering those perplexities which are either expressed or implied.[60] More than that, however, even the event itself is approached wholly from the point of view of the disciples rather than from its relation to the central figure. The subject is not Jesus but the apostles, and in this there is a complete contrast with Luke 24.50–1. In Luke's Gospel, it is Jesus who leads them out to witness something that is to happen to him; in Acts, whatever is to come to pass happens 'when they were come together' and the interest centres upon the onlookers. The description of the actual event is given only as it bears upon the disciples; it is seen in terms of its significance for them. 'As they were looking on' he departs and is removed *apo tōn ophthalmōn*. Even before he is actually gone, the attention is directed to them—'while they were gazing into heaven as he went'. The place of the ascension is mentioned only in connection with their return from it (Acts 1.12).

Acts 1.6–11 is really less concerned with giving an account of the ascension than with the significance of this for the disciples, and with the problems raised by the assertion that Jesus is the glorified Lord. But even the response of the disciples is different in Luke's two accounts. In Acts, unlike Luke 24, there is no exuberance. The reality of the departure, the questions, and even the answers occasions something like perplexity, so that they can only return to the upper room and devote themselves to prayer, for it is not until after the gift of the Spirit that joy comes to them (Acts 2.46–7).

In Acts 1 the ascension is presented as something of an enigma. Though the event is put forward as the glorification of Jesus, this is done in a restrained manner, for it is less concerned with giving

a value judgement upon him than with dealing with the problems
that such a value judgement brings. Acts 1.6–11 could hardly have
been Luke's primary account of the ascension for it does not make
the unrestrained proclamation that such an account required. It
presupposes the existence of Luke 24.50–3 in its longer form and
it needs Acts 1.1–5 with its glance back in verse 2 to the Gospel
record as its immediate prelude. Acts 1.6–11 is of the nature of
supplementary instruction for those who need further assurance
that the judgement of faith expressed in the Gospel account is
still valid in spite of the ambiguity in the events that have occurred
between the time of Jesus and their own day.

Two problems which, though not identical, are closely connected
are to the fore and are expressed in the disciples' question and in
the solace offered by the two men (Acts 1.6, 11). Will Jesus soon
restore the kingdom to Israel and will he really return in glory? In
other words, is the claim that Jesus is both Christ and Lord really
valid? Is Jesus really God's final act, the fulfilment of Israel's
legitimate expectations? Is he really the one to whom Israelite
history was directed? The disciples have addressed him as 'Lord'
(verse 6). Is this expression of faith justified and have events since
the ascension vindicated it?

Jesus himself does not deny the legitimacy of their expectations;
it is only on the matter of the timing that rethinking is required.
The two men vindicate belief in the parousia though they show
that the glorification of Jesus does not depend upon it. The future
expectations are not denied though the emphasis is shifted from
them to the present, to the glorification, to the Spirit, and to the
universal witness. But these are not put forward as substitutes but
as guarantees of their future hopes.

The gift of the Spirit and the universal witness which it em-
powers guarantee the sovereignty of Jesus. They are themselves
eschatological events, the accompaniments, according to prophetic
expectations, of God's final saving action. Since they are completely dependent upon the ascension, they augment the other
means by which Luke brings out the eschatological significance of
that event. The cloud is an eschatological symbol (Dan. 7.13);
Olivet is the place of eschatological expectations (Zech. 14.4);
the ascension is linked directly to the parousia (Acts 1.11); it had
to take place in Jerusalem, for that is the place where God's final
action was to occur (Isa. 2.2–4).

Luke's second account of the ascension is therefore to be understood against the background of his eschatology, and provides a crucial account of the event which is seen to be at the heart of his reinterpretation. It makes the ascension rather than the parousia into the eschatological event which fulfils Israel's expectations in so far as they were true to the prophetic promises. The guarantee that this is so is the gift of the Spirit and the universal witness that it enables; its seal will be the parousia and the restoration of Israel. The story of Acts is told in order to justify this confidence.

The story of the ascension provides the thesis for the book as a whole, the statement which the chapters that follow will justify. Van Stempvoort has called it the ecclesiastical and historical interpretation of the event, and in one sense this is right, for it is the account which looks at the incident from the life of the Christian community and with a perspective controlled by the problems that this faces. It is answering the early Church's questions. But these are more fundamental than the ones van Stempvoort suggests[61] and are concerned, not with the historical problems surrounding the coming into being of the Church and the manner of its early life, but with the fundamental one, which was that of the reality of the lordship of Jesus. If it could find no means of expressing and justifying this, the Christian community would drain away. That it did not do so, at least in one part of the world, is signal witness to the success of Luke's achievement.

ESCHATOLOGY AND HISTORY

If our understanding of Luke has so far been at all correct, it has very definite consequences for the interpretation of Luke–Acts as a whole. In the first place, it means that Luke has not turned his back upon eschatology, that much modern writing which virtually accuses him of abandoning the early Christian outlook in favour of one which came to terms with the world and its history is beside the point, being misled by its inability to accept that eschatology can have anything positive to say to history of any kind. But Luke, in spite of the fact that he wrote history, did not expect the world to continue but, including himself and his contemporaries within the *genea* of Jesus, anticipated the parousia as an event of immediate relevance for them. For him, the world is an alien place, being given into the hands of the devil, its battles reflecting the other-worldly battle between God and Satan and, though the victories in this world witness to the reality of the kingdom of God, the sphere of that realm is the transcendent. The history of God's saving acts has found its climax in Jesus of Nazareth, but Luke nowhere suggests that salvation history is to continue. He talks of witness before the world, but this is not the same as advocating a mission to it. The risen Lord's commands in Luke and Acts (24.47; Acts 1.8) should not be read in terms of that recorded in Matthew 28.19. The 'universalism' of Luke needs careful definition.

By his reinterpretation Luke brings eschatology into the centre of his proclamation, for he emphasizes the ascension in such a way that it becomes the complete eschatological event, in that it is presented as the final act determining the whole of God's saving history, which finds its climax in it and which afterwards is understood as an epilogue flowing from it and witnessing to it. The ascension does not lead into a new stage of history but, rather, history between then and Luke's own time is seen to proceed from it, is controlled by it, and lasts only so long as its witness to that event is required. The universal witness is made necessary by the need to fulfil Old Testament expectations, without which it could only be seen as less than the full eschatological act of God. But again, it is witness to an event rather than a mission to the world, for it is told more for the recognition of the event than for the benefit of mankind at large.

What then is the purpose of Luke's history since the ascension? Certainly it is not to serve the cause of realized eschatology, for the idea of the growth of the kingdom in this world is alien to him. On this point, Ellis seems wrong when he says that 'the Spirit constitutes a continuing presence of the kingdom of God in the post-resurrection Church'.[62] The Spirit witnesses to the exaltation of Jesus, and so to the present fact of the kingdom's existence, but it does not manifest its presence, which is as yet a reality only in the other world. Neither does continuing history since the ascension further the effectiveness of the kingdom in the transcendent realm, for it is the exaltation which has guaranteed and established this, and the miracles of the disciples are now derived from the authority of Jesus by the use of his name rather than presented as contributing further to the overthrow of Satan.[63] But, equally, Luke's second volume is not written primarily in the interests of salvation history, for it is not open-ended, describing a progressive extension of the saving message of God and thereby linking men to Jesus. If that is what Luke is doing, the end of Acts is an anticlimax, for it does not conclude with the arrival of the Gospel at Rome, since he notes that Christianity is already in the city when Paul enters it, and the apostle's preaching there is not represented as a success story.[64] Again, the emphasis is upon witness rather than mission. But salvation history is excluded as Luke's primary purpose by his eschatological emphasis and his expectation of the early return of Jesus. Luke, like the New Testament as a whole, has a place for salvation history, but this is used in the service of his eschatology rather than to the exclusion of it.

Van Unnik[65] offers a different approach when he sees Luke's purpose in Acts as being 'the confirmation of what God did in Christ as told in the first book', and when he maintains that 'the whole book is meant to witness to the truth'. The story of the Gospel is confirmed by the witness of the disciples, by the presence of the Spirit, by the manifestations of God's power, and by the fulfilment of his declared purposes. To see the aim of Luke's second volume in terms of the establishing and proving of what he has proclaimed in his first is a right emphasis. Luke's Gospel is primarily proclamation, and Acts is not of a different kind. But what does it confirm? It is not enough to say that it establishes the story of the Gospel as 'the word for the world' for this makes Acts read more like a success story than it actually is, or rather, it puts the burden of success in the wrong place. The success is not the universal embrace of the Gospel but is found in the universal witness to it.[66] What this universal witness confirms is the authority of Jesus, the reality of his exaltation. Acts therefore is the confirmation, the proof, of the Gospel's assertion that Jesus is the Lord, an assertion that is repeated at the beginning of the second volume in the account of the ascension and to which the rest of the book gives proof as it describes the historical events as witnesses to the fulfilment of God's eschatological promises.

History in Acts does not embrace eschatology, neither does it deny it. It rather proceeds from the eschatological event and bears witness to it. God's convenantal people are re-created in history as the Old Testament promised and they are then made ready for the time when either through death or at the parousia they will enter into the kingdom of God. The events into which history draws them await a future act for their consummation, for that moment when there returns the Christ 'whom heaven must receive until the time for establishing all that God spoke by the mouth of his holy prophets from of old' (Acts 3.20–1).

In the second place, Luke's understanding of the ascension brings to the fore the question of his attitude to the Jews. Old Testament history and Israel's prophetic expectations are taken up into the life of Jesus and find their fulfilment at his ascension and in the history proceeding from that. As the event to which God's earlier saving acts pointed and in which they found their significance, the life of Jesus is linked closely to that earlier salvation history to which it gives approval and meaning. Bultmann has denied that the early eschatological community understood its relation to the Israelite people as one of real historical continuity. 'The continuity is not a continuity growing out of history but is one created by God.'[67] But eschatology does not necessarily pronounce such a negative judgement upon history which has led up to the eschatological event, nor is the apocalyptic view of history, as opposed to the Old Testament view, necessarily the only one which is consistent with a true eschatology. Even the apocalyptists did not entirely opt out of history, for they saw themselves as the heirs of the true religious enthusiasts of old and as the inheritors of their traditions. Their negative approach to contemporary history does not entail a negative view of that history which has led to their own times. As Russell points out: 'They were men of faith who could see within history, through history, and beyond history, the working out of God's triumphant purpose.'[68] The eschatological event can be seen as the climax of a series of events, as the final decisive action of God to which they had pointed forward and in the light of which they were for the first time properly understood. Again, the earlier saving acts have enabled the eschatological event to be understood as such and have caused a group to respond and so to become at least the nucleus of the eschatological community. Even Paul could not have understood Jesus without entering into a dialogue with the Old Testament presuppositions which were not entirely rejected by him. Luke's assessment of Israel's preparation for Jesus is more positive than that made by Paul, but it is none the less viewed in relation to Jesus as God's eschatological act.

Nor does eschatology necessarily place a wholly negative value upon past institutions and saving events but, in presenting a new act of God, invalidates a clinging to the old. It condemns that attitude which Luke describes: 'And no one after drinking old wine desires new, for he says, "The old is good".' As Von Rad puts it, the truly eschatological and revolutionary outlook of the prophets is found when they 'saw Jahweh approaching Israel with a new action which made the old saving institutions increasingly invalid since from then on life or death for Israel was determined by this future event'.[69]

The third result of this understanding of Luke's emphasis upon the ascension issues in the need to re-examine the idea that he set out to write a 'life of Jesus' which was presented as the time of salvation and to which the Christian believer is linked by the period of the Church. Conzelmann has maintained that, whereas for Paul the acceptable time of salvation is the 'now' of the present, for Luke the 'today' of salvation is found in a period of past history. 'Luke sees salvation already as a thing of the past. The time of salvation has come about in history, as a period of time which, although it determines the present, is now over and finished.'[70] The same point is developed by Wilckens: 'The history of Jesus as a historical time is closed with the ascension, and with this, the unmediated presence of salvation on earth.'[71] Now, salvation is achieved only as the proclamation incorporates the believer into the continuing salvation history which is based on the life of Jesus. Only at the parousia will the unmediated presence of salvation again be realized. In one sense of course this is true for, since the time of Jesus, the call to follow him must inevitably be a mediated one. But when this becomes understood as a call to be incorporated into a history which is based upon an event in the past, when the bond with Jesus is seen to be a link through history to a person, present in earlier times but now absent, then this misunderstands the significance that Luke put upon the ascension.[72] For him, the life of Jesus, though important in so far as it was the time when Satan was being overthrown and men recalled to the demands of the God of Israel, was not itself the actual climax of God's saving action but the way to the achievement of that in the ascension. It was the prelude to the exaltation, the means whereby that was made possible. Jesus actually became Lord only at the ascension, and God's saving action proceeds from that. Before then, faced with the presence of Jesus, the disciples misunderstand; the cross is not a past event having saving significance in the present; the eschatological Spirit comes to the disciples only after the ascension.

For Luke, Jesus is not a figure of the past, but the living Lord. The Spirit is not the substitute for the living Jesus but the witness to the fact that he lives and is the present Lord. What Luke lacks is any sense of the indwelling of Christ in the Christian community but this, as we shall see, is the result of his Christology rather than his eschatology. But the power of Jesus is active and his name provides a direct and immediate bond between him and the community for, as Von Rad says of the name of God: 'In it and in it alone lay the guarantee of Yahweh's nearness and of his readiness to help, and through it Israel had the assurance of being able at all times to reach his heart.'[73]

For Acts presents stories of encounters with the living Lord rather than a developing sphere of salvation history. The speeches draw out the significance of the events in which they are set so that they become, not types of early proclamation and thus the guarantees of later preaching, but the means whereby the reader is drawn to make a response to those events and through them to the ascended Lord. The apostles are the nucleus of the eschatological community rather than the guarantees of a link with the historical Jesus; they must be witnesses of his life and resurrection, for otherwise they could not witness to the full significance of the eschatological event through him. They link the life to the exalted Lord and to the post-ascension acts rather than the reverse. For the community is not institutionalized, the ministry is not defined, the understanding of the sacraments is fluid, and the action of the Spirit is thought of in eschatological terms rather than in those of catholic order. It is hard to see Luke in Käsemann's judgement that 'the Word is no longer the sole criterion of the Church, but the Church is the legitimation of the Word, and apostolic origin of the Church's ministerial office provides the guarantee of a valid proclamation'.[74] Luke's narrative suggests a much less clearly defined group, living more expectantly, and open to the ever new promptings of the Lord.

Finally, this emphasis on the ascension shows that his work is very much a proclamation summoning men to a decision. He writes in order to lead them to an enduring faith, to bring them to salvation. This of course is not to suggest that a salvation-history plan for Luke's work would debar him from doing this. Marshall, who rightly stresses the evangelistic concern of Luke, seems to underplay the fact that an understanding of the redemptive act in terms of salvation history can be a real evangelistic instrument.[75] Where it does differ is not in the object of what it hopes to achieve but in the response which it tends to evoke. The salvation history exponents of Luke–Acts tend to think of the evangelist calling out a response which is harmonious, logical, and safe. Resting secure on a past series of events, it plays down the stumbling-block presented by the cross and can view the future with an easy confidence. The eschatological response of early Christianity is seen to be wholly other than this. In the words of Bultmann: 'Christ is the ever-present and ever becoming present eschatological event' so that 'the Now gets its eschatological character by the encounter with Christ or with the Word which proclaims him, because in the encounter with him the World and its history comes to its end and the believer becomes free from the World by becoming a new creature.'[76]

But the response which Luke desires is not far removed from this. He writes to meet the ambiguities in the lives of his readers caused by doubts, persecutions, and disappointments. In this situation he summons them to make an act of faith in the present lordship of Jesus, in the present transcendent reality of the kingdom. Their hopes are removed from this world; they rest on faith in the unseen. Though this world can give evidence for his beliefs through its witness to the universal proclamation of the Gospel, the otherwise unseen nature of much of the eschatological event leaves it open to acceptance or rejection. He writes history, not to immerse them in the world. Historical context for Jesus proclaims him only as a fact for the world rather than of it. But he is not accepted by it and Christians cannot expect a more positive response to themselves.

2

Jesus of Nazareth

Luke's thoroughgoing reinterpretation of the eschatological beliefs
of his predecessors provides the central plank of his theology and
controls his explanation of the whole of God's saving action in
Jesus. It also suggests that his work is best understood as a response to those problems of faith which were arising within the
Christian community rather than as an attempt to persuade non-
Christians to embrace the gospel. Doubtless it was not a matter of
a complete 'either–or', but in general it was the difficulties of those
who were already Christian, but whose faith was coming under
severe pressures, which were the immediate objects of his concern.[1] His aim was to strengthen and confirm, and if need be to
reawaken, faith in Jesus as the present Lord, and it was to this
end that his theological interpretation was directed.

Practical concern however resulted in a skilled and consistent
theologizing. In the first place, his theological understanding of
the centrality of the ascension means that he views the life of Jesus
as a preliminary to that event. At the baptism, the Spirit comes
upon him 'in bodily form as a dove', but it is not until the ascension that he is enthroned as Lord and so becomes fully distinctive
from the saving figures of old. Luke's Jesus is one with them and
his life is seen as a movement towards exaltation, as a progress to
that event which will enable his glorification at the right hand of
God.

But, secondly, if Luke's revised eschatology has this definite
result for his presentation of the life of Jesus, the practical needs
which brought about this revision determine his purpose of showing that the life is capable of bearing the value judgement that the
ascension places upon it. He had to justify the career of Jesus
and the manner of his life in order to prove that this was a fitting
prelude to the exaltation and did not rule it out of court. Rejection,

suffering, crucifixion—these have to be explained if Luke's ultimate claims are to be seen as worthy of credence.

In the third place, therefore, his understanding of Jesus was
dominated by Old Testament categories of thought, for that
source alone could justify Luke's claim that Jesus was God's
final, saving instrument. By necessity, he was compelled to go to
that book to show that Jesus' career was not contrary to its expectations. But, more than that, his use of the Old Testament is
such as to suggest that what began as necessity soon passed into
design, and that he used that source to provide the actual basis for
his whole understanding of the person of the Christ. Luke presents
Jesus in terms which are derived from the Old Testament so that
its expectations and ideas control the Gospel portrait.

THE LORD

The most characteristic title of Jesus in Luke–Acts is *ho kurios*.
At the birth, the angels announce Jesus as 'Christ the Lord'
(2.11); at Pentecost, Peter declares that the exaltation has established him as 'Lord and Christ' (Acts 2.36); at Rome, Paul is able
to teach about 'the Lord Jesus Christ quite openly and unhindered' (Acts 28.31). At these crucial moments in his story
Luke chooses to call Jesus Lord and Christ and, while the latter
is, as we shall see, a matter of dispute to be used as the conclusion
of an argument, it is 'Lord' which is the vehicle of Luke's own
declaration of faith and that to which he summons his readers to
respond.

In his recent essay on the Christology of Acts, C. F. D. Moule[2]
has pointed out that, though Luke, unlike the other Synoptists,
does refer to Jesus in the main body of his gospel as *ho kurios*,
these instances are confined to passages where the evangelist himself is writing as narrator, and that, apart from two places in the
infancy narratives (1.43, 76) and Jesus' own designation of himself as *kurios* in 19.31, 34, Luke refrains from allowing men to
describe Jesus thus until after the resurrection. Professor Moule
himself suggests that this is to be seen as a part of Luke's historical
undertaking—that he was attempting to say how Jesus may have
been understood by his contemporaries—and that he did not think
that they acknowledged him as Lord until after the resurrection.
Another possible interpretation of the evidence could be that the

distinction arises out of Luke's own ideas, that it is to be explained, not by his attempts to say what actually happened, but by what he deemed appropriate, and that the use is as it is because he himself dated Christ's entry into lordship from his exaltation.[3] Either way, the narrative use of *ho kurios* is simply a case of Luke's writing in the light of the whole experience of Christ and expressing his own conviction that the one at its centre is Lord.[4]

However, it is possible that the evidence that Moule puts forward requires neither of these conclusions, which would appear, rather, to go beyond the facts on which they are based. In the first place, can one really make much of the fact that men do not describe Jesus as *ho kurios* during the ministry but that they do so after the resurrection? By its nature, *ho kurios* is an affirmation about Jesus addressed by one person to another. It is either a statement of faith between two or more people who share in a common attitude to Jesus, or it is a proclamation of a conviction about him to those outside. Instances of the former occur at Elizabeth's meeting with Mary: 'And why is this granted me, that the mother of my Lord should come to me?' (1.43, 45), and in the witness of the Eleven to the Emmaus disciples after the resurrection: 'The Lord has risen indeed, and has appeared to Simon' (24.34). In Acts it is found in the rebuke of Simon Magus by Peter: 'Repent therefore of this wickedness of yours, and pray to the Lord that, if possible, the intent of your heart may be forgiven you' (Acts 8.22). The latter use would be found at the end of Peter's Pentecost speech (Acts 2.36) and in his speech to Cornelius—'He is Lord of all' (Acts 10.36). By its very nature the account of the ministry contains little that would be an appropriate setting for either of these uses. The story of the preparations for the entry into Jerusalem is, and here Luke uses *kurios* twice (19.31, 34). Indeed, the second appearance of the term in this episode is peculiar to him, for Mark has simply: 'And they told him what Jesus had said' (Mark 11.6), while Matthew at this point is even more general (Matt. 21.6). There are very few other places in the main body of the Gospel where it could have been used in this way. Luke could, indeed, have introduced it in the narrative of the preparations for the passover, but he retains the Marcan 'Teacher' (22.11). It would hardly have been appropriate, even as a question, in the mouth of Pilate (23.1–5), and, in his account of the appearance before the high priest (22.66–71) Luke, though dividing the use, retains the Marcan titles. Its introduction here would not have been likely in material that was already well formed, and a pointer to its significance is already present in the use of Psalm 110.1. Luke has three christological affirmations in the body of his Gospel—at 7.16 when, after the raising of the widow's son, the crowd says: 'A great prophet has arisen among us', at Peter's confession where the apostle names him 'The Christ of God' (9.20), and at the cross, when the centurion calls him '*dikaios*' (23.47). A fourth comes after the resurrection: 'The Lord has risen indeed' (24.34). These are all functional terms and, though it appears that *ho kurios* is deemed peculiarly appropriate to the resurrection stories and is to be seen as the climax of the christological witnesses, it is nevertheless not thereby suggested that he was not acknowledged as Lord until then. Indeed, its introduction as a simple statement suggests that the faith it expresses is not newly acquired.

A second point also tells against Professor Moule's conclusion, namely the significance to be assigned to the Gospel's use of the vocative, *kurie*. He sees in this only the significance of a respectful address, while Hahn, though describing it as more than a courtesy title, so that it is one by which the speaker admits subordination to the person addressed and puts himself at his disposal, nevertheless, distinguishes between it and the absolute *ho kurios*. The vocative in Luke, he says, is not meant to express the 'predicate of the exalted one'.[5]

There are, indeed, instances where *kurie* contains little more than respect (5.12; 9.59; 18.41). At other times, however, in Luke's interpretation at any rate, the meaning comes very close to the full significance of *ho kurios*. Twice it expresses the full reality of Jesus, once in Peter's response to the first epiphany: 'Depart from me for I am a sinful man, O Lord' (5.8), and once after the return of the Seventy, where it gives their true understanding of Jesus in the light of their mission: 'Lord, even the demons are subject unto us in your name' (10.17). Elsewhere, Luke uses it in an eschatologically controlled passage where the disciples are associated with those of the post-exaltation period: 'Lord, are you telling this parable for us or for all?' (12.41). At other times it expresses a deep relationship to Jesus which is an expression of such as existed in the later Church. Such, for instance, is its use at 11.1: 'Lord, teach us to pray' and its appearance in the passion

episodes (22.33, 38, 49). It expresses the community's response
to Jesus and so comes close to the significance contained in *ho
kurios* in the narrative.

Moreover, at four points in his Gospel, Luke uses *ho kurios* and
kurie in such close proximity that the significance of the former
must be carried over into the latter. At 10.1 he tells how 'the Lord
chose seventy others' and sent them out. When they return, they
acknowledge the significance of the journey in the same terms:
'Lord, even the demons are subject unto us' (10.17). A similar
link is found in the eschatological discussion of chapter 17. At
the beginning, 'the apostles said to the Lord, Increase our faith'
(17.5), while, at the end of the chapter, they ask, 'Where, Lord?'
(17.37). At the prediction of his denial, Peter says: 'Lord, I am
ready to go with you to prison and to death' (22.33) and, when he
denies Jesus: 'The Lord turned and looked at Peter. And Peter
remembered the word of the Lord, how he had said to him,
"Before the cock crows today, you will deny me three times" '
(22.61). Finally, at 19.8, the title and the vocative are found together. 'And Zacchaeus stood and said to the Lord, "Behold,
Lord, the half of my goods I give to the poor." '

The close connection between the title and the vocative use
which is found in the Gospel is seen also in Acts where, in the
description of Paul's conversion, Luke's position as narrator
causes him to use *ho kurios* (Acts 9.1, 10, 15), and where both Paul
and Ananias use *kurie* (Acts 9.5, 13). The vocative is given the full
significance of *ho kurios* for, not only does Paul in his own accounts
of the conversion use it in his address to Jesus after the full impact
of the appearance has dawned upon him, and after he knows the
nature of the one he is addressing (Acts 22.19; 26.15), but it is
used twice by Stephen in his commendation after he has announced the status of the one he has seen (Acts 7.59, 60).

All this therefore suggests that neither Moule's own conclusion,
nor the other possibility that we have put forward, can be drawn
from Luke's use of *ho kurios* in his two volumes. Luke does not
suggest that Jesus was not recognized as Lord until after the
resurrection, neither does it look as though he felt Lord to be an
inappropriate description of Jesus during his lifetime.

But how does Acts 2.36 fit into this conclusion? Are we to see
here the marks of a different belief? Haenchen[6] suggests that Luke
is here taking over an older tradition which is at odds with his

own Christology, while O'Neill sees the Evangelist as making a gallant, but not altogether successful, attempt to reconcile conflicting views.[7] It is doubtful, however, whether such a conclusion is required.

Luke's use of *ho kurios* and *kurie* in the Gospel is essentially an expression of commitment, representing a response of people to Jesus, either of those who were drawn to him in his lifetime, or the acknowledgement by the Evangelist himself of the meaning of the whole of Jesus' career. In any case, however, since Luke is writing to his contemporaries to deepen their loyalty and faith, the usage, even in the Gospel, expresses the response of a community which already knows the power of the Exalted One. The same emphasis is present in Acts. *Ho kurios* is found as the value judgement of Luke as narrator; it is used by Christians to each other to express their mutual understanding of Jesus; it is elaborated to become 'the Lord Jesus', or 'the Lord Jesus Christ'; in the vocative, it is found as the address to the Exalted One. It is significant that the passage in which the designation is found most frequently is that which contains Paul's farewell speech to the Ephesian elders, for it represents the language of one Christian to another giving expression to a common faith, a common acceptance of Jesus' status, and a common loyalty to him (Acts 20.17–35).

The overridingly dominant significance of *kurios* in Luke–Acts is this expression of the community's witness, devotion, and allegiance to Jesus. It is an affirmation of a common belief whereby Christians see themselves as standing under obligation to Jesus. But it is more than a term of devotion. It is also the expression of the finality of God's redemptive act in him and of the conviction that, as the victor over all that denies the power of God, he is installed at the Father's right hand, sharing in his authority and supremacy.

This is what the exaltation has guaranteed and accomplished, and the speech of Peter in Acts 2 is a careful explanation of how Christians can proclaim that he is both their Lord and the Lord over all. In him the hopes of Psalm 110.1 are fulfilled and Jesus is now Lord in the full sense that that psalm expected. In a real way, therefore, Jesus becomes Lord at the exaltation in a manner that he was not so before. Earlier, as is clear from the Lucan account of the call of Peter (5.1–11), his lordship was found in a personal bond between him and his disciples. This still remains, but to it is added a universal sovereignty which has been accomplished through his exaltation. Now, what was a personal recognition is universalized and made actual when Jesus takes up his place at the right hand of God. The proclamation to those outside needs some explanation; the conviction of the Christian group needs some justification if it is to be held in spite of the seeming contradiction provided by later events. This Luke gives by his account of the ascension which is the event which realizes what the disciples had maintained was always true.

For Luke's Gospel presents a path to the establishment of that lordship which the disciples recognize to be his. The Gospel is a journey to Jerusalem where the *exodos* is to be accomplished by which he enters into his glory (9.31; 24.26). The glory which is seen at the transfiguration is a foretaste of that which is to become permanent at the ascension (9.32; Acts 1.9). Until then the Lord is 'constrained' (12.50). It is not until the third day that he is 'perfected' (13.32). The thought of the speeches in Acts which describes Jesus in terms of an inspired man is characteristically Lucan (Acts 2.22; 3.13; 4.10; 10.38). The life of Jesus is a career which leads to his exaltation and makes it possible.

Luke's understanding, however, does not allow for any deification; Jesus does not become other than what he was before. What happens is that his victory is achieved and that his status as Lord over all is accomplished. But he himself remains as he was before, the individual Christ, for the Third Gospel moves wholly within the sphere of Old Testament thought. It is this which fashions Luke's understanding at this point and, more especially, the ideas suggested by Psalm 110.1. This makes it possible for Luke to call both God and Jesus 'Lord', and at times it is difficult to determine to whom he is referring. But this does not mean that Jesus becomes God or that he is given a divine status by Luke.[8] The Psalmist calls both God and the king 'Lord' but he does not give equality to the two.[9] In the same way, Luke sees Jesus as wholly subordinate to the Father,[10] given a share in the Father's authority, but one which is derived from the Father. He is still the instrument of the Father and is still called his servant (Acts 3.26; 4.30).

Nevertheless, there is a clear relationship between Jesus and the worshipping community. Though Luke's exalted Lord remains an individual, addressing the worshippers and standing over against them, and though his real sphere is a heavenly one, there is a firm link between him and those who believe in him. The Lord does not dwell in either the individual or the community, it is true, and the words to Paul at his conversion are not characteristic of Luke's thought, but he appears in visions (Acts 9.10; 18.9; 22.18; 23.11), and adds to the number of the saved (Acts 18.10). Preaching and baptism are in his name (Acts 8.16; 9.29; 19.5), and men call on the name of the Lord (Acts 9.14; 9.21; cf. 7.59). In times of trial, he himself gives 'a mouth and wisdom' (21.15). The spirit is an indirect link between Jesus and the community. It does not mediate him, but too much should not be made of this, for Luke's understanding of the Spirit is almost completely centred upon its function of empowering eschatological witness to the Lord.[11]

Luke's use of Lord allows for an expression of the disciples' response to Jesus and an empowering of their lives by his presence. Though his thought is usually dominated by Old Testament concepts so that he does not always give full expression to the experience of the early Christian community, he does at this point strain his Old Testament vehicles to their fullest extent and his thought about an 'absent Christ' or an 'individual Christ' should not be pressed too far to the exclusion of ideas which suggest a much deeper relationship between Jesus and the Christian community.

THE CHRIST

But if Luke's use of Lord places the emphasis upon the present, exalted Jesus and represents the response of a worshipping community, it is nevertheless imperative for him to show that the Jesus of history is capable of bearing such a value judgement and that the earthly life does not invalidate this but rather demands it. For this reason, the second most characteristic title of Jesus to be found in Luke–Acts is that of 'Christ'. The fact that it never appears as a proper name, however, and that even the name 'Jesus Christ' is used only very occasionally, shows that he deliberately retains its use as a title so that it becomes the explicit statement of his belief in Jesus as the full and complete instrument of God and as the fulfilment of legitimate Old Testament promises. In Luke it retains this technical reference throughout.[12]

However, though he uses it frequently, there is little to suggest that he regards it as in itself an adequate expression of the Christian commitment to Jesus. In his version of the trial before the high priest (22.66–71), he divides Mark's single question into two, so that Jesus' acceptance of the title 'Christ' is seen as only a preliminary which is expanded by him through reference to his exaltation and which then leads on to his recognition as Son of God. So far from pointing to the identity of meaning contained in the titles, as Conzelmann has maintained, this Lucan device suggests that he regarded 'Christ' as in itself unable to convey the full significance of Jesus.[13] Its inadequacy lay in the fact that it was not able to do full justice to the exaltation.

Nevertheless, it was essential for him to establish that Jesus did fulfil messianic expectations, for if he could not be seen to be Messiah, Luke's wider claims would fall to the ground. Luke therefore sets out to describe Jesus as being that supreme instrument of God which is implied by the messianic designation, to show that he really was and is the 'Lord's anointed' (Acts 4.26). What has caused this is the exaltation (Acts 2.36; 13.33), which can virtually be said to be the point at which Jesus became Messiah, not in the sense that he was not Messiah during his time on earth, but in the way that Luke's Gospel describes the earthly Jesus as in the process of becoming what in fact he already was. For Luke's use of 'Messiah', like his Christology as a whole, is primarily functional, and his aim is to prove that the career of Jesus is capable of being accepted as truly messianic. At his birth, angels acknowledge this status (2.11), his suffering fulfils messianic prophecies (24.46), because he is and was Messiah his resurrection was inevitable (Acts 2.31), he is confirmed as Messiah by his exaltation (Acts 2.36), as Messiah he will come again (Acts 3.20). His was, throughout, a messianic career. Even the universal proclamation is drawn into the closest possible connection with his messianic status (24.47).

Luke's usage here is apologetic and is dominated by the fact that he is engaged in polemic which is designed to establish that belief in Jesus as Lord is a rational one. He could be Lord only if he were also Messiah and Luke's aim is therefore to show that the life of Jesus was truly the outcome of messianic expectations. He had to discount any suggestions that there were discrepancies between the expectations and their fulfilment in Jesus. His means of doing this was to take the various stages of the career of Jesus and to show that, being controlled by Scripture, they proved him to be Messiah. He uses Scripture both to determine his description of Jesus and also to guarantee the messianic status of what is depicted. This is seen particularly in his description of the passion.[14] But it is important to note that for Luke himself the title 'Christ' when used of Jesus is a secondary one, being not so much an expression of commitment as a statement of belief arising out of an intellectual debate occasioned by disbelief and doubts.

It is this which causes certain discrepancies. So Robinson argues that, whereas Acts 2 dates the Messiahship of Jesus from the exaltation, Acts 3 visualizes it as something reserved for the future and occasioned by the parousia.[15] Again, O'Neill sees a contradiction between the claim of Peter's speech in Acts 2 and the earlier statements that Jesus was always the Christ (Luke 2.11; 9.20; 24.26).[16] But Luke's thought here is controlled by three things—his emphasis on the exaltation, his idea that the life of Jesus is a progression towards that, and his thinking mainly in functional terms. These three things mean that he sees Messiahship primarily in terms of a career, which has to be proved from its various parts and against which certain incidents seem to militate. He is conducting a disputation in which the various parts have to be put together and seen as a whole. He can remain with the seeming inconsistencies because for him 'Christ' is a secondary term, used nearly always in an *argumentum ad hominem*, expressing the conviction that Jesus is truly God's decisive instrument and that the details of his career prove this rather than confound it.

But the way in which he uses these two titles suggests that his argument is directed primarily towards Christian doubters rather than to unbelievers. *Ho kurios* is the primary value judgement; its use includes a confession of faith and a submission on the part of the user. The fact that he introduces it into the narrative of the gospel suggests that he and his readers already share a common basis of faith, the understanding of which he can take for granted even though he seeks to reawaken their response. *Ho christos* is a supplementary title. Whereas Luke's reinterpretation of Christian eschatology is designed to answer doubts as to the lordship of Jesus in the light of disappointments, his description of Jesus as 'the Christ' is made in order to answer those doubts about his status which were occasioned by the circumstances of his career. The career is not contrary to one who was the 'Christ of God'

(9.20) and is therefore no compelling embarrassment to those who would call him Lord.

THE SUFFERINGS OF JESUS

The crucial problem remains of course the fact that Jesus was crucified, for it was at this point that the stumbling-block to belief was still centred and, if Luke's readers were to be confirmed in their faith, it was essential that some justification for this should be given. However, his apology is not concentrated upon the death itself, the blame for which is often laid firmly at the feet of the Jews (Acts 2.23b; 3.14; 4.10–11), but is concerned rather with the suffering as a whole.[17] Jesus was 'delivered up according to the definite plan and foreknowledge of God' (Acts 2.23). Men united against him, to do only 'what God's hand and plan had predestined to take place' (Acts 4.28). Suffering puts its stamp upon the whole life of Jesus so that it is foreseen in Simeon's witness to the infant (2.35) and is foreshadowed in the prologue to the ministry provided by the rejection at Nazareth (4.28–9). It is a prominent theme in Luke's account of the journey to Jerusalem.

The idea of a journey is, of course, already present in Mark 10, and verse 32 of that chapter points to the suffering and glorification: 'And they were on the road, going up to Jerusalem, and Jesus was walking ahead of them and they were amazed, and those who followed were afraid.' Luke, however, has expanded the significance of the journey so that it takes up about a third of his first volume (9.51—19.44). The reason for this emphasis and expansion is twofold. In the first place, he presents the events in Jerusalem as the outcome of Israel's hopes, the final act of God on her behalf, and the conclusion and climax of his saving work which was begun in the Jewish nation with Abraham and continued with David (1.32–5, 54–5, 73–4). Now is God's eschatological visitation of his people. Jesus is the conclusion of that saving progression which the history of Israel has unfolded. It is therefore both historically and geographically a movement towards the place where those hopes were always expected to be realized. Secondly, Jerusalem is the goal towards which Jesus' own life is directed, for it has to be the place of his glorification, the place where he enters into his kingdom. Jesus' historical progression towards glorification is represented as an actual journey which underlines the necessity and reality of what is to happen in that city. Eschatology is worked out in Jerusalem.[18]

But Jerusalem is also the place of the suffering which, as alone the means to that glorification, is the necessary prelude to it. Suffering and glory are thus inextricably drawn together. Conzelmann, believing that thought about suffering is central here, maintains that Luke's concern is to cast this centrality in the form of a journey.[19] But though this rightly sees the importance of the theme of suffering in this central section, it fails to see the importance Luke gave to it as the journey to the eschatological event and does not give full value to the diversity of the material which it contains.

Luke's apologetic interest in the suffering can be seen at three points. When, in the apocalyptic discourse, at 17.24–5, he brings together the passion and the parousia, this is the only place in the Synoptic Gospels where such a relationship is explicitly established.[20] The historical Jesus and the Christ of faith are fully linked so that, on the one hand, the passion is seen as the guarantee of the parousia and, on the other, the parousia is brought in as added proof of the necessity and validity of the sufferings of Jesus.

Secondly, the problem presented by the suffering of Jesus is emphasized by Luke's stressing that the disciples constantly failed to understand its necessity. While in the first prediction of the passion he omits the Marcan rebuke to Peter (9.18–22 cf. Mark 8.27–33), this is done, not to cover up the disciples' lack of understanding, but out of respect to them. Luke clearly places a premium on them. Nevertheless, at the second and third predictions, Luke emphasizes their complete failure to understand what is being foretold (9.43–5; 18.31–4). Comprehension comes only with the resurrection. At the tomb, the two men remind the women how Jesus had foretold his sufferings, but when the women returned to tell 'all this' to the disciples, 'these words seemed to them an idle tale and they did not believe them' (24.6–7, 11). It is not until they are met by the risen Lord, who repeats his earlier words about the necessity of the suffering, that the penny drops. The suffering makes sense only in the light of the exaltation. When that is accepted, then a rationale of it can be given. Luke undoubtedly writes this up with the problems of his readers very much in mind. He is aware that they are faced, through the sufferings of Jesus with a real *skandalon*; he shows that their problems are not new but were formidable even to the first disciples. It is only when Jesus is first seen as Lord that the sufferings can be seen to make sense.

Finally, at the third prediction of the Passion (18.31–4) Luke adds that what is to happen to Jesus at Jerusalem is to be an accomplishment of what 'is written of the Son of man by the prophets'. 'For he will be delivered to the Gentiles, and will be mocked and shamefully treated, and spat upon; they will scourge him and kill him, and on the third day he will rise. But they understood none of these things; this saying was hid from them, and they did not grasp what was said.' Here we come to Luke's basic reason for the inescapable *dei* of the sufferings and his ultimate justification of their validity, namely that they are required by Scripture and so are to be viewed as the fulfilment of scriptural expectations. This is what Jesus says to the disciples after the resurrection (24.7, 26, 46) and so it becomes the heart of the apostles' own approach and justification after the ascension (Acts 3.18; 26.22–3).

But what Scriptures does the Evangelist have in mind? Overall, in view of this Lucan emphasis, he gives remarkably little explicit reference. He takes over the Marcan use of Psalm 118.22 (20.17, Acts 4.11, cf. Mark 12.10), adds to the Marcan pointers to Psalm 22 in the passion narrative (23.35, 36), and makes use of the allusions to Deuteronomy 21.22 (Acts 5.30; 10.39; 13.29). Fulfilment of prophecy plays a large part in his account of the death of Jesus. The sun is darkened as in Amos 8.9 and Jesus' last saying is given in terms of Psalm 31.5. His words to the women who accompany Jesus to his crucifixion depict the prophecy of Hosea 10.8 as guaranteed by the cross even though its fulfilment remains for the future.

More generally, however, Luke shows that the sufferings are required by the scriptural pattern which can be gathered from the careers of the earlier of God's servants. Suffering was integral to Joseph (Acts 7.9–10), Moses (Acts 7.27–9), Elijah (9.54), Jonah (11.30, 32), and John the Baptist (3.18–20). He emphasizes that the prophets as a whole were persecuted (6.23). Jerusalem killed the prophets and stoned those who were sent to her (13.34). Whereas in Matthew the Wisdom saying refers to the persecution and killing of Christian witnesses, Luke applies it to the prophets and servants of old (11.49–51 cf. Matt. 23.34–6). This pattern determines, not only the career of Jesus, but also that of his followers (Stephen, Acts 7.60; Peter, Acts 12.17; Paul, Acts 9.16) and it is required of all Christians (Acts 14.22). But it is the Suffering Servant pasages to which Luke goes most obviously, for these make this common pattern explicit and by way of them it can be applied most fully to Jesus.

THE SERVANT

Use of Servant imagery is not widespread in Acts, but its appearance in what is to be understood as the definitive apology to the Jewish people in Acts 3, in the apostolic prayer of Acts 4, and in the account of the first tentative evangelistic steps outside Israel in Acts 8, suggests that it occupied an important place in Luke's thought. Though the use of *pais* in the Apostolic Prayer is determined primarily by its liturgical context,[21] the close link in thought between the prayer and the speech in chapter 3 suggests that the Suffering Servant is also in mind, and enables the Servant idea to be something of an umbrella title which makes a link with the Old Testament Servant figures as a whole and, more especially, throws some kind of a bridge between the Servant of Isaiah and the messianic, Davidic Servant.[22] Acts 3 alludes to Deutero–Isaiah, for it refers explicitly to Jesus as one who suffered and was glorified, who was delivered up and denied. His mission is in the first place to Israel, but God's promise to Abraham, which he is said to fulfil, ensures that it does not end there (3.25–6). The explicit condition which centres the Servant imagery in the suffering is important for, as Longenecker points out, though direct quotations from the Servant Songs are applied to him in five places in the New Testament, only the Lucan quotes 'directly connect Jesus with a suffering servant concept as well as a servant motif'.[23] For Luke, the primary (though not, as we shall see, the only) significance of the Servant is to be found in the fact that he suffers. This is clear, not only in his use of Isaiah 53.7–8 at Acts 8.32–3, but also in the direct quotation from Isaiah 53.12 at Luke 22.37. He writes up the episode of the two swords as a fulfilment of this prophecy, and the difficult phrases *hikanon estin* at 22.38 and *Eate heōs toutou* at 22.51 are probably meant to draw attention to this. He brings the Servant idea to the fore in his narrative of the Last Supper and links it to the suffering (22.15, 27) and adds

Servant allusions to his description of the crucifixion (23.32, 33, 34, 41).

At the cross the comment of the centurion expresses the belief that Jesus dies as the Suffering Servant. Luke states that, by his witness, the centurion *edoxazen ton theon* and, since he elsewhere uses this phrase to indicate significant responses to God's action in Christ (7, 16, Acts 11.18), its appearance here suggests that he was underlining the validity of the centurion's value judgement, *ontōs hō anthrōpos houtos dikaios ēn* in 23.47. Kilpatrick suggests that full allowance is made for this by translating *dikaios* as 'innocent', thereby seeing it as Luke's definitive piece of political apologetic which argues that at this crucial point in time the representative of the Roman power was compelled to acknowledge the politically innocuous nature of the founder of Christianity.[24] However, Luke's use of *dikaios* elsewhere suggests that, though it incorporates the idea of innocence, its meaning is not exhausted by this, but that when it is used of individuals it has a religious connotation which describes a piety towards God especially in relation to his revelation towards Israel. In this way, it speaks of Simeon (2.25), Joseph (23.50), and Cornelius (Acts 10.22). Elizabeth and Zechariah were both 'righteous before God, walking in all the commandments and ordinances of the Lord blameless' (1.6). In more general terms it is used of the 'just' in contrast to the disobedient (1.17), of the resurrection of the just (14.14. Acts 24.15), of the ninety-nine who need no repentance (15.7). The parable of the Pharisee and the Publican was told to some 'who trusted in themselves that they were righteous' (18.9). Here again it is a question of what is primarily a God-ward relationship. Only once in Luke is it possible that such a value is not uppermost, when it is used of the spies who *hupokrinomenous heautous dikaious einai* (20.20), yet even here, in view of the fact that their hypocrisy lies in their pretending to seek after the way of God (20.21), the emphasis is still on a piety which is oriented towards God.

This is supported by Luke's use in Acts of *dikaios* as a title of Jesus. In Acts 3.14 it is used to contrast Jesus with one who is a murderer and so contains a declaration of his innocence.[25] Nevertheless, it refers back to the Servant in verse 13, is expanded into 'the Holy and Righteous one', and then is paralleled by the title 'Author of Life'. These things suggest that it therefore points to the full Servant function of Jesus and that the main emphasis of the title is not exhausted by the idea of innocence. It conveys the thought that Jesus is indeed the true agent of God to Israel.

At Acts 22.14 it is not a question of innocence. Here, again, it may have messianic as well as Servant overtones which is probably also the case at Acts 7.52.[26] Since *pais* has overtones of Davidic sonship as well as Servanthood, so *dikaios* has the same double reference. It is precisely this which gives it further appeal for Luke, but, just as in his use of *pais* the Servant motif is fundamental, and gives it its distinctive content, so with *dikaios*, whatever other significance it may contain it is interpreted in terms of the Suffering Servant.

We conclude therefore that Luke means the centurion's witness to be an expression of the Servant nature of Jesus, that his introduction points to it as a definitive statement, and that the translation 'righteous' makes full allowance for this. 'Innocent' is preferable only if the apologetic purpose were uppermost in Luke's mind at this point and, as we shall see below, this is unlikely.[27]

But if Luke turned to the Servant aspect of Jesus in the first instance because it gave a reason for his sufferings which could then be claimed as the fulfilment of Scripture's requirements, his use of the Servant concept does not stop there, but widens out to become his most complete means of expressing the whole significance of the person of Jesus and of God's action through him. For him a Servant Christology is comprehensive. In the first place, it allows the actual history of the Christian mission to be set out as the fulfilment of the divine plan. Simeon witnesses to Jesus as

> a light for revelation to the Gentiles,
> and for glory to thy people Israel (2.32).

Isaiah's songs proclaim both the restoration of Israel and the wider witness to the nations. Jesus' ministry is therefore directed in the first instance to Israel, but his death enables a declaration of faith to be made by one who is not a Jew. His exaltation accomplishes the restoration of the people of God. This is proclaimed to the Jews first (Acts 3.25). The first outside preaching is by witness of the Servant songs (Acts 8.32, 33) and from them Paul justifies his concern with the Gentiles (Acts 13.47)[28]

Secondly, the Servant career provides a programme in the light of which the ministry of Jesus can be presented and clarified. Here Luke's source is Isaiah 61.1–2, which Jesus quotes at the beginning of his ministry (4.18–19) and which Luke of course would have understood as part of the whole Servant description. This passage presents a Spirit-filled prophetic figure who is the proclaimer of God's salvation, and it is in these terms that the distinctive element in Luke's portrait is constructed. Jesus' birth is the action of the Spirit (1.35), and his baptism emphasizes the complete and objective nature of his inspiration (3.22). After the baptism, the Spirit leads him into the wilderness for the temptation (4.1), his ministry begins in the power of the Spirit (4.14) and at the synagogue at Nazareth he announces it in these terms (4.16). Acts 10.38 tells how 'God anointed Jesus of Nazareth with the Holy Spirit and with power' and that this issued in a ministry of preaching and healing. Actually, however, Luke's references to the Spirit-inspiration of Jesus, though distinctive in the gospels, are less than might be expected for, in keeping with the clearly-defined understanding of the Spirit's function which he shows in Acts, he places the emphasis, not so much upon the Spirit-possession of Jesus throughout his ministry as upon seeing the Spirit as the sign of the eschatological action of God in Jesus and the means whereby he is empowered to be it. The Servant idea as a whole increases the concentration upon Jesus as the instrument of God and Isaiah 61 emphasizes the centrality of the preaching of the reign of God which Luke presents as so important a part of Jesus' ministry (4.43 cf. 4.15; 9.1; 10.9).

Finally, Luke's portrait of Jesus in terms of Servant gives full scope for him to emphasize the centrality of the idea of the exaltation and so to lead into the ministry which is to proceed from that. Isaiah 52.13 has talked of the glorification of the Servant, from which there is envisaged a successful ministry of near-universal proportions. (Isaiah 52.13–15; 53.11–12a.) Luke takes this up and uses it as the means of linking the career of Jesus before and after his exaltation so that his ministry in Palestine becomes truly the *archē* of something which he continues through his followers.[29] The active effective ministry of Jesus is taking place in the present (Acts 13.26 cf. 5.31).

THE CROSS

But the very fact that Luke has made such a comprehensive use of the Servant figure, so that the career of Jesus is seen predominantly in its terms, makes it all the more surprising that he avoids all reference to it at just that point where he might be expected to have found it most helpful. He does not go to the Servant Songs to explain the death of Jesus and he firmly avoids any mention of the vicarious benefits of the Cross. This can only be deliberate on his part for, as we have seen, his interest is in the sufferings of Jesus in general and he does not concentrate upon the death. Quotations from the Songs give no hint of its redemptive value, and in his use of Mark he omits those passages which give a specific evaluation of its significance. Mark's *lutron anti pollōn* is replaced by 'I am among you as one who serves' (Luke 22.27 cf. Mark 10.45). This may be because some other source was preferred to Mark, though even then one of the reasons which made for this preference must have been his desire to avoid Mark's phrase.[30] It is more likely, though, that he modelled his account in chapter 22 on the lines of Mark 10, that he transferred it to this crucial setting in order to enhance the Servant character of the sufferings, and that he shortened the episode in order to describe the Servant career in such a way that its significance, though culminating in the death, is not to be found in that alone. For Luke omits not only *lutron anti pollōn* but also the reference to the cup and baptism of Jesus, for these savour too much of sacramentalism whereby a disciple is incorporated into Christ through his death. In Luke, the Lord and the disciple stand over against each other. Jesus is baptized by death (12.50) but the Evangelist places no special saving significance upon that, and he is reticent about the death of the martyrs. It is the witness of Stephen rather than his martyrdom which enables him to have a preview of the Son of man (Acts 7.55).[31]

The same reason suggests that Luke wrote the account of the Last Supper in the form of the shorter text. (22.14–19).[32] The climax of the meal comes in the breaking of bread, which is seen as the guarantee of the presence of the exalted Lord, who is to be made known in this action (22.19; 24.35). The meal therefore looks forward to the breaking of bread in the early Church (Acts 2.42, 46; 20.7) where the presence of Christ is guaranteed and where the emphasis is upon the anticipation of the eschatological banquet which it provides (22.16, 18). Luke does not see the eucharist's witness to salvation as forging a link with a past event but as guaranteeing the presence of the living Lord who grants its participants a future membership in the kingdom of God.

Only on one occasion, that of Paul's farewell speech to the elders of the Ephesian church, does Luke give any saving value to the death of Christ (Acts 20.28). This speech, however, contains not only Luke's testimony to his hero, Paul, but also the apostle's witness to the Church of Luke's day. It is Luke's defence of Paul against those who have been belittling the apostle and as such is an accommodation to Paul's beliefs rather than an expression of his own theology.[33]

But why has Luke avoided all references to the redemptive significance of the death of Jesus and the vicarious expressions that should have been suggested by his use of the Servant idea? Lampe has pointed out that the Septuagint version puts less emphasis here than does the Hebrew,[34] but 1 Peter 2.24, using the Septuagint, comes out with a very strong statement.[35] The reason can only be that Luke's thinking here is controlled by his Christology which has its emphasis, not on the past life of Jesus, but in the present reality of the living Lord. He does not look back to any event in the life of Jesus to give a guarantee of salvation but finds it in the contemporary activity of the Lord whose name brings redemption. For Jesus saves by virtue of his exaltation and it is from this that his saving work proceeds as it enables men to come under his sway in the present. The cross is not the means of salvation; what comes nearest to being that is the act of exaltation accomplished at the ascension. But even the ascension as a past event has saving significance only as it accomplishes the present status and activity of the Lord. Because Jesus is Lord, men can now live their lives under the shadow of the kingdom.

But this does not mean that Luke takes a negative view of the cross or that he does not find a place for it in his theological understanding of God's action in Jesus.[36] His theology of the present redeeming Lord means, indeed, that he can put no saving value upon it as a past event. He therefore uses it to bring out the folly and disobedience of the Jews. Nevertheless, it must not be allowed to go against the claims made on behalf of Jesus, and so it is included firmly within those things which were decreed by God about the Messiah. It is the climax of the sufferings. But its positive value lies in that it alone made the resurrection, and consequently the ascension, possible. Through it, Jesus was able to enter into his glory (24.26), to be raised as was expected of the Messiah (Acts 2.31) and so to be enabled to sit at God's right hand. Suffering and glory are inextricably interwoven in Luke so that his understanding of the cross underlines its reality and necessity in the life of Jesus, and also provides a pattern which Christians are called upon to follow (Acts 14.22). Suffering, culminating in death, becomes the means of glorification. For Christians, the suffering, crucified Messiah alone gives meaning to the lives they are compelled to lead; for Jesus himself, the cross is the link which brings his whole career into a unity by which Jesus of history and the Lord of glory, the Christ of faith, can be held together. It alone enables the one to flow into the other and for the whole to make sense.

THE PROPHET

Since Luke sees the earthly life of Jesus as the preliminary to the ascension, he is able to describe it in terms of the lives of the Old Testament servants of God for, though Jesus is the culmination of their line, until the exaltation he is not other than them. His life and activity could be described in their terms, and it is this which determines the Evangelist's presentation of Jesus as a prophet. Though his taking over of the transfiguration story from Mark, and his use of Deuteronomy 18 at Acts 3 and 7 suggest that he was familiar with the tradition which saw Jesus as the eschatological prophet of the End-time, there is little to show that this is the primary idea he wished to convey when he describes Jesus in prophetic terms.[37] His use seems to be less in order to present him as the eschatological prophet of a particular expectation than to describe him as a prophetic person whose history is bound up with the Old Testament prophets, who is one with them, whose person is described as being like theirs, and who represents the climax of God's continuing saving activity through them. In Luke's account of the transfiguration, Moses and Elijah are associated with the glory of Jesus and point him towards his *exodos* (9.31-2). Jesus is closely linked to these earlier prophets who are involved in his destiny and in some sense determine it. In Acts 3,

Jesus is one with the prophets in that he fulfils their expectations (verses 18, 21 and 24), and is of the same kind as the prophet Moses (verse 22). Since those addressed are described as the 'sons of the prophets' (verse 25), they should respond to the one who is the climax of the prophetic line and hopes. Deuteronomy is again quoted in Stephen's speech (Acts 7.37) but once more, it is not primarily to present Jesus as the eschatological prophet but to link him to Moses and, through him, to the prophetic line. The whole passage is concerned to account for the rejection of Jesus by the Jews and the reason for the inclusion of the Deuteronomic reference is to show that this was of one piece with the Jewish rejection of Moses who, though approved by God, was cast aside by the rebellious, disobedient chosen people (7.35, 39).

Luke therefore does not use the prophet of the End-time as a technical description of Jesus. His interest is rather in describing Jesus as a prophetic person whose ministry and person are one with those of the prophets of old. At Emmaus, the two describe his life as that of 'a prophet mighty in deed and word before God and all the people' (24.19). Jesus speaks of himself as a prophet (13.33) and, since Jerusalem kills the prophets, she will kill him also (13.34). At Nain, in response to the miracle, the people glorify God saying, 'A great prophet has arisen among us' and 'God has visited his people' (7.16). Ellis interprets this as an inadequate response,[38] but it is unlikely that Luke himself understood it thus. It echoes the words of Zechariah (1.68): in this episode, Luke for the first time calls Jesus Lord (7.13); it provides the basis for Jesus' witness of himself to John (7.22). The irony of 7.39 shows that Luke regards the prophetic character of Jesus, when recognized, as affording a true description of him.

In particular, Luke links Jesus to Moses and Elijah. Like Moses, he is a spirit-filled figure (4.14), chooses out seventy (10.1), takes part in an exodus (9.31), and is rejected by those to whom he is sent (7.23).[39] Like Elijah, he goes outside the confines of his own people (4.25), raises a widow's only son (7.12), has the ability to call down fire from heaven (9.54), and at the last is carried up into heaven, from where his spirit comes upon his followers.

But in all this, Luke describes Jesus in terms of Elijah and Moses rather than as a new Moses or a new Elijah, for he does not see him as taking the place of the old but as linked closely to it. He is careful not to present him as a new Moses either superseding the Law or giving it a new, fuller interpretation. The Matthaean picture of Jesus deepening the Law and even pointing out its inadequacies is totally absent in Luke, and he is not presented as establishing a new covenant, but rather as bringing the old to fulfilment.[40] Again, Luke does not put him forward as the eschatological Elijah, the fulfilment of Malachi 4.5. It is true that he avoids the Marcan presentation of John the Baptist in these terms (Mark 9.13) even though he shows himself aware of this identification by describing John as working 'in the spirit and power of Elijah' (1.17). But, equally, this explicit identification is not made of Jesus. His use is more fluid and is designed to link Jesus to Moses and Elijah as the supreme representatives of the prophetic line. He is one with them rather than superseding them, and Luke implies that at the transfiguration Peter is right to suggest that three tabernacles should be made, for the three are linked in a permanent bond (9.33).[41]

Luke then sets out to present Jesus as a prophetic person and his ministry as the fulfilment of those of the earlier prophets. This means that Jesus is linked to them in the closest possible way and that their ministries are given a saving value. What differentiates Jesus from them is his exaltation, but even then he is not wholly other than the glorified Moses and Elijah (9.31–2) Even then his unity with them is not broken (Acts 3.22). Luke's Jesus is controlled by Old Testament categories which are used to present him as the climax of Israel's saving history.

THE OLD TESTAMENT

All this points to the crucial part which the Old Testament played in determining the way Luke chose to present Jesus of Nazareth. Its influence dominates his outlook so that it controls, and at times even restrains, his account of salvation through Christ.[42] The reason for this was, in the first instance, the sheer practical necessity of bringing conviction to his belief that Jesus was the Christ. Schubert has shown that proof from prophecy played a fundamental part in Luke's writings, so that the relation between prophecy and its fulfilment in Jesus became one of the determining factors in his work.[43] This of course centred around the cross, but it embraces the birth (1.70), the course and nature of his ministry (4.18–30), the progress to Jerusalem (13.33), the resurrection (24.46), the ascension (Acts 2.34–5), the gift of the Spirit (Acts 2.17–21), and even the universal mission (24.47). All these things are seen as the fulfilment of prophetic expectations but, since they are this, they are controlled by those expectations and described in their terms. While these provide a fair enough means for an approach to the person of Jesus during his earthly life, they are limited as vehicles for expressing the full reality of the Christian experience of Jesus as the glorified Lord. They do in fact inhibit a complete description of the experience of the indwelling of Christ and of the Spirit. Though, as we have seen, there is more thought in Luke on the present activity of the ascended Christ than is sometimes allowed, his descriptions here are not always happy, because he has not let the instruments of the new dispensation break through the limitations imposed upon them by the expectations of the old. Luke would perhaps have been on firmer ground here if he could have learned from Paul a little more about the tensions between promise and fulfilment. But it is important to note that any inadequacy on this score is to be accounted for, not by any accommodation to the political or intellectual requirements of the time, for Luke was not trimming his sails and producing an emasculated version of Christianity, to appeal to upholders of the Roman power, but because of his involvement in the Old Testament.[44]

For here again, though the necessity to prove Jesus as the Christ from the Old Testament was increased by the circumstances of the times in which he was writing, it would be to misunderstand Luke completely if it were felt that this necessity was the cause of his concern with the Scriptures. The depth of the Old Testament's influence upon him suggests, not that he came to it by way of Christ so that he used it primarily as a source-book to support his beliefs, but that it had a deep and abiding significance for him, and that when he found Jesus, he saw him as the fulfilment of promises which were already real to him, and as the climax of a saving activity which had already embraced him. For the most distinctive thing about Luke's use of the Old Testament is that from it he gained a theology of history which saw world history as being open to the promptings of God, and that of Israel as being the sphere of God's activity which was destined to have a universal significance. Luke writes his own history in terms of Israel's history and represents Jesus as the climax of God's action

in that. Luke's infancy narratives witness to this; his story of the
progress of Jesus to Jerusalem links him to the history of Israel;
his account of the ministry is determined, not by its being the
prelude to early church history as it is recorded in the Acts of the
Apostles, but by its being represented as the climax and fulfilment
of the history of the Jewish people. Luke's life of Jesus is controlled
by its relation to the history of Israel. Acts does not present the
Jesus of history but the exalted Lord, for it is the exalted universal
Lord who now saves, not the prophet of Galilee and Jerusalem.
The Jesus of history makes the exalted Lord possible, and is
remembered as showing who the exalted one is and what God's
salvation through him really means. Only because the Lord is
Jesus can men have hope and knowledge that salvation brings
love, peace, and forgiveness. Only because Jesus found men like
Zacchaeus, women like the one who was a sinner, and declared
that through his ministry God was seeking the prodigal, only
because his was the life of a servant, can they come to have joy in
the Lord. Nevertheless, for Luke the time of salvation is now. The
past is its basis and it remains its guarantee, but salvation is found
not by linking up with a person of the past but by submitting to
the Lord of the present. The 'now' of Jesus at Nazareth is the
present of Luke's contemporaries. Schweizer, in a welcome corrective to much recent explanation of this passage, notes that Luke
says, 'Today, in your hearing, is this scripture fulfilled' (4.21), and
comments: 'Luke therefore looks upon the sacred event as a
message event, that is, as an event that cannot simply be noted
objectively and made a fact of history; it is an event one must
confront as a listener.'[45]

Luke's account of Jesus has its historical dimension because he
sees it as the fulfilment of God's actions in Israel. Jesus' progress
to his exaltation is the last stage of Israel's journey to her eschatological event which is accomplished through the ascension. His
life belongs firmly to the period of Israel and for this reason Luke
can describe him in terms of Israel's earlier witnesses to the
action of God in her midst. This is a basis for a true typological
understanding of Jesus which is controlled by Luke's theologically motivated historical outlook.[46] Typology becomes a wholly
adequate vehicle for his Christology. Elsewhere in the New Testament the Servant figure is not found as an expression of the
person of Jesus, as opposed to an explanation of his work, for its

inadequacy in this direction was all too obvious. Whereas Luke
is happy to call Jesus a prophet, the other evangelists do not see
the term as a suitable description of him for, as Cullmann points
out, whereas the New Testament places the centre of the faith of
the early Church upon the exalted present Christ, the idea of
Jesus as prophet 'actually excludes a continuation of his work in
the present. The exclusively preparatory character of the prophet
of the End-time simply makes a prolongation of his function impossible.'[47] Because of Luke's peculiar concern with the exaltation, this presents no problems for him. Jesus can be completely
at one with the Old Testament saving acts, and typology can become an adequate explanation of the Jesus of history, for the
ascension provides the perfect bridge whereby the Servant and
the Prophet can become the Lord. But nevertheless, Luke's
understanding of Lord remains to safeguard the continuity of the
ascended one with the figure who walked in Palestine, and to see
him still in Old Testament terms.

Luke's typology then is determined by his Christology. In
Matthew Jesus is a new Moses, compared and contrasted with the
Moses of old, but Luke presents him rather in Mosaic terms and
the contrast is lacking. Whereas in Matthew the relationship is
largely controlled by the urgent problem of the Christian's attitude
to the Law, in Luke it is used simply in the service of his theology
of history.[48]

Just how deeply this outlook is embedded in his thought can be
seen from his handling of the transfiguration story (9.28ff). We have
seen how he strengthens the links between Jesus and Moses and
Elijah. He has revised Mark's account in order to view the scene
in the light of Moses' experience on the Mount of God as that is
recorded in Exodus 24 and 34. Whereas in Mark 9.4 it is 'Elijah
with Moses' who appears, Luke 9.30 has 'Moses and Elijah'. The
episode is introduced by the Septuagintal expression *Egeneto
de meta tous logous* (cf. Exod. 34.29). The Lucan account suggests
a more extended period of time than does its Marcan counterpart
(9.28b, 31, 36). In Luke the episode is centred strictly around
Jesus. He takes the disciples, but it is Jesus alone who *anebē eis to
oros*. Here the language reflects Exodus 24 where, though in
verse 13 it is said *Kai anastas Mōusēs kai Iēsous hō parestēkōs
autō*, Joshua falls aside so that the verb in verses 15 and 18
becomes *anabē*. In Luke too the disciples fall aside; they sleep, so

that the emphasis is upon the speaking of Moses and Elijah to
Jesus rather than upon their appearance before the disciples. In
the actual account of the transfiguration, Luke omits Mark's
metemorphōthē and uses *To eidos Tou prosōpou*, so recalling the
description of Moses in Exodus 34.29, 35. His use of the definite
To oros and his mention of the disciples' fear continues the thought
of the Sinai theophany, as does the use of *exodos*. In the salutation,
hō eklelegmenos in place of the Marcan *agapētos* reflects the description of Moses in Psalm 104.26, while *autou akouete* (a trans-
position of the Marcan order) is probably a reminiscence of the
actual text of Deuteronomy 18.15 which played a large part in
Luke's thought.

The pervading influence of the Septuagint upon Luke's writing
has often been pointed out. Schweizer says that he 'practically
speaks the language of the Greek Old Testament, loves phrases
from his Greek Bible, even where he does not refer to them directly
or, as he often does, quote them.'[49] More dispassionately, Sparks
has called him 'an habitual, conscious, and deliberate Septu-
agintalizer'.[50] Less frequently, however, is it suggested that this
is part of his wider use of the Old Testament and that it appears
wholly in the service of that. In other words, his use of the
Septuagint and the way he allows it to come through and shape his
writing is determined less by his dramatic interest—by his sense
of the appropriate, of atmosphere, of what is becoming to any
particular incident—than by his theology which is, as we have
seen, largely determined and controlled by his involvement in the
Old Testament. More especially is this a theology of history which
sees Jesus as the fulfilment of God's saving action in the Old
Testament, the point at which the actual history of Israel finds
its focus and culmination. It is Luke's theology of history which
causes the uneven appearance of the Septuagintalisms. He introduces them at significant points, when he is wanting to emphasize
the solemnity and mystery of what he is proclaiming and its
importance in the history of God's redemptive acts. When Luke
at 9.51–3 begins his account of the journey to Jerusalem, he points
out the reality of the new step in the career of Jesus by bringing
together an 'unusually strong concentration of biblical idioms'.[51]
The account of the ascension at the end of the Gospel has been
called 'one of Luke's most beautiful Septuagintalisms'.[52] The
words of God and of the risen Jesus in Acts are always in a biblical

mould.[53] The final episode of Paul at Rome, his interview with
the Jewish community there, is reported in a manner that is
strongly biblical in tone. The biblical style of these passages links
them firmly to the mystery of God's whole redeeming activity.

But Luke's theology of history is even more clearly apparent in
the way he has allowed his biblical style to be used in its service.
His infancy narratives read like a piece of Old Testament history,
thus linking the birth of Jesus firmly to Israel, but, since they so
clearly portray the fulfilment of Old Testament hopes and
promises, they see him as the eschatological event for the Jewish
people. The life of Jesus presents him in these terms. Luke's
Septuagintalisms in the first part of Acts are again in the service
of his theology, for these chapters present the eschatological renewal of Israel, the appeal to the Jewish people to respond to this,
and the inclusion of representatives of the nations in it.[54] Fulfilment is the prime message that Luke wishes to convey, so what
could be more natural than that he should choose to present it in a
biblical manner? The speech of Peter in chapter 3 is the definitive
appeal to the Jews, and its difficulties are caused by the piling up
of Old Testament imagery, as Luke tries to give value to Jesus
and his significance in terms and ideas derived from the Scriptures
which have found their final meaning in him.[55] The second half
of Acts contains fewer Septuagintalisms because the drama of
salvation now spreads to the Gentile world. The eschatological
event has been detailed. What is now being described is not that
but a secondary testimony which proclaims it and witnesses to
what has already been accomplished.

Luke's theology of history determines also the manner in which
he makes use of Old Testament quotations. These are usually
taken from the Septuagint, though Wilcox has shown that a
number of them have a community of tradition with Targumic
and Samaritan sources (e.g. Acts 7.3, 32; 13.22).[56] It is possible
that Luke may be using forms that have come to him from the
Antiochene church. Yet there are a number of quotations which
are not so easily paralleled, and this suggests that he exercised
some freedom in bringing more unity between the quotation and
its fulfilment in Jesus than its original form allowed. Rese has
shown that Luke does not regard the original form of the text as
sacrosanct, but alters it so that it becomes a more adequate vehicle
for a theological explanation of the person of Jesus.[57] So at Luke

4.18–19 Leaney points out that 'it is surprising to find that a passage introduced specifically as a quotation is in fact composite, made up of Isaiah 61.1; 58.6; 61.2'.[58] This is Luke making Scripture conform more fully to its fulfilment in Jesus. Perhaps the other most important illustration of this is his Pentecost quotation from Joel 2 where he brings out the eschatological significance of what he is describing.[59]

Equally important here is the unity of outlook between the quotation and the episode or speech in which it is embedded, for the quotation usually has a decisive theological influence upon the ideas which Luke expresses. His quotation from Isaiah 61 is a definitive expression of his understanding of the person of Jesus; his idea of the exaltation is controlled by Psalm 110; his thought of the Spirit depends upon Joel 2. The quotations are not peripheral, nor are they 'picture fulfilments' alone, but flow into and control the theology of Luke.

One last influence of the Old Testament upon Luke remains to be noted, namely, its understanding of God, which determines his whole outlook upon the salvation achieved through Jesus. Luke's God is the transcendent creator whom he calls *ho despotēs*. 'Sovereign Lord who didst make the heaven and the earth, and the sea and everything in them' (Acts 4.24 cf. Luke 2.29). Though this may be a Hellenistic form of address, nevertheless, since on the two occasions when he uses it he is writing in a biblical mould, the ideas it conveys are those of the Old Testament.[60] The thought of the transcendent creator comes out strongly in the two speeches before Gentiles, but the contrast between him and the idols continues the thought of Deutero-Isaiah, and the idea of the supreme independence of God is closely paralleled in Stephen's speech (7.41, 48–50), while assertions of his control of the nations is illustrated by Luke's descriptions of the relations of the Roman state to Jesus and his followers.

But Luke's God, though he is the one before whose messengers men respond in fear, is nevertheless himself the Saviour (1.47). The Benedictus proclaims that God himself has visited and redeemed his people by raising up 'a horn of salvation for us, in the house of his servant David' (1.68–9). The source of salvation is God himself who, now as always, redeems his people by raising up men to be his instruments. Jesus is the last and greatest of Israel's line.[61]

It is this understanding of God, grounded completely in its Old Testament proclamation, that is ultimately responsible for the subordinationism and lack of metaphysical speculation which is rightly seen to characterize Luke's Christology.[62] In his earthly life Jesus is wholly obedient to the Father's will (4.43), at his death he commends his spirit into the Father's hands (23.46), it is the Father who raises him (Acts 3.26) and exalts him at his right hand (Acts 2.33), so making him Lord and Christ (Acts 2.36). But though he is Lord, and Stephen, at the point of death, commends himself to him (Acts 7.59, 60), though Christians are those who call upon his name (9.14), he remains subordinate to the Father to whom the Christian's prayer is addressed (Acts 4.24–30). Conzelmann has maintained that this understanding of Luke is focused in his thought of the resurrection. 'The raising of Jesus from the dead is clearly characterized, not as a resurrection, but as an act of "being raised".'[63] This, however, is to go too far. In the first prediction of the Passion he does alter Mark's *anastēnai* to *egerthēnai* (9.22 cf. Mark 8.31). Too much should not be made of this, though, for in the third prediction, where Matthew again has *egerthēsetai*, Luke follows Mark and uses *anastēsetai* (18.33, Matt. 20.19, Mark 10.34). Perhaps more significantly at 24.7 and 24.46, which he appears to regard as fundamental statements, he uses *anastēnai*. In Acts 10.40–1, he can use *ēgeire* and *anastēnai* in close proximity. Nevertheless, in the speeches as a whole, Jesus is almost always treated as the object of an act of resurrection which is accomplished by God. We may therefore go so far with Conzelmann to say that, while Luke does talk of Jesus' 'rising' and does not deliberately avoid such thought, nevertheless, it is more characteristic of him, when he is setting this event within the total saving action, to emphasize it as an act of God which retains the idea of the instrumentality of Jesus. Once more, this is primarily because of the Old Testament's influence. It was this source which determined his presentation of Jesus whom he saw as God's final act for Israel, one with the instruments of the old covenant, and the fulfilment of their hopes. In him, Israel's history reached its eschatological climax.

3

His People Israel

Though Luke's approach provided his contemporaries with an answer to those problems which were caused by the delay of the parousia, and his description of Jesus enabled them to accept his career as messianic, it nevertheless raised in its most acute form the dilemma posed by the failure of the Jews to respond to Jesus. If Jesus really was God's eschatological act for Israel, why had the nation as a whole turned its back upon him? If he really was the Christ who fulfilled scriptural expectations, why did the experts in those Scriptures fail to acknowledge him? If he really was the climax of Israel's history, why was she even now a divided, defeated people? Didn't the failure of the Jews to submit to the Jesus who was proclaimed in the Christian kerygma negate Luke's whole theological position and militate convincingly against his claims? This for Luke is the ultimate paradox—that Jesus is linked firmly to the Jewish nation and yet that nation is still consistent in its refusal to acknowledge him, and he can neither share Paul's hope that the ingathering of the Gentiles will cause the return of Israel, for history has so far shown the emptiness of such speculations, nor can he share the belief of later Christians that the Jews were never really God's people, since Luke's Jesus stands too close to the Jewish nation for him to say that.

Luke's approach is more complex. In some ways he provides a perspective rather than gives an answer to the problem. Nevertheless, in his two volumes, by taking the relations between Jews and Christians as one of his major themes, he shows that the Jewish denial of the Christian claims does not invalidate them, and he presents a way in which Christ's close relationship to the Jewish people and the Jewish refusal of him can be held together, albeit in a somewhat uneasy alliance.

Basically, Luke's perspective here is conditioned by a number

of underlying beliefs which both determine his approach to the
Jewish problem and also shape the telling of his history. These
may be summarized under five heads:

1.   Jesus is the climax of God's saving actions as these were described in the Old Testament. In Jesus, God's promises under the
old covenant were fulfilled. Old Testament history was taken up
into him, and he was controlled by Old Testament expectations
and beliefs.

2.   The true in Israel acknowledged this and saw their piety
leading them to him. Law and Temple were preparatory to him
and pointed to him. Those who were true to the old covenant
were led inevitably to Jesus; those who refused him were showing
their blindness to the instruments of the old Israel.

3.   It was therefore only the disobedience and obstinacy of the
Jews which caused their failure to acknowledge the claims of the
ascended Christ. Such perversity was characteristic of them—it
happened throughout their history, it happened at the crucifixion,
it happened at the time of Paul, and it continues to happen as
Luke writes.

4.   In the work of Jesus, Israel was remade and renewed. God's
eschatological act brought confirmation of the promises but it
also caused divisions within Israel. It was an act whereby Israel
herself was judged as well as confirmed.

5.   Nevertheless, as God's eschatological act to Israel, Jesus was
the fulfilment of God's promise to Abraham. This was not
annulled. The remade Israel does not turn aside from the old
which still has claims upon her. The relationship is still open-
ended. Though there may be little positive hope that Israel as a
whole will repent, the relationship is not closed and Christianity
has not turned aside from its source.

As an assessment of Luke's approach to the Jewish–Christian
problem, these five points make him take a more positive attitude
to Israel than current discussions of his theology tend to attribute
to him.[1] However, they arise from, and are consistent with, two
further points, which have already been discussed, and which are
the basic beliefs against which the rest of his ideas are developed,

namely, his fundamental use of, love for, and assimilation of the Old Testament, and his understanding of the ascension as God's eschatological act which was for Israel and, through her, for the nations. His absorption of the Old Testament, of its history, promises, and expectations, means that he sees Israel as having some permanent validity within the sphere of God's covenantal people. Whether Luke was himself a Jew must remain an open question. At any rate, however he must have been one who was influenced supremely by the Jewish faith, one who loved 'our nation', who was moved by its law and captivated by its Scriptures, one who was led to see in Jesus a fulfilment of its hopes and a widening of its promises. It is scarcely conceivable that one such as Luke who was so immersed in the Old Testament could ever have turned his back upon the nation whose hopes it recorded.

Luke's understanding of Jesus and of God's eschatological act through him means that he cannot be divorced from the history of the Jewish people. Since he is the climax of their history and the fulfilment of God's promises to them, he is not to be separated from the period of Israel, but rather must be understood as both its culmination and its acceptance. He and Israel are bound closely together. But again, since the saving history after the ascension proceeds from it and witnesses to that event, this is not a new period either but the confirmation and establishing of what the ascension has achieved. The ascension binds the whole of God's saving history into a single action and gives meaning to it in its totality. This is the fulfilment of God's promises.[2]

The fact that the eschatological event is an event in time determines the historical mould of his writing. He must take history seriously because, of itself, it could either witness to, or make nonsense of, his claims on behalf of Jesus of Nazareth. Since the movement of Luke's story is therefore important, any attempt to understand his theology must be made, not by taking his episodes in isolation, but by relating them to the place they have in the total work, and the part they play in the overall development. As O'Neill puts it: 'His theology must be looked for primarily in the movement of his history.'[3] This is especially important in attempting to evaluate his attitude to the Jews. For us, however, his history is controlled by his understanding of the ascension, which gives the work its perspective and in relation to which the single episodes must be interpreted.

THE INFANCY NARRATIVES

Conzelmann's neglect of the infancy narratives and his assertion that they contain a theology which is not in keeping with that found in the rest of Luke–Acts[4] brings to the fore the question of the significance of these early chapters of Luke's work. Whatever sources may underlie them, and whatever their original purpose, as they now stand they present a consistent story, and, since Luke was not a slave to his sources, he must have seen them as correct vehicles for his thought. And that there is an overall unity between the theological ideas expressed in them and in the rest of the work seems clear. The titles of Jesus, the way in which he is regarded as God's instrument, the interest in the Old Testament, the presentation of Jesus as God's final promise to Israel, the use of typology, the emphasis upon the Spirit and the understanding of his mode of activity, and the universal outreach of these chapters, all suggest the hand of Luke at least in their final shaping.

Nevertheless, there are tensions between them and the work as a whole. In them, Jesus is assigned a position and titles which, as the total work understands them, are not really his until the exaltation; in them, the Holy Spirit is active in an outpouring which is not elsewhere considered appropriate until after Pentecost. The early chapters have a universal setting and outlook which do not make themselves felt again until the exaltation of Jesus is accomplished.

Yet within these differences, there remains a unity of theological understanding of the nature of Jesus and his work. What really distinguishes the infancy narratives from the rest of the work is the fact that they do not fit into the scheme of gradual historical development that is so apparent in Luke–Acts as a whole. They are not just one episode which begins the narrative, but, instead, view the birth in terms of the total activity of Jesus, and in such a way that the whole career is telescoped into one event. Because of this, the birth is itself described as the eschatological event. The activity of the Spirit, the awakening of prophecy, the presence of angels and of miracles, and the outbursts of joy, all combine to give these narratives a thoroughly eschatological dimension. The birth of Jesus is the outcome of the Spirit's agency, since the very fact of his bestowal is seen as God's final work for Israel. The birth thus sums up the career of Jesus and is given a significance which elsewhere is assigned only to the exaltation.

The infancy narratives are therefore to be seen as Luke's prologue to his whole work and, as such, there is no inconsistency between them and the rest of Luke–Acts. They are the declaration of God's work, the value judgement upon the whole career of Jesus. In them is proclaimed what in the narrative is then justified and explained. If they bring together events which in the narrative are separated because of Luke's theory of progression through history, they are not contradictory to it, but see the work of Jesus in its totality and regard the whole as a single work which is to be included within the sphere of the eschatological. The prologue and the narrative are not to be set over and against each other. In the evaluation of Luke's thought, the infancy narratives cannot be ignored, but neither can they be forced into a pattern derived from the narrative alone.[5] On the contrary, they must exercise some control over the interpretation of the narrative, which has to be understood in the light of them and in such a way that Luke's work is seen to give expression to a unified theology.

The basic purpose of these narratives is to set forth Jesus as God's final action for Israel. In him God has confirmed his earlier promises, met Israel's longings, and brought her history to a triumphant climax. Atmosphere, style, and outlook combine to give an Old Testament setting against which these beliefs can be declared. The canticles proclaim Jesus as the realization of Old Testament expectations as a whole;[6] the promises to Abraham are said to be fulfilled in him (1.54–5, 73–5), thus stressing the permanence of God's presence with the Jewish people (1.55), and Israel's hope, partly personified in David, finds realization in him. This strong assertion of Israel's national hope is implicit in the actual account of the birth of Jesus (2.4, 11), while in the annunciation to Mary the nationalistic expectations are given explicit recognition:

He will be great, and will be called the Son of the Most High; and the Lord God will give to him the throne of his father David, and he will reign over the house of Jacob for ever; and of his kingdom there will be no end' (1.32–3).

From the Temple, when the requirements of the Law are being

carried out, Jewish piety, speaking with the voice of prophecy and inspired by the Spirit, is made to pass its true value judgement upon the child. Temple, Law and prophecy witness to the out-pouring of the Spirit which accompanies the birth of Jesus, so enabling representatives of what they have produced to acknow-ledge Jesus as the answer to those 'looking for the consolation of Israel' and 'to all who were looking for the redemption of Jerusalem' (2.25, 38). This episode shows Luke's belief that the instruments of the old covenant, when they are rightly under-stood, should gather up their adherents and lead them over to Jesus, in whom they find fulfilment and before whom they recognize their role to be but preparatory, but this same episode shows too that Luke sees Jesus as in some sense bound to the Jewish covenant so that he is controlled by its expectations which are to find their realization in him. Luke sees him as being a 'light to the Gentiles' but it is in connection with the universal meaning of Jesus that the 'glory of Israel' is also to be achieved (2.34f). The narratives of the circumcision and of the presentation of the child in the Temple suggest that Jesus himself is accepting his role in the Jewish covenantal community, and the full significance of his mission is acknowledged for the first time at just that point where (as Luke emphasizes) the requirements of the Law are being fully enacted and when he is being incorporated within the sphere of God's initial covenant with his people. In Jesus God takes over the obligations that he laid upon himself under the old covenantal promises.

But though the bond between Jesus and Israel is so close, in that Jesus takes over God's promises to his people and that the representatives of that people acknowledge him—while the instru-ments of the old covenant show that their value lay in pointing to him—nevertheless the infancy narratives show that divisions within Israel are to follow because of the child. Hints of future conflict are never far below the surface. Zacharias must go outside established customs and name his son 'John' (1.61–63); Jesus is laid in the manger because there is no room for him in the inn (2.7); it is shepherds alone who are acquainted with his birth (2.8). At the age of twelve, in the Temple, he is beginning to go beyond the understanding and expectations of the doctors of the Law (2.46–47); it is only those who have entered into a real under-standing of the hope of Israel who acknowledge him (2.25, 38).

The Magnificat speaks of both an exaltation and a rejection, and it is most likely that Luke meant this to include divisions within Israel (1.46–55).[7] Above all, it is Simeon, in the infancy narratives' final and most complete witness to the child, who speaks most definitely of a judgement that is to come upon Israel through Jesus. 'This child is set for the fall and rising of many in Israel' (2.34–5). Jesus will provoke hostility both towards himself and his followers and will be a cause of judgement upon those who are faced with him. Even Mary herself, whether as an individual or as the representative of Israel, is not to escape it.[8] Here for the first time we get a definite assertion by Luke that Israel is not necessarily to be equated exactly with the nation that bears the name. His interest in Abraham allows God's initial covenantal promises to widen out beyond the Jewish people,[9] and to suggest that all within Israel are not automatically included within its embrace.[10] Judgement has always been a feature of God's covenantal promises in the Old Testament whenever the requirements that accompanied the promises were not met. God's covenants with Abraham and David required a response of obedience that was not fundamentally different from that required by Sinai, and judgement is endemic to both types.[11] In seeing Jesus as bringing judgement upon Israel, Luke is being faithful to his Old Testament understanding as well as to the requirements of early Christianity. Nevertheless, his emphasis remains upon a covenantal continuity which is guaranteed by Jesus as the fulfilment of the promise to Abraham, and which is enshrined within a nucleus of the people of Israel.

The same emphases are present in Luke's account of the birth of John the Baptist. By giving a consistent and well-ordered statement of the relations between John and Jesus, these throw light upon the Evangelist's understanding of Israel when she stands before the fact of Christ. The Christ and the immediate forerunner are brought into the closest possible connection and, so closely is John linked with God's activity in Jesus, that the events of his own birth are brought firmly within the sphere of the eschatological. Eschatological elements that surround his birth are to be found in the presence of the Spirit (1.15, 67), of prophecy (1.67), of joy (1.14), of angels (1.11). John is linked with the eschatological return of Elijah (1.17) and is described as the means of the rebirth of prophecy (1.76ff). His birth is closely tied to the birth of Jesus and is itself both a sign of God's final action in that birth and also a part of its eschatological happening (1.35-7).

Nevertheless, John is also placed firmly within the context of Old Testament history and faith. His father is of the temple staff; his birth is announced during the fulfilling of the sacrificial requirements of the old covenant; he himself stands within the line of those earlier enthusiasts for Yahweh whose task it was to recall Israel to her role as his people. His word is to be performed 'in the spirit and power of Elijah' and his birth is described in terms of that of Samson (Judg. 13). John therefore becomes the bridge which binds together Jesus and the Old Testament history of God's action. He emphasizes the incomplete nature of the old covenant unless it leads on to Jesus, but he is also the link through which the expectations of the old covenant control and restrain Luke's understanding of Jesus. Because of John, Jesus and the Old Testament history belong inextricably to each other.

But John's role is clearly subordinate and preparatory. He is the 'prophet of the Most High' (1.76) in contrast to Jesus, 'the Son of the most High' (1.32);[12] he will 'make ready for the Lord a people prepared' (1.17), in contrast to Jesus to whom 'the Lord will give the throne of his father David' (1.32). John will be 'filled with the Holy Spirit even from his mother's womb' (1.15). He is the Spirit-filled prophetic figure whose significance will lie in his proclamation. Jesus, on the other hand, is born by the action of the Spirit (1.35). His birth is itself the significant event. So, when the unborn John hears the voice of the bearer of Jesus he leaps for joy as he acknowledges that action (1.44). When all the narratives surrounding the birth of the herald are told, he himself 'was in the wilderness till the day of his manifestation to Israel' (1.80) and Luke goes on to give undivided attention to the birth of the Messiah.

John's task therefore is to prepare Israel to meet her Messiah and thus enable her to accept him (1.17, 76, 77). So the theme again comes to the surface that not all the historical Israel is thereby God's Israel. John is to restore Israel to her vocation as the people of God, to recall her to her history and to God's covenantal promises. Israel is thereby acknowledged to have fallen away from the path to which God had called her and John's message is to bring her back into the way of obedience:

And he will turn many of the sons of Israel to the Lord their
    God,
and he will go before him in the spirit and power of Elijah,
to turn the hearts of the fathers to the children,
and the disobedient to the wisdom of the just,
to make ready for the Lord a people prepared (1.16–17).

Once more Luke links Jesus and the old covenant together in a
close bond. For the people to accept Jesus, they must accept their
history. If this is done they will inevitably be led to him. Conversely,
a rejection of Jesus means a turning aside from John and from the
Old Testament expectations which produced him. Though Luke's
emphasis is upon the positive work of John in preparing Israel to
accept Jesus, and though Jesus is presented once more as the hope
of Israel, representing God's continuing activity in her so that the
atmosphere is one of expectancy produced by the coming restoration of God's people, his presentation of John's role carries forward the theme that God's eschatological act to Israel results in
divisions within the chosen people because of their disobedience
and inability to respond to God's messengers. Their reaction to
Jesus will not be different from, but will be dictated by, their
reaction to the earlier agents of God's gracious activity among
them.

In the light of the infancy narratives, Conzelmann's belief that
Luke envisaged a change of aeons between the ministries of John
and Jesus must be modified. Luke's Gospel is to be interpreted as
a progressive unfolding in historical form of the themes which the
infancy narratives proclaim. The history is dominated by the
thought of Jesus' progress from his beginnings in Israel's history
to his exaltation, and if, in the scheme of things, the ministries of
Jesus and John seem to be separated in time, the division is of the
same kind as that which later causes Luke in his narrative—though
by no means always in his proclamatory statements—to distinguish between the resurrection and the ascension. Luke uses
history for a progressive unfolding of his beliefs. If he had a fault,
it was that at times he could become a slave to a good idea.

Seen in this way, Luke–Acts as a whole does not contradict
the infancy narratives. In Luke 3, John's ministry follows the
secular dating of the period of salvation which it opens (3.1–2).
As in the infancy narratives, John appears as the immediate pre-

cursor of the Christ though, as in them, he is definitely preparatory to him, presenting a people to Jesus and linking him to
Israel. Luke 16.16 hardly bears the weight that Conzelmann puts
upon it.[13] Luke has taken it from its Matthaean setting (Matt.
11.12–15) because there he wanted to include the additional
verses which take up his theme of the people's acceptance of
John in contrast to the leaders' rejection of him (7.29). The different context of Luke 16.16 means that the verse is no longer concerned primarily with the place of John but is included here in a
section which, though emphasizing the inclusive nature of Jesus'
mission (15.1–2, 7, 10, 32), warns, nevertheless, of the need of
vigilance (16.8–13) and of law (16.18). The new freedom does not
dispense with the Law (16.17); the good news of the kingdom of
God does not bring to an end the Law and the prophets which
reached their climax in John. Verses 16 and 17 together show that
grace and demand are not to be set in antithesis to each other but
that Jesus' preaching of the kingdom completes the old dispensation which runs into it.[14] John, though he is quite definitely preliminary to Jesus, represents the continuity between Jesus and the
old dispensation rather than marking a change of aeons. He does
not proclaim the kingdom because in Luke this has primarily a
transcendental rather than an apocalyptic character and is therefore
properly only the subject of the preaching of Jesus and his
disciples who are able to announce its reality only because of the
events of the ministry of Jesus and its culmination in the ascension.[15] He is not described as Elijah, because Luke does not think
primarily in terms of a new Elijah, the significance of whom is
centred in an apocalyptic function. Jesus himself is described in
terms of Elijah. The changes that Luke makes are accounted for
by his theology of the person of Jesus and of the kingdom rather
than by the demands of salvation history.

The same outlook is found in the references to John in Acts.[16]
In Acts 10.37 the place of John is determined by his part in Jesus'
progress to his exaltation rather than by his witnessing to a change
in epochs. He marks the beginning of Jesus' ministry. In Acts
13.34–5 he is the one who, by linking Jesus to Israel's history,
shows him to be the culmination of it. The episodes of Apollos
and of the Ephesian disciples (18.24—19.7), by their descriptions
of Apollos (18.25) and of the twelve (19.1) suggest a contrast
between a pre- and post-Pentecostal situation rather than between

John and Jesus. The emphasis is wholly upon the bestowal of the Spirit, but Apollos, in spite of his knowing 'only the baptism of John', is already virtually within its sphere.

The use of the infancy narratives modifies Conzelmann's theory of periods in redemptive history so that Luke is seen as having a more positive attitude to the Jews than Conzelmann himself would allow. Jesus is linked firmly to the promises of the old covenant and to the saving work of God which was begun in Old Testament times. The Old Testament expectations retain a controlling influence over the unfolding of his work. More value is then given to the Old Testament period, which is seen not merely as preparatory to Jesus, but is endowed with saving significance. It begins what is completed in Jesus. Finally, such a view means that Israel is still seen as the people of God. Though she must be summoned to become what she is in a message which, on the one hand, brings divisions within her and, on the other, widens her embrace, nevertheless, the Church has not replaced her. There is an uneasy relationship, as both stand within the sphere of God's covenantal promises.

In the infancy narratives, the mission of Jesus is seen in terms of the Servant of Isaiah 42 and 49. There, the Servant, who is himself called Israel, is to restore Israel to the obligations and blessings of her covenantal relationship with Yahweh. There is tension between the nucleus and the whole. The small group has not taken over the privileges of Israel to the exclusion of the rest but, in becoming the firstfruits of Israel, is the means of the restoration of the ethnic group. The infancy narratives suggest that this is how Luke envisaged the relations between the Church and Israel after the flesh. The narrative will unfold how the eschatological event in Jerusalem brought about the first stage of the renewing of Israel, how the mission to Israel was undertaken, and the varying nature of its success. It will maintain that the lack of overall success does not deny the reality of the message, and, when it leaves Paul at Rome, it will have enabled the readers to understand the situation of their own day.

JESUS AT JERUSALEM

Luke casts over a third of his first volume in the form of a journey by Jesus to Jerusalem (9.51—19.44). Since the geographical notices are of the vaguest kind, it must be seen as an artificial construction designed to present Jerusalem as the determined climax of Jesus' ministry for which everything else is preparatory and to which it all leads. The reason is that the eschatological event must take place there, but such an emphasis links the happenings to the history of Israel so that the journey is seen to present the events in Jerusalem as the climax, not only of the life of Jesus, but also of God's covenantal activity in the Jewish people.[17]

Though the elements of confrontation which are so clear in Mark are not altogether absent from Luke, the emphasis rests primarily upon Jesus' taking possession of the city which, in the person of his followers and, in the earlier part of the week, of the crowds, acknowledges him. Thus, in Luke, the entry takes on regal proportions. What in Mark is presented as a somewhat *ad hoc* collection (Mark 11.8–10) becomes a whole multitude of disciples, praising God and acknowledging, not some future messianic kingdom, but the entry of Jesus into the heavenly sphere. Jesus is seen as taking over Jerusalem; the disciples are the true in Israel who acknowledge this and, had they failed in their recognition, the very stones would have cried out in honour of the one in whom their history found fulfilment (19.37–40).

Luke's considerable shortening of the Marcan account of the cleansing of the Temple and his omission of the episode of the cursing of the fig-tree empties the event of the element of rejection.[18] Jesus does not appear as hostile to the Temple; instead, he takes possession of it. Now, he teaches daily in the Temple (19.47; 20,1, 9,45). Whereas in Mark, Jesus is not really at home in the Temple (compare Mark 11.27 with Luke 20.1), in Luke Jesus gives his authoritative teaching there with the freedom of one who is in his rightful place. The people hear him willingly (19.47–8; 21.38). The Temple, rightly understood, makes way for him who is the outcome of its life and piety. The eschatological chapter is spoken in the Temple rather than over and against it.

Nevertheless, Jesus provokes opposition, which causes divisions within Israel. Even at the triumphal entry into the city, the opposition cannot be silenced, but finds expression in the complaints of the Pharisees (19.39). Thereafter, opposition comes from the Jerusalem leaders (19.47; 20.1, 19). In these verses which contrast their opposition with acclamation accorded him by the crowds, Luke clearly distinguishes between the people and their leaders with whom the real confrontation occurs. In Luke, the parable of the Wicked Husbandmen is told to the people against the scribes and the chief priests (20.9, 19). If verse 18 heightens the note of judgement, it is nevertheless, a judgement directed against them rather than against the nation in general. There is no parallel to Matthew 21.43, which talks explicitly of the rejection of the Jewish people as a whole. The same approach is probably to be seen in the Lucan parable of the Pounds (19.11–27). Set in the context of the acceptance of Jesus by Bartimaeus and the people (18.43), of Zacchaeus (19.9–10), and of the disciples (19.37–8), it contrasts the rejection by the chief priests and the leaders of the people (19.39–40, 47–8). The citizens stand over and against the servants; it is the enemies who are destroyed (19.27), and nothing is said about the destruction of the entire city. In 20.45–7 the scribes are attacked by Jesus in a discourse which, though delivered to the disciples, is overheard by 'all the people'.

Luke is clear that Jerusalem will be destroyed because she 'did not know the time of her visitation' (19.44). Yet he is careful to avoid saying that it is God who will do this. Though in 19.41–4 he uses phrases clearly taken from Isaiah 29.3, his changes mean that the enemies rather than God are to be the cause of the destruction, and it seems that he sees this prophecy fulfilled in the events of A.D. 70.[19] Unlike Isaiah and the prophetic tradition, however, he does not suggest that God was actively at work in such an event, or that the destruction fulfilled God's purposes. Jesus does not reject the city, but rather the city's rejection of him causes him to weep for it. The destruction is not willed by God, but is the inevitable outcome of the city's refusal of him.

Likewise, Jesus' lament over Jerusalem and its Temple in 13.34–5 is not in itself hostile. If the shout of welcome is to find its fulfilment at the Entry (19.38), the pericope sees the situation primarily in terms of the life of Jesus, whose eschatological visitation of Jerusalem restores meaning to the Temple for the first time since its destruction in 586 B.C. If, as is more likely, the oracle is seen from the post-resurrection perspective, it refers to the fact that the Temple then has validity only in so far as it points to Jesus. Since it has failed to do so, it is forsaken as the place where God's glory is manifested to the nations. The forsakenness is probably seen as occurring with the destruction of A.D. 70. But, in any case,

the quotation from Psalm 118.26 refers to some future visitation
at the return of Jesus when the restored Israel would acknowledge
her Lord.[20] God is not said to have initiated a destruction of the
Temple, towards which there is no hint of hostility.

Jesus' reply to the women who accompany him to his crucifixion (23.28–31) again does not suggest any destruction by God.
Whatever their original motives, Luke presents them as true
'daughters of Jerusalem' who weep for their Lord, as earlier the
faithful in Israel had wept for David at his rejection (2 Sam.
15.30–1). But Jesus tells them to weep instead for the destruction
that is coming upon Jerusalem for 'if they do this when the wood
is green, what will happen when it is dry?' These words, though
sometimes seen as dependent upon Isaiah 10.16–19 and Ezekiel
20.47, are scarcely influenced by ideas from them. In Isaiah and
Ezekiel the judgement is a divine visitation. In Luke, this is not so.
The agent is not God but the Roman power. If the Romans have
dealt thus with the innocent Jesus, how hardly will they deal with
those who are guilty? Again, however, the concern is for Jerusalem's suffering the inevitable consequences of her folly, expressed in her rejection of the Christ, rather than for the divine
judgement upon her. Here, the Romans are not praised but
criticized, and this must see their action dissociated from God's
purposes. In 21.20–4 this prophecy is seen to be fulfilled, but the
event is denuded of its Marcan eschatological reference, and the
action is therefore dissociated from the purposes of God.

Luke then does not picture Jesus as hostile either to the city or
its Temple. Nevertheless, in his account of the cleansing, he
omits Mark's use of the Isaianic prophecy which foresees the
Temple as the place of prayer for all people (19.46 cf. Mark 11.17,
Isaiah 56.7). Luke deliberately avoids making the Temple the
place where the nations will come to worship Yahweh. This may
be because he is writing after the fall of Jerusalem, so that he is
forced to alter the centripetal expectations of the prophets into a
centrifugal mission from Jerusalem to the nations. Theologically,
however, this emphasis ties up with Luke's understanding of the
place of the Temple in the divine scheme of redemption. It gives
place to Jesus. After he takes possession of it at the immediate
prelude to the exaltation, it ceases to have any validity of its own,
but rather gives place to him who is now seen as the bearer of the
divine glory. It is not to the Temple that men go to see the divine

glory but to Jesus. So long as it witnesses to him and points men to Jesus, so long as its place is seen to be preparatory to him, Christians can continue to worship there. But it is no longer essential and, though its destruction is not willed by God, it arises inevitably out of the Jewish nation's rejection of Jesus. Its destruction however is no longer within the sphere of the eschatological happenings, and, as an event, it is of no significance for faith.

In line with this, Luke omits the Temple accusation found in Mark 14.57–61 from his account of the appearance of Jesus before the Sanhedrin. In doing so, he avoids any possibility of a suggestion that Jesus' words or deeds may have given grounds for any such accusation and so divorces him from any anti-Temple bias.[21] It is true, of course, that since Mark emphasizes that the witnesses are false, he also may have played down any such bias. Since, however, at the cleansing, Mark himself appears to be against the Temple, it is possible that he calls them false, not because he is favourable to the Temple, but in order to emphasize his hostility to it. They are false because, by presenting a garbled version of what Jesus actually said, they made him out to be a traditional messianic figure who, through an act of Temple destruction and renewal, seemed to give a permanent place both to the Temple and to the nation which it embodied. The witnesses therefore were forcing Jesus into current Jewish nationalistic-particularistic expectations.[22] For Mark, this was entirely false. For him, Christianity gave no permanence to such Temple belief. At the death of Jesus the rending of the Temple veil witnesses to its supersession, and its total destruction is taken up into the final eschatological event. For Luke, however, this is not so. The Temple, it is true, has no permanence, but Jesus is not hostile to it. In playing its part in the divine plans, it has led to Christ and found its fulfilment in him.

Such emphases serve to bring to the fore the problems raised by the Jewish rejection of Jesus and by the part the Jews played in his crucifixion. Luke approaches these from two angles. In the first place, as we have already seen, he emphasizes the necessity for the death of Jesus, showing it to be in accordance with God's will as that was determined and revealed in the Scriptures. However, whereas such an approach provides a perfectly reasonable explanation of the crucifixion, it does little to account for the attitude of the Jews of Luke's own day. He therefore describes Jewish action at the trial of Jesus in such a way as to throw light on their later lack of response to the Christian proclamation. This second purpose is served by emphasizing the part the Jews played in the death of Jesus and by showing that, at this focal point of history, they displayed that same disobedience and hardness of heart to God's actions as were to characterize their reaction to the Christian message. Luke therefore describes the trial with the situation of his own day in mind. The blame for the death of Jesus is made to rest firmly upon the Jews, who occasioned it by the same obstinacy that they revealed in Luke's own times.

Jesus' appearance before the Sanhedrin, which in Luke loses any appearance of a trial that may have been left to it in Mark, is a stark attack upon him.[23] No witnesses are called, for the council is itself the prosecution; no verdict is given, for the issue is already decided by them; no horror is shown at the alleged blasphemy, for any pretence of good motives on their part is gone. In Luke there is no question of a failure to understand that Jesus was the Messiah. It is rather a case of deliberate refusal to accept what is acknowledged; what is evoked is a calculated rejection. Jesus' reply to their demand to tell them if he is the Christ suggests that any answer on his part would be merely superfluous, since they are neither prepared to accept the truth from his lips, nor are they capable of summoning up true belief from their hearts. They know that he is the Christ, but they refuse to act upon their knowledge (22.67, 70).[24] Nevertheless, Jesus makes his claim that he is about to be seated at the right hand of God. They recognize the meaning of this and ask: 'Are you the Son of God then?' Jesus' reply is no disclaimer; it is not even a modification of their expectation.[25] It is rather an acceptance of the title, originally given by the angel at the annunciation to Mary (1.35). The Jews recognize Jesus for what he is, and so the wilfulness of their rejection is underlined.

Luke's rewriting of the trial before Pilate has often been noticed.[26] He makes the Jews accuse Jesus in terms which, though explicit, are obviously false (23.2 cf. Mark 15.3). Three times Pilate declares Jesus to be innocent (23.4, 14, 22); he is attributed with the desire to release him (23.20). On the other hand, the Jews are represented as obstinately determined upon his destruction (23.5, 18, 21, 23), and it is their voices rather than Pilate's objective judgement which prevail (23.24). Pilate acquiesces and delivers up Jesus 'to their will' (23.25). Luke omits the Marcan account of the mockery by the Roman soldiers (Mark 15.17–20) and this enables him, not only to spare the Romans such an indignity, but also and more important, to give the impression that the Jews were actually the agents at the crucifixion (23.26). From first to last, the responsibility is laid firmly at the feet of the Jews. Luke had earlier, at the arrest, made the chief priests come out themselves against Jesus (22.52 cf. Mark 14.43); Luke's whole account of the passion is an explanation of how it is their 'hour and the power of darkness' (22.53).

Political apologetic does not of itself supply sufficient motive for these changes. Pilate does not appear as an impressive figure and, since he does give way to Jewish pressure, Roman discrimination and justice are hardly presented as a matter in which confidence can be placed.[27] In Luke 13.1 Pilate is presented as tyrant and, though in Acts 3.13 he is described as wishing to release Jesus, this fact is brought out only to emphasize the obduracy of the Jews. On the other hand, in Acts 4.27 he is named among the opponents of Jesus. In Luke, the Romans alone actually condemn Jesus and the final responsibility is very definitely stated to be theirs (23.24–5, and compare 18.32–3 with Mark 10.33–4). Jesus' words to the weeping women do not suggest confidence in Roman integrity (23.31), and Luke 21.24 gives to Rome's destruction of Jerusalem the horror of a political event. Apologetic motives are secondary here, and Luke would seem to have scarcely more desire to vindicate Pilate than he would have to present Herod in a favourable light. The reason for his changes can only be that he wishes to lay the blame for the death of Jesus firmly upon the Jews.

The Jews are presented as being wholly responsible for the crucifixion. Their leaders took the initiative at his capture; they were the prosecutors at his trial; recognizing him for what he was, they nevertheless deliberately turned their backs upon him; they constrained the weak political power to hand him over to them; and they are virtually stated to have crucified him. Pilate remains a secondary character. He is necessary, indeed, to account for the actual crucifixion of Jesus but, as far as Luke's interest is concerned, he is irrelevant.

The Lucan speeches have the same bias. On the way to Emmaus, though it is admitted that the Jews delivered him up to the

Romans to be condemned to death, it is nevertheless stated that they themselves crucified him (24.20). In the earlier speeches of Acts they take the initiative in his death and are held responsible for it (Acts 2.23; 3.13–15; 4.10; 5.30; 10.39; 13.28). They are once declared to have acted in ignorance (Acts 3.17), and a distinction is at one point made between the people of Jerusalem and their rulers (24.19–20). More often, however, they are all seen as acting as one body, a fact that accords with the Lucan account of the scenes before Pilate where, in contrast to earlier episodes where people and their leaders are frequently distinguished, the total *laos* rejects its Messiah.

Yet, even as they reject the Christ, the Jews are acting as the covenantal people of God in whose purposes they are, albeit unwittingly, co-operating. If the speeches in Acts unite in emphasizing the responsibility of the Jews and the blame incumbent upon them, to the virtual exclusion of the part of Pilate, they nevertheless include even that in the purposes of God for the chosen people. Paradoxically, the Jews, as God's people, reject the Christ, but even in their rejection they witness to the fact that they are God's instruments. At the crucifixion, Rome was irrelevant; it was merely doing what God's purposes required of it. It was the chosen people who were being used to further the saving action of God in the world. Jesus was 'delivered up according to the definite plan and foreknowledge of God' (Acts 2.23 cf. 3.18). Without knowing it, they were doing God's will, for 'they who dwell in Jerusalem, and their rulers, because they knew him not, nor the voices of the prophets, fulfilled them by condemning him' (Acts 13.27).

The Lucan crucifixion scene is, therefore, not one of wholly unrelieved gloom. The leaders remain hostile and now even come to mock at the crucified Messiah (23.35), but the people 'stand by watching', not joining in the abuse offered by their leaders but, later, having witnessed what has taken place, return home beating their breasts (23.35, 48). They are not entirely insensitive to what has happened. Jesus' words from the cross are cries of hope both for himself and others. His plea, which in the light of its immediate context does not contain any reference to the Roman soldiery, is one of forgiveness for the Jewish people (23.34). It is they who 'know not what they do'. Though this agrees with Acts 3.17 where, in the appeal to Jerusalem, the Jews are offered ignorance as an excuse, it seems to represent a different attitude from that shown in Acts 13.27, where their ignorance is described as culpable. It is unlikely that these differences are to be accounted for by supposing that Luke is in Acts 13.27 following some source, while in the other passages he is expressing his own opinions.[28] Rather, these verses are to be interpreted in the light of their contexts. Luke 23.34, occurring before the resurrection which alone established the indisputability of the claims of Jesus' Messiahship, is therefore understandable. The sin against the Holy Spirit is not yet (12.10). Again, Acts 3.17 represents the initial appeal to the Jewish people to accept what the resurrection proves. Acts 13.27, on the other hand, reviews the whole of Jewish history in the light of the rejection of the risen Christ and comes to the conclusion that it is all of one piece.

Luke's passion narrative ends with the witness of the centurion to Jesus (23.47). In contrast to the mockings of the Jewish leaders, the uncertainty of the crowd, and the doubts of the disciples, the Gentile, seeing all that had happened, responds with a true statement of the significance of the person of him who hangs upon the cross and of the significance of his being there.[29] Nothing could more effectively underline the blind stupidity of those who should have seen but did not.

THE RECONSTITUTION OF ISRAEL

When, at the ascension, the disciples ask Jesus: 'Lord, will you at this time restore the kingdom to Israel?' (Acts 1.6), the hope that underlies the question is not denied, even though it is suggested that the desire to know the time of such a restoration is wrong. Nevertheless, Jesus goes on to give a new direction to the disciples' hopes, which are to be realized, at any rate in the first instance, not in the way they expect, but are to be viewed in terms of the gift of the Spirit and of the universal witness it makes possible (1.8). In the light of the disciples' question and of the comments of the two witnesses of the Ascension (1.11), the Spirit and the universal mission, which in terms of the answer alone could be taken as a substitute for the disciples' hopes, are to be understood rather as a guarantee that those hopes are not false. They are a pledge of the return of Jesus and of the restoration of Israel of which they are the first-fruits. Israel is now being restored and awaits the gift of the kingdom.

There is, indeed, a reinterpretation. The restoration of Israel is seen to have meaning only in the light of its universal significance; the gift of the Spirit, since it witnesses to the exaltation of Jesus, means that Israel's claim to be the people of God depends upon her response to him; the postponing of the parousia suggests that Israel's renewal is immediately effected in obedient response to God's initiative rather than in any visible glorification of her people. All this suggests that there will inevitably be divisions within Israel. Israel to be herself as the covenantal people of God must be renewed through the events proceeding from the exaltation of Jesus.[30]

However, before the actual reconstitution of Israel can take place, the gap in the Twelve caused by the apostasy of Judas must be filled. This is done through the election of Matthias (Acts 1.15–26). Some recent discussions of this episode, denying that Luke saw any eschatological significance in the Twelve, have, in the light of Acts 1.21, suggested that he envisaged the apostles primarily as the link between the early Church and the time of Jesus which, as the period of salvation, had become a thing of the past. 'For Luke the apostle is neither the eschatological ruler in the coming kingdom, nor the person called by the risen Lord to be a messenger. He is the eyewitness of Jesus' earthly life and work, and only as such is he called to witness.'[31] It is true, of course, that Acts 1.21–2 does regard eyewitness of Jesus' ministry as an essential part of the qualifications of an apostle, but this would appear to be not in order that the apostle might link the Church to the life, for there is little overall reference to the ministry in the early speeches, but that, by having known him in the flesh, the apostle might be an irrefutable witness to his resurrection. This is what the speeches emphasize as the apostolic work (Acts 2.32; 3.15; 5.32; 10.41; 13.31); reference to the ministry finds its importance as it shows that the life of Jesus was in accordance with the Scriptures and of such a kind that the claims regarding his exaltation are seen to be reasonable (Acts 2.22; 10.38–9; 13.26–9). Luke emphasizes the Twelve as a group within the larger body (6.13 cf. Acts 6.2, 6). His accounts of their mission and of that of the Seventy (9.1–10; 10.1–20) suggest that he saw little difference between the qualifications and work of the two groups; the risen Jesus appears to men outside the apostolic band (24.28 ff); and the very fact of the existence of Matthias and Joseph (Acts 1.23) suggests that there were many others whose qualifications were as good as those of the Twelve if their work was primarily that of providing a link between Jesus and the Church. But this is not how Luke understood their distinctiveness. They were called by Jesus to perform a particular function and, since it is marred by the apostasy of one of their members though not by the death of another (Acts 12.2), that function is specific and is not given to a body which is self-perpetuating. Their importance can only lie, not in their persons, but in their number. The fact that their number must be made up in Jerusalem, between the eschatological act itself and the application of it to the covenantal community, means that they are seen by Luke as having eschatological significance which continues what is inherent in Jesus' initial choice of them. Their presence challenges Israel to accept her renewal, to see the significance of the Christian group, and to join the reconstituted people. They act as the rulers of the renewed Israel which is derived from the eschatological event. The Lord's promise at the Last Supper (22.29–30) is not yet fulfilled, for the kingdom is not yet, but it is anticipated as the earthly Israel is renewed through the Pentecostal outpouring. So long as the community centres upon Jerusalem, the Twelve are its rulers, but they disappear as soon as the centre of interest passes into the Gentile world.[32] The Twelve are the foundations of the re-made Israel—which is always wider than they—and they enable the renewal of Israel to be achieved.[33] The community centred upon them is the eschatological community, owing its existence to the exaltation, created by the outpouring of the Spirit, living a life of unity and controlled freedom, and waiting expectantly for its completion at the parousia.[34]

Luke emphasizes the outpouring of the Spirit as an eschatological event[35] by associating it with prophecy, which he equates with speaking with tongues in order to give it a universal significance, with tongues of fire which have something of the nature of the phenomena foretold by Joel, and with the world-wide gathering at Jerusalem. As an eschatological event he sees it derived from the exaltation of Jesus—which for that reason is treated in Peter's speech as separate from the resurrection—and also as the proof that Jesus is now empowered as Lord and Christ. Since the exaltation is seen as the climax of Israel's history, Pentecost is understood as the renewal of Israel; because it is the result of prophecy, it is related to prophetic hopes for the chosen people; as the fulfilment of the Baptist's expectations, it is understood in terms of God's continuing activity in the Jewish nation.[36]

Whatever its further implications, Pentecost is first and foremost an event for Israel. Though it has a wider significance (Acts 2.6, 39), it is with the Jews that it is primarily concerned. Those who are present are Jews or proselytes (Acts 2.5, 10); they are *eulabeis* which, used only in the New Testament by Luke, for him means those whose piety is nurtured by the Jewish faith;[37] Peter's speech is directed to 'men of Judaea and all who dwell in Jerusalem', to 'men of Israel', and so to 'all the house of Israel' (Acts 2.14, 22, 36).[38]

It is therefore unlikely that Luke describes the event in terms of God's reversal of his act at Babel (Gen. 11.1-9).[39] Though there are parallels of language which may suggest that he was not entirely unaware of this wider implication, this was not his immediate concern. Neither is it likely that Luke was interested in it as the giving of a new law.[40] The story of Acts 2 shows little influence of the Sinai tradition.[41] Luke does not speak of a Spirit-law contrast, he nowhere talks in terms of a new covenant, and for him the old law is not superseded (Luke 16.17, Acts 15.21; 21.20). He does indeed bring out the covenantal significance of the gift of the Spirit, but it is seen as the eschatological renewal and quickening of the initial bond rather than as the introduction of a new covenant.[42]

But though Luke does not envisage Pentecost as the start of the world-wide mission, for that is portrayed as developing from the initial stage of the apostolic witness, he does nevertheless give a universal significance to the miracle. The messianic prophecies which are fulfilled in Jesus assign him a universal meaning in so far as those who are called into obedience to him are to include peoples from the Gentiles and as the nations as a whole are to witness the sovereignty of the Christ. Hence Luke's use of Psalm 110 and his enumeration of the nations of the world point to the belief that the world will see the renewal of Israel, while Peter's hopes in 2.39 express the belief that others besides Jews will be called. But the point nevertheless is that the event is concerned primarily with the renewal of Israel, and that this will cause others to be joined to her, while yet others will see the mighty hand of God in their midst.[43]

Because the appeal of Peter is separated from the speech (2.38–40), it allows the speech itself to be a statement of the significance of Pentecost in such a way that it becomes the thesis which the rest of the book will justify. Of Dodd's parts of the kerygma[44] it lacks only the reference to the return of the Christ, but this is unnecessary here, since the relation of the gift of the Spirit to the return has already been fully established in the Lord's own ascension speech (Acts 1.7–8). But the appeal itself testifies to the significance of this re-making of Israel which the chapter describes. The reconstituted Israel is no longer to be identified with the nation that bears the name. Israel's inclusion is not automatic but, like others to whom the appeal will eventually go, it depends upon repentance, which is the necessary pre-condition for the reception of the Spirit's renewal (2.38). Though Israel remains the nucleus of the people of God, though others do not take her place to her own exclusion and though others enter only by incorporation into her (15.14–18), she, as a whole, is not automatically within the sphere of the eschatological community. What is her opportunity, what is virtually hers by right of the covenant with Abraham, can become hers in fact only as she acknowledges the sovereignty of Jesus.

REJECTION BY JERUSALEM

Of crucial importance for the understanding of Luke's attitude to the Jewish nation is the speech of Stephen which stands at the first significant turning-point of Acts when the appeal to Jerusalem is brought to a close and when what is ultimately to become the world-wide mission is begun. Inevitably the question arises whether the martyrdom of Stephen inaugurates a turning away from Jerusalem, and whether the speech represents an attack upon the heart of the Jewish faith.

Luke of course was writing at a time when the Jews as a whole had turned their backs on the Christian proclamation and when Jerusalem had been destroyed by the Roman power. His account is therefore coloured by these factors in such a way that he uses the Stephen speech both to explain the fact of the Jewish rejection and also to describe the significance assigned to the

Jerusalem Temple in the light, not only of the Christ, but also of the coming disaster. Nevertheless, though the martyrdom does represent a new stage in his work, and though it brings to an end any hopes which his narrative may seem to suggest of the conversion of Jerusalem as a whole,[45] the speech does not necessarily express the hostility to the Jews and their institutions which is often assigned to it.

In coming to a correct appraisal of the speech two factors seem important. In the first place, it is linked to a particular episode in Luke's work and can only be understood in relation to that. Though the speech may have little actual historical connection with the event to which it bears witness and though as a report of what was actually said at the time it may carry little credibility, it is nevertheless a significant comment by the author upon the event to which it is attached when that event is seen as occupying a particular place in the development of the narrative as a whole. To attempt to interpret it without relating it to the martyrdom of Stephen and the place it occupies in the book is to do despite to the method of historical writing which Luke has used.[46] In the second place, because Luke has chosen to write history, the significance of the event which the speech is describing can only be ascertained by considering the historical episodes which lead up to it and follow from it. Luke is unlikely to have included a speech which ran counter to the narrative in which it is embedded. The speech then must be understood, not merely in the light of the theological ideas underlying the historical narrative, but also against the background of the historical narrative itself.[47]

The episode of Stephen comes at the end of a section which describes the appeal to Jerusalem to accept Jesus as the Christ and which recounts the developing hostility of the city to such preaching. The Pentecost episode has given a statement of the significance of the exaltation of Jesus and its result as seen in the renewal of Israel. Chapter 3 then records the appeal to Jerusalem to enter into this new era. The miracle in the Temple points to the fulfilment of its life in Jesus so that now the 'name' of Jesus brings that salvation to which the manifestation of the divine name in the Temple had been a pointer. The speech is closely linked to the event upon which it is a commentary. *Onōma* occurs in verses 6 and 16; *estereuthēsan* in verse 7 is picked up by *estereōse* in verse 16; *thambous* in verse 10 is taken up by *ti thaumazete* in verse 12;

the use of 'Jesus Christ' in verse 6 is justified in verses 18 and 20.
It is also styled to make it an appeal to Jewish devotees. So great
is its piling up of Old Testament imagery and ideas that the resulting artificiality has often been accounted for by the hypo-
thesis of an Aramaic source.

As an appeal to the heart of Jewry, the speech emphasizes
Jesus as the fulfilment of Jewish expectations, which are therefore
given positive value. The one who has glorified Jesus is the 'God
of Abraham and of Isaac and of Jacob, the God of our fathers'
(3.13). 'These days' were foretold by the prophets (3.24). Those
who accept Jesus would be truly within the prophetic faith and
the Abrahamic covenant (3.25). Jesus is therefore described in
terms of the Old Testament figures. He is God's servant (3.13,
26), the holy and righteous one (3.14), the author of Life (3.15),
the Christ whom the prophets foretold would suffer (3.18), the
prophetic figure whom Moses foresaw (3.22).

As the fulfilment of the Abrahamic covenant, Jesus has a universal significance (3.25) which is achieved, however, only through
the posterity of Abraham, so that the first object of the preaching
must be the re-making of the Jewish people by their acceptance
of Jesus as Christ. The priority of the Jews is unquestioned (3.26).

Nevertheless, the blame for the death of Jesus is laid wholly
upon them (3.13), but, since this had been foretold in the Scriptures, the calamity of this is modified (3.18) and, because the
speech represents the initial appeal to Jewry, both the people as a
whole and the rulers are offered the excuse of ignorance (3.17).
But this only emphasizes the urgency of the situation which they
now face. The past is dead—at any rate as far as the apportioning
of blame is concerned—but it does have a bearing upon the gravity
of the appeal in the present which demands a clean break with the
past record. Of the seriousness of the present there can be no
doubt, for 'it shall be that every soul that does not listen to that
prophet shall be destroyed from the people' (3.23).[48]

The Jews must therefore repent. This is no new situation for,
in Luke, John the Baptist had preached a 'baptism of repentance
for the forgiveness of sins' (3.3) and Jesus himself had proclaimed,
'unless you repent you will all likewise perish' (13.3). Now, however, the Jews are called upon to respond in repentance to the
whole eschatological act, and the radical change which is needed
is underlined by their part in the crucifixion.

If they do repent, there will come 'seasons of refreshing from the presence of the Lord' (3.19–20). In the light of the rest of the verse and of Luke's theology as a whole, this is most likely to be understood in terms of the present gift of the Spirit and incorporation into the eschatological community. The return of the Christ is then anticipated but is, nevertheless, dependent upon their repentance.[49] When he does come, there will be 'the *apokatastasis* of all that God spake by the mouth of his holy prophets from of old'. In the light of the use of *apokathistaneis* at Acts 1.6, *apokatastasis* here would refer to the restoration of the kingdom to Israel in terms of the Davidic promise of the annunciation (1.32–33). These two verses then repeat and expound the answer of Jesus to the disciples at the ascension and see the present activity of the Spirit as restoring the covenantal people, witnessing this to the nations, and becoming the prelude and guarantee of the restoration of Israel's kingdom, of which it is also the necessary precondition.

We have examined this speech at length because, being given in the Temple, it relates Jesus most closely to Jewish hopes. Jesus stands wholly within the framework of the covenant with Abraham and confirms the promises which were explicit in it. As in the infancy narratives, the Temple leads to Jesus so that, finding its fulfilment in him, it acknowledges that it is not in itself that the promises to Abraham are to find reality. The Temple must lead men to Christ if it is to have any further usefulness; it must lead men to repentance, for it is now only through the name of Jesus that God's name is to rest upon them. The fact of Jesus brings meaning to the Temple, but it also emphasizes its inability to make the Abrahamic covenant a reality unless it leads to him.

The following chapters, however, show the increasing hostility of Jerusalem, first in the persons of the leaders of the community as distinct from the people (4.1–2; 5.17; 5.26), but, by the time of Stephen, of the people also (6.12).[50] The story of Stephen is used by Luke to summarize the rejection of the gospel by Jerusalem as a whole (so that the persecution following his death is represented (8.1) as a persecution of the whole Church 'except the apostles') and the speech, explaining why this should have happened, shows where the Jews went wrong in their attitude to the Temple which is seen as the focal point of their rejection. It is a speech commenting on the fact that Jerusalem preferred to remain with the

Temple and to regard that as the final mark of God's favour, rather than let it lead them to Jesus to whom it pointed.

But before the speech itself can be considered, one further point in Luke's history should be noted. Both before and after the martyrdom of Stephen, Luke points out that many in Jerusalem did accept the Christian proclamation (Acts 4.4; 5.12–16; 9.26–8; 11.2, 29–30; 12.25; 15.22; 21.20) and remained as loyal adherents of the Temple which they frequented regularly (2.46; 3.1; 5.12; 21.26–7; 22.17; 24.12). Jerusalem is not written off, neither is its Temple neglected by those who have been led to follow Jesus. Moreover, though Jerusalem is no longer the scene of the Christian proclamation, it does, nevertheless, control the mission which moves out from the city and is drawn into its embrace by the subordination of the missionaries to the control of the Jerusalem church. In this, the Lucan bias is clearly to be seen. The mission becomes the extension of the renewal of the true Israel which is centred in Jerusalem; by means of the control exercised by Jerusalem, the mission to the Gentiles is seen as a guarantee that Jerusalem has been renewed and its earlier history taken up into Christ. The Jews in Jerusalem who reject Jesus are open to the strongest criticism, for they are denying all that their history has signified. Nevertheless, the criticism is of the people rather than of the instruments of Israel, since those instruments have led to Jesus and continue to be respected by his adherents. After all, Luke does say that those who maintained that Stephen had spoken against the Law and the Temple were quite definitely 'false witnesses' (6.13–14).

The main point of the speech is to show that the hostility of the Jews to the Christian proclamation is of one piece with the hostility to the purposes of God which is characteristic of their history. As Haenchen maintains: 'Stephen will owe his death to a state of mind which has long been a recurrent feature in the history of Israel'.[51] Joseph and Moses, as types of Jesus, were rejected by those whom they benefited. The Jews refused the living oracles which Moses received for them (7.38), and instead chose to worship the calf, the 'work of their hands' (7.41). Moses looked to Jesus, and the treatment of both was of the same order.

So far, the speech is clear and provides a reason for the rejection of the Christian proclamation by Jerusalem which successfully counters any claim that such rejection invalidates the truth of the message. As such, its purpose is less to launch an attack upon the Jews than to make a defence of the rejected gospel. Difficulties of interpretation arise, however, in the speech's treatment of those subjects which are said to be the matter of the false witnesses' attack upon Stephen.

The speech makes little reference to the Law, but it clearly regards the Jews as a whole as disobedient to the Laws and hostile to the commandments of Moses (7.38-9, 53). The climax of this disobedience came in their rejection of the Righteous One (7.52). It is possible that the speech, by making a distinction between 'our fathers' in verses 44 and 45 and 'your fathers' in verses 39 and 52, and by including a line of the faithful in Israel in contrast to the unfaithfulness of the vast majority of the people, has something of the idea of the two Israels, the true and the false within the one nation.[52] But such thought should probably not be pressed too hard, for it is the apostasy of the people as a whole which is the primary concern of the speech. There are not clear lines of demarcation, and Luke's thought is still concerned with Israel as a whole where there is not a definite separation between the two groups and the false have not yet been cut off from the nation.

But however that may be, the Christians who have accepted the Righteous One are the true in Israel and the heirs of the promise. By their acceptance of Jesus they have shown themselves to be faithful to the Law of Moses which pointed to him, to the prophets who foretold him, and to the Spirit who inspired him (7.51-3), while those who reject him reject all these, and with them the God of Abraham. The immediate occasion for such an overall attack upon the Jewish people is the mention of the Temple which, in some way, is clearly seen as the focal point of Jewish disobedience. The question of importance is whether this disobedience is found in the very existence of the Temple or in the Jewish attitude to it in the light of the appearance of the Christ.

On the whole, the majority of commentators have maintained that Stephen's speech is an attack upon the Temple as such. So Cullmann writes that it regards the construction of the Temple 'as an act of the worst unfaithfulness',[53] while Simon says that 'the building of the Temple by Solomon seems to stand on the same plane as the making of the golden calf'.[54] Certainly the language used about Solomon's house is harsh, and were the speech taken in isolation felt to contain a complete statement of an outlook upon the Temple, then one would have to accept that it did express out-and-out hostility which saw its building as due to a complete failure of understanding and obedience. So, doing this, Simon has to explain the speech as being taken over by Luke from a source which is at variance with his own ideas upon the Temple,[55] while O'Neill, seeing the speech as a quintessence of Luke's thought upon the subject, is forced to make the Lucan writings as a whole take a hostile stance towards it.[56] Yet, as we have seen, Luke's two volumes cannot be made to express such an outlook.

As it now stands in its place in Acts, the speech explains why the Jews rejected the Christian proclamation. It discusses the Temple in the light of that rejection which, because they failed to see the Temple as leading to Jesus, has caused an 'either–or' situation to arise in which they are using the Temple to take the place in God's designs which is legitimately occupied only by him. The Jews rejected Jesus and chose to find the fulfilment of their covenantal status in that complex of hopes and beliefs which centred on the Temple, which was therefore given permanence by them and which, even after the fall of Jerusalem, was the central point of their eschatological expectations. Jerusalem rejected Jesus because she preferred the Temple, saw that as the fulfilment of God's promises to Abraham, and failed to realize the preparatory nature of her own institutions.

The speech therefore is an attack, not upon the Temple itself, but upon an attitude which assigned permanence and finality to it. It is a discussion of the Jews' attitude to it in the light of their rejection of the Christ. In contrast to Jesus, the Temple is but *cheiropoiētos* (7.48). Though this comes close to the description of the idol that was made in the wilderness (7.41), the question here is not one of worship, and so of idolatrous activity, but rather of a man-made institution which, by seeking to express some claim upon God, limits the divine freedom and so impairs the divine transcendence. When Luke uses the same word again in Acts 17.24 he is not being derogatory about the Athenian temples, since he sees them as representing a religious attitude which is met by Christ, but he is pointing out their limitations and, when they are compared with the fact of Christ, their imperfections.[57] The word is used to express the finality of Christ; any judgement upon the Temple is made only in the light of Christ and in comparison with him (cf. Heb. 9.11, 24).

The Old Testament itself contains ample warnings of the dangers inherent in a wrong emphasis upon the Temple which makes for a denial of the transcendence and freedom of God. I Kings 8.27, as an integral part of Solomon's dedicatory prayer, comes close to the thought of Stephen's speech.[58] This represents Deuteronomic theology which, though not against the building of the Temple in a way that is found in the original version of Nathan's oracle (2 Sam. 7), nevertheless adds a note of caution to the more extravagant claims made on its behalf and, emphasizing the transcendence of Yahweh, reinterprets its significance in order to safeguard this.[59] The Temple is no longer regarded as the necessary means of Yahweh's approach to his people, the guarantee of his presence, or the symbol of the permanence of Yahweh's relations with Israel. Yahweh and the Temple are not yoked in a matrimonial alliance of eternal validity. What guarantees the unity of Yahweh with Israel is rather his promise which, by maintaining his freedom and graciousness, safeguards his sovereignty and puts no external restraint upon his transcendence. The Temple does not guarantee God's promise to David, far less does it enshrine it, but rather points to the source of that promise as being something other and greater than itself.[60] This thought is continued in Stephen's quotation from Isaiah 66.1–2 which again is not an attack upon the Temple, but an expression of the freedom of God which is neither limited by nor dependent upon the existence or non-existence of any building.

In Solomon's dedicatory prayer, the word of God's promise to David is greater than the house which stands as a witness to that promise but which does not itself guarantee it (1 Kings 8.22–7). In this, it agrees with the Nathan oracle of 2 Samuel 7.[61] The guarantee of the promise is simply Yahweh's word (verse 8); the content of the promise, the means whereby the promise itself is accomplished, is the house that Yahweh will make for David. As it now stands, it is allowed that what was forbidden to David—the making of a house for Yahweh—is accepted from his son. The reason for this can only be that the divine promise to David was emphasized as being independent of any temple. The Temple is acceptable so long as it is realized that it does not enshrine the promise, which was prior to it and so independent of it. The promise was fulfilled and guaranteed in the Davidic heir, not in any building which remained ancillary to the covenant. The promise of 'the house for Jacob' (Acts 7.46) is realized, not through the Temple but in the son of David. The Temple, given as a place of prayer and worship, the place for those who look for the fulfilment of God's promises, is not itself the fulfilment but the pointer to the Son of David in whom the promises are to be established. It is this thought which finds expression in Stephen's speech in verses 46–7. The point of the contrast between David and Solomon is not to suggest that Solomon's action was wrong but to show that the promise to David was prior to the building of the Temple, was independent of it, and was fulfilled, not through the house that Solomon built for God, right in its place though that action was, but in the House built by God for David—a house, not made with hands but created by God in the Davidic line fulfilled in Jesus as a result of promise.

The point of the speech then becomes that the promise to David—and through that the promise to Abraham—is realized not through the Temple, but through Jesus to whom the Temple points, but before whom it gives place. The theme of promise finds its fulfilment in Jesus and in nothing else.[62] The speech therefore offers a history of Israel which is designed to show this. In this, perhaps the closest model is provided in the Psalm 78, where the history of Israel is unfolded in such a way as to show the building of the Temple as the climax of Israel's history which finds a unity and purpose in that event to which it leads.[63] It is that event alone which gives significance and meaning to the seemingly purposeless meanderings of Israel's past and shows that even the murmurings and rebellions of the people contribute to the fulfilment that the Temple provides. Stephen's speech follows the same pattern and certainly takes no more hostile a view of the Israelite people than does the psalm. Its difference is rather that it includes the attitude of the people towards the Temple within its condemnation, and, whereas the psalm sees the Temple as giving fulfilment and meaning, the speech plainly reduces the Temple to a preliminary role in God's plans for his people, and sees their refusal to accept such a status for it as the culmination of Israel's disobedience. It is just in the speech's attitude to the Temple that the contrast with the psalm is to be found, and it is therefore small wonder that it is at this point that Luke makes the

crowd burst out in fury. But it is the attitude to the Temple
rather than the fact of the Temple which is singled out for condemnation. The speech does not present a theology which is at
variance with that found in Luke–Acts as a whole.[64]

LUKE'S PAUL

It is generally recognized that a certain tension exists between the
understanding of Paul that is to be gained from the epistles and
that which is given in the Acts of the Apostles. Though such an
opinion is not universal, there is enough divergence to suggest
that in Acts there is to be found, if not necessarily a picture of
Paul as a later generation thought of him,[65] at any rate an understanding of him that is largely shaped by Luke's own convictions.[66]
There emerges a picture of the apostle to the Gentiles which fits
into the Lucan unfolding of history in such a way that a careful
and consistent portrayal of the unity of the early Christian outlook
is achieved, and Paul himself is seen to be the vehicle of Lucan
beliefs as they have already appeared in the two volumes. In particular, for our immediate purpose, significance appears in the
way Luke describes Paul's approach to the Jews and also his
account of Paul's understanding of his Christian beliefs as they
are related to their Jewish antecedents.[67]

Acts shows Paul as having a constant concern with Jews which
is expressed in an active mission to them and one which frequently takes its beginning from the synagogue. It is just at this
point where the Lucan bias is usually found. The measure of this
bias depends, of course, upon the extent to which Luke's picture is
thought to diverge from that culled from the epistles. Schmithals,
on the basis of a strict interpretation of Galatians 2.9, makes
Paul's contacts with the synagogues a complete fabrication on the
part of Luke, who uses it in the service of his own aim to present
Christianity as the true Judaism.[68] On the whole, however, it is unlikely that Paul in his missionary concern cut himself off completely
from the Jews. Not only is it inherently likely that natural ties and
sheer convenience led him to make contact with his own nation
on his various journeys, but passages in his epistles such as
1 Cor. 9.20, 2 Cor. 11.24, and 1 Thessalonians 2.16 suggest that he
did not sever his links with them completely.[69] Gal. 2.9 is prob-

ably to be seen as defining the main areas of concern rather than laying down restrictions,[70] while Paul's own assessments of his situation such as that found in Romans 11.11–15 express an outlook forced upon him by his own failure to win Jews, a failure which no doubt sharpened both his attitude to the Law and the lines of his understanding of justification by faith.

Nevertheless, even though Luke's description of Paul's contacts with the synagogue cannot be dismissed as being determined entirely by his theological interest, he has given to these contacts a pattern and significance which are the expression of his own theological concern. He gives Paul a very definite mission to the Jews and to the synagogue (Acts 13.5; 13.14; 14.1; 17.1; 17.10; 17.17; 18.4, 5; 18.19; 19.8). Luke's own interest lies in the first instance in these contacts so that the initial account of Paul's conversion states that he was charged to go to Jews as well as Greeks (9.15). Only at Lystra (14.8–20), Philippi (16.12–40), and Troas (20.6–16) is there no mention of Paul's work among Jews, but even here Luke is not going against his usual practice. The episode at Lystra is closely linked to that at Iconium which controls it by supplying both its prelude and sequel and the mission to the Jews is undertaken there (14.1). At Philippi, though there is no mention of a synagogue, Paul 'on the sabbath day' joins a gathering (16.13), while those who oppose them identify them as Jews. Troas sees no missionary activity undertaken. Its importance for Luke lies in the miracle occurring at the meeting of the local church. Hence even these three episodes do not break the general pattern of Luke's presentation. Even at Athens, before the Areopagus sermon, in a verse which obtrudes into the general flow of the story, Paul is said to have argued with Jews in their synagogue (17.16–17).

Schmithals, however, has claimed more than this here, and has maintained that Luke presents Paul as going to the Gentiles only because the Jews rejected him[71] while, in a similar vein, Bornkamm says that Luke presents Paul's Jewish and Gentile missions as successive stages in which the Gentile enterprise only takes place when the Jews have rejected the missionary appeal.[72] This, however, goes beyond the evidence of Acts as a whole and systematizes the Lucan presentation in too exact a manner which is over-dominated by the rejections at Antioch, Corinth, and Rome. Important though these are, they nevertheless can be understood only against the total presentation which, as a whole, does not bear out such a clear scheme.

As we have seen above, at Lystra and Philippi there are no records either of a mission to the Jews or of hostility on their part. At Athens, no rejection by Jews precedes the delivery of the Areopagus speech. At other times, successes among Jews are recorded. At Antioch of Pisidia (13.43) it is not a case of total failure, and much the same situation prevails at Iconium (14.1), Thessalonica (17.4) and Beroea (17.11). At Corinth, even after the rejection by Paul (18.7), he does not sever connection with the Jews, and the ruler of the synagogue and others believe. Gallio regards the matter as one of divisions within the Jewish community (18.12–17). At Ephesus, even after the withdrawal from the synagogue, many Jews believe (19.10, 17). Paul's farewell speech indicates that the ministry to the Jews was not entirely without success (20.21). Many passages refer to successes among both Jews and Greeks (14.1; 17.4; 19.17; 20.21) in such a way as to suggest that there was a church as a result of Paul's work which broke through the Jewish–Gentile barrier.

Even though Luke sees the preaching to the Gentiles as the climax of Paul's work, he does not envisage this as taking the place of his concern with the Jews, which he does not reduce to a preliminary stage of Paul's missionary activity.[73] As he makes clear in Paul's speech at Antioch of Pisidia, Luke regards the witness to the Jews as being the first charge upon the missionary preaching since Jesus fulfils Jewish history and witnesses to God's completion of his covenantal promises (13.46). In this, Paul is made to pursue a course determined by the same theological considerations as have inspired Peter, Stephen, and Jesus himself. The renewal of Israel, leading to the incorporation of the Gentiles, remains the predominant theme.

Nevertheless, Luke knew that Paul had been rejected by the Jewish people as a whole so that his work could only be represented as a comparative failure. Having emphasized the activity of the apostle to the Gentiles amongst the Jewish people for the sake of his own theological considerations, Luke had to explain the rejection of him by his own people in a way that would throw light upon their continuing hostility in his own day. He does this by emphasizing the hostility and perversity of 'the Jews', who are presented as the undying opponents of Paul (17.5; 21.27; 23.12),

by making Paul issue three clear rejections of them:[74] and by
contrasting their enmity with the willingness of the Gentiles to
believe. By linking the disobedience of the Jews to the willing inclusion of the Gentiles, Luke is able to emphasize the sheer
perversity of the Jewish people and also to put forward the Gentile
witness as a proof of the claims of the reality of the Christian
proclamation.

Luke's picture of Paul's relations with the Jews is not part of a
plea for the treatment of Christianity as a *religio licita*[75] and it
does not explain Christianity's relationship with Judaism in terms
of a *Heilsgeschichte* which envisages successive phases within God's
continuing historical enterprise.[76] Though it may be seen as
giving a historical explanation of the emergence of the Christian
Church as distinct from Judaism,[77] this is unlikely to have been
his ultimate purpose, which remains much more one produced by
theological rather than historical considerations. He is concerned,
not to explain as such the historical reasons for the failure of the
Jewish people to embrace Christianity, but to counter the real
theological difficulty that such a failure presented to Christians.
What was at stake was the credibility of the Christian proclamation which saw Jesus as God's eschatological act for Israel. It was
this that the Jewish refusal to believe threatened to show up as
completely false. How could the Jews have failed to acknowledge
God's eschatological act? That was Luke's problem and, in his
description of Paul, he deals with it as he has dealt with it both at
the passion and at the martyrdom of Stephen, by emphasizing the
sheer perversity and obstinacy of the Jewish people as a whole,
and by placing over against that the impact of the proclamation
upon the Gentiles.

Luke's Paul is therefore made to present Christianity as the
fulfilment of all that was best in Judaism which, as the pointer to
Christianity, is given the highest possible value, Paul is a good Jew
who circumcises Timothy (16.3), delivers for observance the
apostolic decisions regarding the keeping of the law (16.4), takes
on Jewish vows (18.18; 21.26), and is proud of his ancestry
(21.39; 22.3; 23.6). God, 'the God of our fathers', has led him to
embrace Christianity, which is the culmination of his earlier life's
devotion (23.1), the fulfilment of his Jewish hope (26.6), and what
Moses and the prophets had looked for (26.22). 'According to the
Way, which they call a sect, I worship the God of our fathers,

believing everything laid down by the law or written in the
prophets, having a hope in God which these themselves accept,
that there will be a resurrection of both the just and the unjust'
(24.14). Jesus is the Christ foretold by the Scriptures (17.2-4)
and, as such, is the realization of that salvation which was partially bestowed through the instruments of the old dispensation.
Paul therefore shows his respect for both the Law and the Temple
in such a way that the accusations of the Jews are obviously shown
to be false (21.21, 28; 24.5-6). His presence in the Temple was
out of piety. He is an upholder of the Law, which is seen by him
to find fulfilment in Jesus. Jesus completes what is partially realized in the Law, and since he remains complementary to it, he
does not, in Luke's Paul at any rate, abrogate it (13.39).[78] Paul's
mission to the Gentiles, so far from being a turning aside from the
instruments of the old covenant, was instituted by an immediate
appearance of the Christ himself at a time when Paul was praying
in the Temple (22.17-21).

The embrace of Christianity is therefore but a little step for
those whose understanding of Judaism is correct. Luke's Roman
officials see very little difference between the two and regard
points of conflict as of minor significance (18.15; 23.29). The
heathen are not able to distinguish between Jews and Christians
(19.33-4). This again, however, though it shows Luke's bias, is
not determined by *religio licita* considerations but by his theological convictions.[79] The Jewish faith finds its natural fulfilment
in Christianity, for which it was a fitting prelude and preparation.
Paul's conversion is no traumatic experience by which his former
life stands condemned. Instead, it is a dawning of the truth, a
realization of what before was veiled, but so natural is the development that the converted Paul is unable to understand why the
truth should not be perfectly clear to his Jewish hearers and why
they should regard it as in any way a betrayal of their inheritance
(22.18-20).[80] The differentiating factor is that the belief in the
resurrection of the dead is fulfilled in the resurrection of Jesus
(23.6; 24.15, 21; 26.8, 23; 28.20) by which the general resurrection is guaranteed. Luke's Paul knows of no tensions caused
by such a belief and his statements of the relations of Christianity
to its Jewish antecedents 'obscure the essential difference from
Judaism, its law and its hope which went with belief in Jesus as
Messiah'.[81]

Nevertheless, in spite of all this, there still remains the possibility that Luke represents Paul's last journey from Jerusalem to Rome as the final appeal to the Jews which, when it is rejected, occasions their abandonment, the end of any hopes for their conversion, and the movement of the gospel into the Gentile world unimpaired by its associations with the Jewish people. So Lampe sees this last episode of Acts as the decisive confrontation in which the last chance to repent is rejected by the Jewish leaders. Acts represents 'an apostolic testimony IN Jerusalem to the self-styled leaders of Israel until they finally reject it, and an apostolic testimony FROM Jerusalem to Rome and the Gentile world of Luke's own day'.[82] O'Neill makes the break even more complete: 'The Gospel was breaking out of its entanglement with organized Judaism and becoming free to be the universal religion. Jerusalem is left behind and Rome is entered.'[83]

But did Luke mean the last chapters of Acts to represent a break which is as decisive as these estimates suggest? Is his interest in the Jewish people in the greater part of his two volumes merely a prelude to emphasize the gulf which is finally seen to exist inevitably between them and the Christian Church? Is his concern to show the Jewish correctness of Paul merely to bring out the obstinacy of the Jews in their refusal to accept his preaching? It is, of course, possible that this was Luke's aim, yet it drives such a wedge between the end and the beginning of the two volumes as to make little sense of the hope of the early chapters. It is true, of course, that since Pentecost those who have accepted the Christ are the real successors of the prophets, the heirs of the covenant with Abraham. Yet the fact that Jesus is presented as the fulfilment of God's promises to Abraham and David suggests that Israel is still his concern and that she is not abandoned. It is true also that there are divisions within Israel but these divisions are, in essence at any rate, internal and there still remains the thought of Israel as a whole as summoned to respond to her covenantal status which Jesus has confirmed.

Ultimately, however, the significance of these last chapters will be determined by the understanding of Luke's theological position and his purpose in the total work. If his work is conceived in terms of *Heilsgeschichte* which is developed against an abandonment of eschatology and a belief in the continuing historical process of history, then an abandonment of Jews in a movement

of thought which finds its outcome in the later catholic attitude
becomes inevitable. If, on the other hand, eschatology is not
abandoned, if Jesus is seen as God's final act in the history of
Israel, if the Old Testament beliefs and promises are taken seriously by Luke, and if he is convinced that the outpouring of the
Spirit 'in the last days' has begun, then his concern is not with
continuing history as such so much as with the establishing of his
readers' belief in the lordship of Christ, a belief which, against
such a background, must take Israel's denial seriously and in such
a way that God's promises are seen not to be nullified. What Luke
does is to try to account for Israel's disbelief in a way that does
not cause a denial of her history and which leaves open her contact
with God's promises.

Paul's last journey from Jerusalem to Rome is therefore to be
understood as a confirmation of the earlier attitudes rather than
as an abandonment of those principles which we have seen to
motivate the earlier episodes of Acts. Paul is still represented as
a loyal Jew whose adherence to Christianity is the logical outcome
of his earlier piety (22.3; 23.5; 24.11-16). His concern is still very
much with his own nation (21.23; 23.11; 24.17; 28.17). The
enmity of the Jews is both illogical and perverse; their accusations
are obviously false (21.28; 24.5-6).

His final journey is the result of his pious act in going to Jerusalem (20.16; 24.17); the final attack upon him comes because of
his willingness to embrace the law (24.18). His last visit to the
Temple is described against the background of a speech that proclaims that his initial mission to the Gentiles was the result of a
piety that had led him to that place (22.17-18). That earlier mission
had not resulted in his turning aside from the Temple, and Luke
means to suggest that this later journey derives from Paul's temple
piety rather than witnessing to an abandonment of it. Luke's
whole account of Paul's last visit to Jerusalem is determined by a
positive attitude to the Temple which enables Paul to preach at
Rome.[84] Even Jewish hostility has this positive result.

The final episode at Rome is to be understood as a justification
of Christianity in spite of its refusal by the Jews rather than as a
turning aside from them. Paul's work among the Jews at Rome is
not a total failure (28.24). Jewish disbelief is denounced in terms
of Isaiah 6, which makes even their rejection of Christianity the
outcome of prophecy, so giving further proof that it is not a

falsification of the Christian claims. Nevertheless, Christianity is still put forward as the 'hope of Israel' (28.20), a designation that suggests that even now the Jews are unlikely to be abandoned. Paul announces the Gentile mission: 'Let it be known to you that this salvation of God has been sent to the Gentiles; they will listen' (28.28). This is less a programme for the future than a justification of what has happened, where the Gentile mission and their response is used to contrast their attitude with that of the Jews and so to witness to the truth of the proclamation. As such, Paul's final statement is not a rejection of the Jews. Rather it is a commentary in the light of Scripture upon a situation which has arisen out of the Jewish refusal of the gospel and its ready acceptance by the Gentiles. Emphasis is upon Jewish perversity rather than upon a rejection by Paul, and upon the witness of the Gentiles which is not, however, said to take the place of concern with the Jewish people. The priority of the Jews remains; their refusal presents a problem which cannot be solved by its dismissal but which can be approached in the light of Paul's address to Agrippa: 'To this day I have had the help which comes from God, and so I stand here, testifying both to small and great, saying nothing but what the prophets and Moses said would come to pass; that the Christ must suffer, and that, by being the first to rise from the dead, he would proclaim light both to the people and to the Gentiles' (Acts 26.22–3). Paul's final journey does not cause the abandoning of that standpoint.

4

To the End of the Earth

A strong clue to the purpose of any literary or historical work is nearly always provided by its ending, so that the point down to which the author carries his account and the manner in which he brings it to a conclusion will often give a fair indication of his interests. To this general guide Acts is no exception. Any attempt to determine the purpose of the work as a whole must bear Luke's final episode strongly in mind and will, indeed, not go far wrong if it starts looking for explanations at just that point where Luke breaks off his story.

But the significance which Luke gives to his concluding narrative is by no means easy to determine. As Lampe points out,[1] Paul at Rome is something of an anticlimax. The successes of his earlier exploits are not crowned by an equal triumph at the capital. Most of the episode is taken up with an altercation with the Jews, and Paul remains a prisoner of the imperial power, a captive to Jewish hostility and calumny. The reader can only be conscious of his impending martyrdom.[2] Nevertheless, the final verses of the book present a triumphant conclusion. 'He lived there two whole years at his own expense, and welcomed all who came to him, preaching the kingdom of God and teaching about the Lord Jesus Christ quite openly and unhindered' (28.30, 31).[3] With that, in some way, the Lord's promise at the ascension is illustrated and in part fulfilled: 'You shall receive power when the Holy Spirit is come upon you; and you shall be my witnesses in Jerusalem and in all Judaea and Samaria and to the end of the earth' (1.8). The missionary enterprise has been described in terms of this programme, and Paul at Rome represents its establishment among the Gentiles at the ends of the earth.

Nevertheless, the significance of the event cannot lie just in the gospel's coming to Rome, for Luke admits that Christians are already there. Haenchen's assertion that Luke hides the Roman congregation from view in order to allow Paul to introduce Christianity to Rome is refuted by verse 15.[4] Had Luke wanted to make Paul the first to proclaim the gospel in that city, he could easily have omitted to mention that Christianity was already established there, for, as Lampe points out, Acts as a whole does not lead the reader to expect such a thing.[5] But the fact that he mentions in such a casual manner that Christianity was already in Rome shows that his aim was not to record the first preaching of the gospel to that city. Equally, his lack of interest in the initial establishing of the gospel in the capital of the Roman empire and so the heart of the world suggests that he was not concerned to present that city as 'the new focal point of the world-wide mission'.[6] He is not, as it were, indicating the successful conclusion of one chapter as a basis from which new chapters can unfold and develop. His climax is not to be found in the fact that the gospel as such is in Rome, but in the fact that Paul is there. At Rome, Luke is not concerned to describe the general growth of the Church, but rather, his interest centres upon a particular aspect of the Church's existence in support of which he has chosen to write the large part of his second volume around the person of Paul.

This point has been seen clearly by O'Neill, who quotes Overbeck's judgement: 'We are not told how the gospel came to Rome, but how Paul came to Rome.'[7] Less likely, however, is O'Neill's own suggested reason for Luke's approach—that he used Paul to show the necessity of the break between Christianity and Judaism, and that Paul at Rome witnesses to the fact that Jerusalem is left behind. 'Luke's thesis is that the gospel is free to travel to the ends of the earth only when it is free from the false form which the Jewish religion has taken. Paul is the one figure in the early Church who saw the issue clearly, and that is why Luke makes Paul the central figure in the latter part of Acts.'[8] However, as we have seen, Luke's theology as a whole takes a much more positive attitude towards the Jewish religion than such a view maintains. Paul's last journey from Jerusalem does not represent a final rejection of the city, and Paul himself is consistently presented as a loyal Jew. Luke's Paul is unlikely to have learned the lessons that O'Neill's Luke would have taught him.

Yet it is specifically in Paul at Rome, rather than in the general establishing of the gospel at Rome, where the significance of Luke's

E

final episode is to be found. At Rome the purpose of Paul's conversion is achieved. The Lord had declared to Ananias that Paul was 'a chosen instrument of mine to carry my name before the Gentiles and kings and the sons of Israel' (9.15). His mission there resulted from a vision of the glorified Christ and is confirmed by a further vision as his last journey to Rome begins: 'The following night the Lord stood by him and said, "Take courage, for as you have testified about me at Jerusalem, so you must bear witness also at Rome" ' (23.11). Paul witnesses at Rome in spite of the hostility of the Jews and in spite of his being a prisoner of the imperial power. Neither Jewish hostility nor the restraining might of the Roman state can impede his progress, which is attributed to the direct empowering of the exalted Christ. Indeed, Jewish national susceptibilities and Roman rule both contribute to the accomplishing of the divine will which is that he should witness at Rome; their hostility or indifference have only furthered his progress and the ascended Christ's designs. When he sees the Church at Rome, he therefore thanks God and takes courage (28.15, cf. 23.11). His being there fulfils the Lord's promises which are confirmed by his witness from prison. It is Paul's free witness from prison which makes the joyful climax of the book, a witness which is important in itself as the fulfilment of earlier declarations rather than as the establishing of the gospel in the city.

Paul comes to Rome in fulfilment of the promise of the exalted Christ. He does so in spite of Jewish hostility and Roman imprisonment. By the very fact of his being there as much as by his preaching he proclaims the truth of the Christian assertion that Jesus is Lord. This is not disproved by the Jewish refusal to believe, for their unbelief is effectively countered by the acknowledgement of the Gentiles. St Paul at Rome becomes the definitive witness to the exaltation of Jesus and to the truth of the power of the Christian proclamation. Luke does not leave him at Rome gathering a kind of first-fruits of the Christian universal mission. The continuing witness to the Gentiles becomes an auxiliary guarantee of what Paul has done, but Luke is presenting evidence of a past achievement, the fruits of which are still manifest in the present, rather than a programme or even a vision of future action.

The latter half of Luke's second volume is in the form of a biography of Paul because he sees that apostle as the living proof of what his total work proclaims—that Jesus is Lord, that Jerusalem has seen the eschatological event in his ascension, that his lordship, which is acknowledged by the best in Jewry, is valid in spite of the refusal of Israel as a whole, that its guarantee is the universal witness to the gospel, a witness that is epitomized supremely in the work of Paul. It is not hard to see why Luke has chosen the form he has for the second part of Acts, for Paul was not merely the apostle to the Gentiles but was also the theologian of the Gentile mission and the one who dealt most fully, in both practice and theory, with the Jewish refusal to accept the gospel. Luke–Acts as a whole is not necessarily inconsistent with having been written by one who was a companion of the apostle of the Gentiles. He views the history of the apostolic times through the eyes of faith; the dilemmas of Paul are no longer faced in the heat of passion, and the hard lines of Paul's theology are smudged and not fully appreciated. But the themes with which Luke wrestles are precisely those which were brought to the fore by the ministry of Paul and are never uninfluenced by the apostle's thinking, even though Luke has not entered into those particular insights which were the result of the apostle's own history and personality. It is perhaps only Paul the complete existentialist and Luke the out-and-out purveyor of salvation history to the exclusion of eschatology who could never have been companions.[9]

ACCORDING TO THE SCRIPTURES

Luke sees the arrival of Paul at Rome as the supreme example which guarantees the reality of the Christian proclamation of the lordship of Jesus, and what is true for Paul in particular is true also of the whole Christian enterprise which has caused the Gentiles to acknowledge this fact. He does not describe the Gentile mission primarily because he wishes to be the historian of the early Church but because he sees it as visible proof that, in Jesus, God's final salvation has been revealed. His interest in the mission is subservient to his desire to set forth Jesus as God's eschatological act for his people and, through them, for the world.

In the Lord's speech at the ascension as it is reported in Luke 24.46–7, Scripture is said to determine not only the suffering and resurrection of the Christ but also the preaching of repentance and forgiveness of sins 'in his name' to all nations 'beginning from

Jerusalem'. This connection of the universal mission with the fulfilment of Scripture is new to Luke and seems almost certainly to have arisen from his own insights, for the concern to make the whole action of God in Jesus conform to the scriptural pattern is fundamental to him.[10] Nevertheless, it was not such a new departure, for the mission to the nations was often given an eschatological significance in early Christian thought and, as such, was seen as the fulfilment of scriptural requirements. If Luke was influenced at this point by the thought of Mark 13.10, he was not breaking away from its eschatological setting but, in relating it to the ascension of Jesus, was being true to his reinterpretation of early Christian eschatology.[11]

Dupont has shown how strongly Luke allowed his understanding of the Christian mission as being determined by Old Testament expectations to influence his writing of Luke–Acts.[12] This insight determined both the need for a description of the world-wide spread of the gospel and also justified the course of the mission as he unfolded it. But there is even more behind Luke's emphasis than this. By describing the universal spread of Christianity as the successful realization of what Scripture expected, Luke presents it as proof that the hand of God was behind it and, since it was determined by the ascension, he uses it to establish the truth of his claims on behalf of the exaltation of Jesus of Nazareth. Scripture shows, not merely that the life of Jesus of Nazareth proves him to be the Christ, but also that the universal mission, undertaken in his name, declares him to be the Lord. By it, the Christian witness is seen to have passed the test laid down for it by Gamaliel: 'If this plan or this undertaking is of men, it will fail; but if it is of God, you will not be able to overthrow them. You might even be found opposing God' (Acts 5.38–9).

Luke would seem to have two groups of prophecies especially in mind. Dupont points to the influence upon him of passages found in the second part of the book of Isaiah. In his account of the appearance of John the Baptist he extends the Marcan quotation from Isaiah 40 to enable a universal reference to be included, 'and all flesh shall see the salvation of God' (Is. 40.5). More specifically, he sees Paul's work among the Gentiles as carried out in fulfilment of Isaiah 49.6. 'I have set you to be a light for the Gentiles, that you may bring salvation to the uttermost parts of the earth' (Act 13.47). In the infancy narratives, Luke has already applied this passage to the work of Jesus (Luke 2.32), and it may well be the universal vocation of the Servant which in part accounts for his liking to describe Jesus in Servant terms. But the fact that he can apply this passage to Paul as well as to Jesus suggests that he sees its emphasis as pointing in the first place, not so much to the person of Jesus, as to the saving work of God which is accomplished through him. It is the salvation of God which is his chief concern (Luke 2.30; 3.6). That salvation is God's action which, directed specifically to Israel (Luke 1.69, 77), is witnessed by the nations (Luke 3.6), and into the sphere of which others are brought as they are incorporated into the people of God (Luke 19.9). The rejection of this salvation by a large part of the Israelite nation will be compensated for by the obedience of the Gentiles (Acts 28.28). His use of Deutero–Isaiah has caused Luke to invest the idea of salvation with an eschatological significance and, at this point, it is this aspect rather than the thought of the Messiah which predominates.

A second group of passages which has influenced Luke is that which talks of the incorporation of the nations at the time of the renewal of Israel. James quotes one such passage from Amos 9.11–12 at the Council of Jerusalem (Acts 15.15–18) and, since it appears in its distinctive Septuagintal version, it seems likely to owe its inclusion to Luke himself[13] who, at this crucial stage of his work, uses it to explain the significance of the conversion of Cornelius and also that which he assigns to the Apostolic Decree. Though this prophecy does not itself talk of the pilgrimage of the nations to Jerusalem, it does refer to the renewing of the house of David, and other such passages link the incorporation of the nations, not merely to the renewal of Israel but also to the restoration of the city (Is. 2.2–4; 55.5; Zech. 2.10–11; 8.20–3; Joel 2.32).

Luke's use of the Old Testament has caused him to see the salvation of the nations as a necessary part of the eschatological action of God. They point less to the thought of a Messiah than to God's final act for his people into which representatives from the nations of the world are incorporated. This accounts for his making the mission centre entirely around the ascension and its results. The speeches at the ascension, both in Luke 24 and in Acts 1, direct attention to the universal mission and, since it cannot take place until then, in the Gospel itself, there is what King calls a 'partial crypsis of his universalism'.[14] Only with the eschato-logical event can the wider significance of the work of Jesus be realized and, even then, the priority of Israel is, as in the Biblical pattern, always maintained. The continuing priority of Israel means that the narration of the universal outreach cannot start until the proclamation has been fully made to her. Even though Jerusalem as a whole rejects the proclamation and even though she scatters the Christian community in that city, the Twelve remain (8.1) witnessing to her eschatological renewal and quickly re-establishing the Christian community there (9.26–30). Only after the new community has been extended to incorporate the area of the old Israel can the proclamation to the Gentiles begin (9.31).[15]

But though Deutero–Isaiah can be used to justify a mission which goes out from Jerusalem, and Isaiah 2.2–4 says that 'out of Zion shall go forth the law and the word of the Lord from Jerusalem', nevertheless the basic thought of Old Testament prophecy points to a movement of the nations to the city and their incorporation into a restored Israel centred upon Jerusalem.[16] Jewish disobedience has caused the prophetic expectations to be only partly realized and the risen Christ, because of his own re-jection brought about by that disobedience can therefore turn the prophetic hopes into a new direction. Nevertheless, just as the rejection of him by Jerusalem furthered the progress to his exaltation and made it possible, so now the continuing hostility of Jerusalem actively furthers the spread of the gospel and the sway of the glorified Lord (Acts 8.4).

Luke uses the Cornelius episode to justify this new mode by which the Gentiles are incorporated into the eschatological Israel. Since the time of Dibelius the fundamental importance of this event for Luke has been recognized as lying in its pro-clamation that 'the incorporating of the Gentiles into the Church without subjecting them to the Law originated neither with Paul nor with Peter, but with God'.[17] For Luke, the emphasis upon the divine initiative is paramount, but, important though this is, the full significance of the result of that initiative is to be found in something even more fundamental than the question of the Gentiles and the Law. For him, the event expresses the reality of the Gentiles' incorporation into renewed Israel, and so witnesses to the fact that, because of the exaltation of Jesus, Israel has truly experienced the full eschatological promises of God. The Cornelius episode is described as an extension of Pentecost, and it is the significance that Luke has applied to Pentecost in describing it as the eschatological renewal of Israel which determines the significance he assigns to the Cornelius episode. The Spirit comes in the same way, manifesting the freedom of the divine initiative, resulting in the same tongues, and issuing in the same praise of God. On both occasions amazement fills those who are present (2.12; 10.45). At Jerusalem, wonder is caused by the fact that the men are Galileans; at Caesarea by the fact that they are Gentiles (2.7; 10.45). Only the mockery is absent from Caesarea, since those who watch are all too well aware of the significance of what they are witnessing. Luke himself frequently points out the exact parallelism between the two occasions (10.47; 11.15; 11.17; 15.8), and, since Pentecost is seen by him as the eschatological renewal of Israel, the outpouring of the Spirit upon Cornelius and his companions becomes therefore a sign of their incorporation into this renewed community, based on Israel and centred upon Jerusalem, but now widened beyond Israel and geographically established away from Jerusalem. It was not the re-made Israel's initiative but, as in Jewish eschatological expectations, God's which caused the Gentiles to be included in a manner which was indeed unexpected but which was compelled by the disobedience of Jerusalem as a whole. Nevertheless, even here the centrality of Jerusalem and its place in the divine plan is not forgotten and there are signs that Luke has emphasized the agency of the eschatological Israel in the person of its chief apostle, Peter. The outpouring of the Spirit is the confirmation rather than the cause of Peter's contact, so that the incorporation of the nations, though carried out by the divine action, results from God's renewing of his people. Peter's vision, which is quite possibly a Lucan addition,[18] brings out the importance of Peter's realizing the full significance of Cornelius's summons and also makes possible a second Lucan addition which is most likely to be found in Peter's speech.[19] In his account of Peter's report of the happenings to his critics, Luke emphasizes this initial vision and the preaching to Cornelius which it alone made possible (11.5–15; 15.7). In his assessment of the meaning of the event, the gift of the Spirit is seen as the outcome of Peter's preaching (15.7; 10.44; 11.15).

Luke uses Peter's speech to bring out further certain aspects of the significance of the occasion as he understands it. God's concern is universal and he accepts all. Jesus is not only Lord over all men (10.36), but God 'shows no partiality' (10.34). It is unlikely that Haenchen is correct when he maintains that this later expression is a denial of Israel's election, which Luke is elsewhere anxious to maintain.[20] Rather, in its context, it states that God's concern is not limited to Israel but that other nations are embraced by it. But it nevertheless does not deny the priority of Israel. What it does deny is that Israel's position is exclusive. Her election issues in a wider significance and in the face of the Christian message, Israel too must repent. The Jews of Jerusalem are blamed for the death of Jesus, and, after the resurrection, Jesus does not appear to all the people, but only to witnesses who are to summon the people to repentance. But the Jews are still the people of God (10.42), Jesus went first to Israel (10.36) and she is not rejected. Cornelius is a godfearer. Both this, and the fact that Luke puts into the mouth of Peter a speech which follows the same pattern as those made in Acts to Jews, rather than being on the lines of those given before Gentile audiences, shows clearly Luke's idea that the renewed Israel is extended as Gentiles are incorporated into her.

THE ESCHATOLOGICAL COMMUNITY

This understanding of the mission in terms of Israel's eschatological expectations is underlined by Luke in three ways, namely by his account of the Apostolic Council, by his emphasis upon the supremacy of Jerusalem, and by his concern with the unity of the young Church. At the Apostolic Council, the heart of the matter for him is to be found in the speech of James. Since the use of biblical ideas to frame the theology of the speech is in accordance with his practice, and the general theological insights agree with his overall presentation of the Gentile mission, it is most likely that here we have Luke's own voice (Acts 15.13–21).[21]

In accordance with this, the speech of James relies wholly upon the episode of Cornelius rather than upon any success experienced by Barnabas and Saul. The decision to be arrived at is in no way influenced by pragmatic considerations but is based entirely upon the proved will of God as it has been experienced in the out-

pouring of the Spirit upon Cornelius which, in the light of Pentecost, can be seen as the fulfilment of prophetic expectations.

The Gentiles are to be incorporated into the renewed Israel and
so the continuity with God's initial covenant is to be maintained.
Of that there is no doubt, for there is no hint in James's speech
that the Church has taken over from Israel the privilege of being
the people of God. She is not yet seen as a *tertium genus*, alongside
Israel and the Gentile world.[22] Nevertheless, within the continuity
there is a discontinuity which, theologically, is justified by the
Cornelius episode and, practically, is expressed in the abandonment of the requirement of circumcision for those Gentiles who
enter the eschatological people. They do not enter by way of the
old Israel for she stands under condemnation and, like the rest of
mankind, has need of repentance (Acts 2.38; 3.19; 13.46), but
what they enter is Israel renewed and restored (15.14, 16–17),
Israel whose Temple and circumcision are no longer the final
signs of God's favour since they have been superseded by the
Christ, but nevertheless who gives identity to the new people of
God as they enter into her covenantal life.

Luke therefore understands the four requirements of the
Apostolic Decree as both concession and obligation. They are
concession in so far as Gentiles are no longer compelled to enter
the eschatological community by taking over the ultimate marks
of the old Israel, but they are obligation in that they recognize
that the new community arises out of the old Israel and is based
upon those who come from her. The holiness of the group is to
be maintained and the position of the Christian Jews is secured.
The decree is therefore understood by Luke as Mosaic regulations
for Gentile Christians which enable them to take their place
within the eschatological Israel. The covenantal community is
continued, the holiness of the total *Laos* is secured, and God's
action in the history of Israel is recognized (Acts 15.29).

It is unlikely that Luke regarded the four requirements as a
matter of table-fellowship.[23] Not only are they inadequate of
themselves for this purpose, but the episode of Cornelius had
settled that question once and for all. Luke could neither have
envisaged nor recounted anything that suggested a partial acceptance of Gentiles, and for him the matters of circumcision and of
table-fellowship were one and the same, as the fact that these two
matters are not divided in his accounts of the significance of the

Cornelius event shows (11.3, 17; 15.1). Table-fellowship provided no theological problem for him, and the speech of James shows that he gave the decrees a theological significance. It is possible that the requirements come from Diaspora Jewry, for Schoeps notes their relevance to such a group who would be loyal to the authority of Moses and from the ranks of whose *Sebomenoi* the Church probably gained a large number of adherents.[24] If this is the case, then it seems that Luke regarded the regulations as putting Gentile Christians into much the same relationship with the Jewish community as was Cornelius. They would recognize the priority of the Jewish nation as the people of God, accept their dependence upon that community, and enter into obligations derived from it. Like Cornelius, they were incorporated through the Spirit into the eschatological Israel, and their acceptance of the decree was their witness to the source of their salvation.

Acts 21 therefore becomes Luke's reminder to his readers of the significance of the decree as he understood it and the introduction of Paul's final episode in its terms. Jewish Christians in Jerusalem remain zealous for the Law and loyal adherents of the Temple (21.20). Jews of the Diaspora do not abandon the Law once they become Christians but, on the contrary, remain loyal to it (21.21), a position which is exemplified by Luke's Paul. Gentile Christians, though released from the obligation to these things which have been superseded by the exaltation of Christ, nevertheless accept the requirements of the decree which enable them to respect those who come to Christianity by way of the Old Israel and which at the same time cause them to acknowledge the true nature of the new community.

Luke then manages to retain respect for the Law by showing Christians in Jerusalem and Paul in particular as the apostle to the Gentiles as loyal advocates of it. Gentiles who become Christians are exempt from circumcision, but this setting aside of the Law occurs only as the result of the direct intervention of God himself. The grand nature of the cause of the exemption indicates respect for the Law rather than its belittling.

Luke's Jesus was himself under the Law (Luke 2.21, 22); he shows respect for its regulations (5.14) and the keeping of it leads to eternal life (10.26). It is true that he breaks the current interpretation of the Law of the sabbath, but this is because the marks of the old dispensation must give way before him since 'the Son of man is lord of the sabbath' (6.5). In doing so, however, he points out their misinterpretation of the sabbath law in such a way as to bring out its real significance (6.9). He therefore acts with no disrespect towards the Law even though he shows its limitations and reveals its fulfilment in himself. Luke omits any hints of criticism of the Mosaic Law which could be read into the discussion on marriage and divorce (Mark 10.1–12, Matt. 19.1–9) or into the Matthaean deepening of the Mosaic commands as they are found in the Sermon on the Mount (Matt. 5.21–48).[25]

Paul at Antioch, it is true, does declare the limitations of the Law when it is compared with its fulfilment in Jesus (Acts 13.39–40), but though he uses Pauline terminology here, it remains most likely that Luke is expressing his own understanding which is a belief, not in the total inability of the Law to secure forgiveness for its adherents, but in its partial and limited success. It was inadequate rather than impotent; it is taken up into the event of Jesus rather than brought to an end by him.[26]

Only once does Luke appear to be hostile to the Law. This is in Peter's speech at the Apostolic Council where he talks of circumcision and the Law as a 'yoke' which 'neither our fathers nor we have been able to bear' (Acts 15.10).[27] Here, he comes closer to Pauline thought, though it is contrary to the Paul whom he describes, but, by expressing it through Peter he frees the sentiment from excesses which might have been unleashed had he put it in the mouth of Paul. Perhaps Luke here is led into an attitude that is stronger than the one he usually takes because of the link with the episode of Cornelius. There, the question of the Law is largely one of circumcision which sums up the Law and expresses its full rigours. Cornelius, a God-fearer, had shrunk from its harsh demands, and it seems here that Luke is making Peter look at the situation through Cornelius's eyes. Is it too much to wonder whether Luke's picture of Cornelius is very much a self-portrait and that in Peter's speech here we have undiluted Luke?[28]

But respect for the Law is uppermost, and it is this which is expressed in the last verse of James's speech (15.21). James reiterates that concern for the Law which is implicit in the regulations when they are regarded from the point of view of both concession and obligation. The *gar* of verse 21 picks up not only the decrees but also the *me paremochlein* of verse 19. Verse 21 justifies the latter by showing that the concession does not imply

any disrespect to Moses since the full Law is universally proclaimed in the synagogues and those who would be able to
identify themselves completely with the Jewish nation can still
enter the Christian community by that way. But the verse, in also
giving a reason for the decrees, explains that Moses is still an
authority for Christians. His Law which, in its universal proclamation, is a partial fulfilment of the Amos expectation, still has
meaning for them, and the acceptance of the decrees witnesses to
the fact that they are not turning away from the old covenant.[29]

The dispensation of grace has neither abandoned the Law nor
turned aside from the history of the Jewish people. That is
Luke's message in Acts 15 and his theme is worked out in his
account of Paul and of his dealings with the church at Jerusalem.
The cry of the Jews of Asia against him is obviously false (21.28)
and Paul's defence of himself is equally obviously true (22.3;
23.5; 24.14; 26.5–6). Luke 16.16 has maintained that the Law
and the prophets have led into the time of the proclamation of the
kingdom. With Jesus, the dispensation of grace has begun. But
Luke 16.17 immediately goes on to speak of the abiding nature of
the Law. The new dispensation has not brought the old to an end,
but has taken it up into itself and given it fulfilment.

Luke's concern to show the early Christian mission as the
fulfilment of Jewish eschatological expectations is illustrated,
secondly, by his emphasis upon the centrality of Jerusalem. In
his story of the developing Christian witness to the exaltation of
Jesus, that city has a twofold function. In the first place, though
she does not inaugurate the succeeding stages of the mission, it is
her approval which regularizes them, and, secondly, their relationship with her alone secures their incorporation into the renewed people of God.

Every stage in the development of the mission has therefore to
be accepted by the Jerusalem church. In accordance with this,
apostles must be sent by her to establish and regularize the
mission to Samaria (Acts 8.14–16). Paul after his conversion,
when he has to leave Damascus, comes at once to Jerusalem to
receive the approval of the leaders there (Acts 9.26). The conversion of Cornelius happens through Peter and it is only after
the Jerusalem church has witnessed to the significance of the
event that Luke goes on to record the extension of the preaching
to non-Jews (11.20). This new stage, however, only gains real

direction when Barnabas and Paul arrive, as the direct result of the intervention of the Jerusalem church, to turn what began as a spontaneous enterprise into a determined mission (11.21–6). Once it is established, this new community acknowledges its links with Jerusalem and its dependence upon her by sending relief to the church there by the hands of Barnabas and Saul (11.30).

As a result of the first missionary journey of Barnabas and Saul, the rift between the new community and the old Israel is magnified by the widening hostility of the Jews and the influx of the Gentiles to such an extent that the continuity of the covenantal community is in danger of being lost. For Luke, this problem is resolved wholly by the authoritative decision of the Jerusalem church in answer to Antioch's request for a ruling (15.2). The Apostolic Decree results, not from discussion, but from theological reflections of the Jerusalem church which are entirely uninfluenced by any pragmatic considerations that could be drawn from the experiences of Barnabas and Paul. When the decree is issued, it bears the character of a decision of the Mother church which requires only acceptance on the part of the Christians at Antioch and which is communicated to them, not by their own representatives, but by envoys from Jerusalem itself (15.27).

Luke's story now centres upon Paul who goes out virtually as a delegate from Jerusalem, 'delivering for observance the decisions which had been reached by the apostles and elders who were at Jerusalem' (16.4). That city is his base. His work inevitably links the newly-founded churches to her, and through him her influence is extended. If 18.22 is to be seen as a visit to Jerusalem, Knox is right to describe Acts as envisaging Paul's travels in terms of a 'series of movements from Jerusalem and back again'.[30] Nevertheless, since Luke gives to this visit the barest of mentions, it is perhaps better to see 15.30—21.15 as a single section which both begins and ends in Jerusalem and to which unity is given by the mention of the Apostolic Decrees at both its beginning and end (15.30; 21.25). Luke then sees Paul's preaching as an extension of the community which he describes as existing in Jerusalem, for his interest in the widening movement does not cause him to turn aside from the developing life of the church at the centre. Jerusalem remains the focal point of the renewed Israel, the gatherer of representatives from all parts of the earth and the legislator for the life of the eschatological community.

Paul's journeyings join the churches to her and enable her to fulfil her prophetically-foreseen function of uniting people of all nations to Yahweh.

That Jerusalem is the goal of Paul's journeyings is suggested as early as 19.21[31] and, from this time on, she is kept constantly before the reader (20.16, 22; 21.11–12, 15). His final visit to the city allows him to offer the nations to Yahweh. As the place of his suffering, she enables him to achieve his glory through the accomplishment of the exalted Lord's purpose for him in his witness at Rome. But his preaching there is still seen as the outcome of his relationship with the Jerusalem church, for it is his response to James's advice which causes him to be in the Temple and so leads him to that city. Paul comes to Rome still as the subordinate of the Jerusalem church, and his preaching there is the final witness that her eschatological role is fulfilled. So far from being the break with the Jerusalem church that O'Neill suggests, Paul is really her representative. At Rome, he has neither turned his back on the Jewish nation, nor has he broken away from the church in that city and from its place as the witness to the fulfilment of the promises of old.

Neither the destruction of Jerusalem nor the scattering of the Christian community there can undermine this triumph nor annul the fulfilment of the promises. Continuing Jewish disobedience has brought about the destruction of Jerusalem which, by the time of Luke's writing, is certainly an event in history. But though Luke is well aware of the tragedy of this happening (Luke 13.34–5; 21.20–4), for him it has no significance in God's plans for salvation. Nevertheless, its destruction is not the last word. In Jesus, the promises to David have received their guarantee (1.32–33) so that the restoration of the kingdom to Israel is still part of the Christian hope (Acts 1.6). At the moment, Jerusalem's house is forsaken (13.35), but this is only until 'the times of the Gentiles are fulfilled' (21.24) when, at the day of her restoration, she will cry, 'Blessed be he who comes in the name of the Lord' (13.35). The destruction of Jerusalem in no way contradicts Luke's theme, for he is confident of her restoration and future supremacy.

Finally, Luke's understanding of the eschatological nature of the Christian community has led him to emphasize its unity. This is his reason for the obvious idealization of the early Church which appears in Acts. The Spirit-filled church of Jerusalem is 'of one heart and soul having all things in common, filled with joy, cease-less in worship, having favour with all the people' (Acts 2.43–7; 4.32–7). As in the days of the conquest, any action in the com-munity which mars that relationship must be ruthlessly extermi-nated. The deaths of Ananias and Sapphira are necessary lest the nature of the new community be forgotten. 'And great fear came upon the whole church and upon all who heard these things' (5.11). Divisions within the group are limited to matters of administration and these are easily settled (6.1–6). When persecu-tion comes, it is directed against the whole Church (8.1).

Later, when the community goes out into the Gentile world, there is no hint of divisions or of those problems which threatened her very life. Paul is wholly at one with the apostles, and willingly subordinate to the elders of the Jerusalem church. That church maintains her own unity of outlook, which is disturbed only by the excesses of some who are quickly won over by the rest (Acts 11.2; 15.1, 5), so that no real divisions or opposition of any stand-ing remains (Acts 11.18; 15.22). The conversion of Cornelius leaves no room for differences of interpretation. Paul and Barna-bas, it is true, part company, but there is no hint that real divisions on any weighty matters underline their disagreement (15.39).[32] James's final declaration to Paul puts out a picture of peace and harmony (Acts 21.20–5).

But this is not just a matter of idealizing the beginnings of the Church's existence. It is not merely a simplified presentation in the interests of the edification of later generations, nor is it done in order to emphasize a unique period in the life of the Church. Conzelmann's view that its uniqueness is accounted for by the presence of the witnesses takes no account of the disappearance of the apostles from the scene once the theological basis of the Gentile mission has been established.[33] Rather is the picture subservient to Luke's desire to present the early Christian groups as truly the eschatological community, the people of God ful-filling in its life the best of the prophetic expectations. God's final action has taken place in Christ, and the universal spread of the Gospel, exemplified by Paul's appearance at Rome, witnesses to this fact. Later events such as the fall of Jerusalem, the failure of the Jews to respond, the occurrence both of divisions and persecutions, cannot belie this fact. Luke encourages his readers to see what actually has happened and to understand the true nature of that community of which they are now a part.

Giving substance to Luke's claim about the nature of the new community which he describes is his emphasis upon its inspiration by the Holy Spirit. Three things need to be said as preliminaries to an assessment of his thought on this. Firstly, as we have seen, the Spirit does not constitute the kingdom but is rather a sign of its reality. For Luke, the kingdom is a fact of the other world rather than an entity in this, so that the Spirit does not bring it about but witnesses to it. But, in the second place, the Spirit is nevertheless part of God's eschatological activity, for it is a sign of his final work in Jesus. It is the witness to his exaltation and the sign that the new community that is thereby brought into being is truly the community of the End-time. Though not itself the actual eschatological event, it nevertheless enables that event to happen and then witnesses that it has taken place. There is therefore no justification for Conzelmann's denuding the Spirit of eschatological significance[34] or for Schweizer's assertion that it 'ushers in a new age, but not *the* new age'.[35] Luke's final period in redemptive history is itself the eschatological age. But, thirdly, because Luke's understanding of the Spirit is subordinate to his eschatology and revolves around that alone, attempts to use his thought as a basis for determining the Spirit's sacramental significance and its relation to baptism and confirmation are unlikely to be successful.[36] As we have seen, Luke is writing a tract for the times rather than a history of one period of Christianity which has an illustrative significance for the continuing history of the Church, and liturgical influences from Luke's own days, though undeniably present, are submerged in his theological concern.

In the light of this, his thought upon the Spirit is seen to gather around two foci. In the first place, he understands its presence as a pointer to the eschatological character of the community it calls into being, and, as that community is extended, as the mark of incorporation into it. Pentecost, as we saw above, is the eschatological renewal of Israel, and this is proved and made possible by the presence of the Spirit. The Spirit occasions the renewal, but its ultimate source is the eschatological event accomplished at the ascension, which enables the Spirit to be poured out (Acts 2.33). It is from the ascension that the Spirit proceeds. Afterwards, the presence of the Spirit brings about the extension of that initial community. Samaritans are incorporated into it by its bestowal through the token of unity afforded by the laying on of apostolic hands (Acts 8.17), and Gentiles are included through its miraculous presence at the house of Cornelius (Acts 10.44). The Spirit, given through the hands of Ananias (Acts 9.17), links Paul to the eschatological community (an action which is absolutely vital for Luke to describe in the interests of his presentation of the relations between Paul and Jerusalem), and later the gift of the Spirit to the Ephesian disciples (Acts 19.1–7) marks their inclusion within the people of God which has been brought into being as a result of the eschatological event. The special mention here of the bestowal of the Spirit through the laying on of hands is to emphasize this transition from a preparatory stage into full membership of the community of the End-time.

But if the presence of the Spirit is the sign of the reality of the eschatological people of God, it is also the supreme witness to the fact that what has enabled this is the ascension which it reveals as God's ultimate saving deed on behalf of his people. The Spirit set apart Jesus as God's final instrument and sent him out on his progress to his exaltation. This emphasis in Luke accounts for the fact that extra reference to the Spirit's action upon Jesus appears only in the early chapters of his narrative of the ministry (4.1, 14, 18).[37] The Spirit is that which initiates Jesus' progress to the eschatological event. At Pentecost, it witnesses to this as it is accomplished at the exaltation (Acts 2.36) and, afterwards, Luke describes its presence mainly in relation to the widening sphere of the Christian community, for he concentrates his understanding of its activity around certain special endowments which make possible the extending witness to God's final saving act.[38] It is Luke's emphasis upon the Spirit as the enabler of the witness to this which causes him to think of it in *ruach* terms, and to give expression to its intermittent activity rather than describing it as a permanent personal indwelling within believers. Luke is less the theologian of the Holy Spirit than is sometimes suggested. It is true that he makes frequent mention of it and that it plays an important part in his overall work, but his theology of it is not embracing and is not fully worked out. Luke shows himself to be aware of the deeper implications of the presence of the Spirit and of the community's experience of its dwelling in both the group and in individuals, but his own interest does not lie here. His thought is circumscribed by his concentration upon the Spirit's presence as the proof of the claims that he is making and of its significance for his reinterpretation of eschatology. The price he paid is seen in the fact that, in any discussion of Luke's understanding of the Spirit, the pronoun used must be 'it' rather than the fuller and more adequate 'he'.

CHRISTIANS AND ROME

So far, it has been our thesis in this chapter that the account in Acts of the extension of Christianity from the Pentecostal experience in Jerusalem to the preaching of Paul at Rome was designed by Luke to witness to his assertion that in Jesus the prophetic expectations were fulfilled and that God's final promises to the Jewish people, and through them to the nations, were being realized. We have seen that Luke–Acts as a whole most probably resulted from a crisis in Christianity that was brought about by the failure of the parousia to materialize and by the failure of the Jewish people to acknowledge Jesus as the Christ of God. Luke's two-volume work is an attempt to confirm a faith that was in danger of faltering and to encourage a return to the enthusiasm of his readers' initial conviction that 'Jesus is Lord'.

If this is so, then it at once raises the question of the apologetic concern of Luke for, as a recent writer has expressed it: 'It is admitted by everybody that Luke wants to represent the Roman government as neutral, and as just, towards Christianity,'[39] and the usual reason given for this outlook is that his work contains a political apologetic which is designed to acquit Christianity on any charge of hostility towards the state and is calculated to encourage a favourable attitude towards it on the part of convinced upholders of the Roman power.[40] Such apologetic interest would of course mean that, seen from this angle at any rate, Luke was concerned to address a non-Christian public, and, even if such a thesis be modified, it at least means that Acts was designed to win individual non-Christians for the cause of Christ.[41] If the latter be the case, then Luke was, as it were, fighting on two fronts.

However, it is open to question whether Luke's undoubted interest in the relation of the Roman powers to the spread of the Christian proclamation was motivated by apologetic concern but rather whether it is to be accounted for by interests which are more directly linked to his main purpose. That some doubt may be placed upon Luke's alleged apologetic interest is suggested by the way in which he ends his work.

As Hanson has recently pointed out,[42] the ending of Acts presents an unresolved difficulty to those who assert that Luke had such a concern. Why does he not say something about the result of Paul's appeal to Caesar? If Paul was condemned and executed as a result of that appeal, then any attempts on the part of Luke to present Rome as just and fair-minded would be severely undermined. His earlier protestations would sound empty and vain. On the other hand, if Paul had been acquitted and Luke had an apologetic concern, he could hardly have failed to mention the fact since it would have set the seal on his case with such conviction that any later condemnation by Nero could then have been presented as an unfortunate aberration by an evil and out of character ruler.

Hanson's answer is that Luke's readers knew the rest of the story and therefore had no need to be told of Paul's fate. Nevertheless, however this may be, and even Hanson himself is not entirely happy with this solution, it does not lessen the problem posed by the ending if Luke had apologetic in mind. Even if Luke's apologetic motives were subordinate to his other concerns, and if Paul at Rome provided such a climax to these that apologetic considerations had to take a second place and here, at any rate, go by the board, Luke could not have given away his case so easily as he must have done if his readers knew that Paul was condemned, or have allowed it to go by default, as would have been the case if Paul had been acquitted, if he had treated it earlier with the seriousness that the upholders of this theory assume. Moreover, Paul comes to Rome prepared for martyrdom and the awesomeness of the future events throws its shadow over his last journey (Acts 20.25, 29, 37–8; 21.11–14; 28.17–20). Acts as a whole would seem to support the view that death awaited Paul at Rome and that Luke's concern was neither with Paul's condemnation nor acquittal but simply with the fact of his being there.[43]

We must conclude then that the ending of Acts suggests that Luke was not primarily interested in making an apology to Rome —either to the state as a whole to achieve the acceptance of Christianity as a *religio licita* or to individual Romans who, feeling that Christianity might be hostile to the state, could thus have

been put off from embracing Luke's beliefs. The only likelihood
on these lines is that Acts might have been written as a defence at
Paul's trial. The ending then would at least not sabotage the main
purpose of the work, but such a purpose for Acts, let alone for
Luke–Acts as a whole, leaves the vast amount of its contents
wholly without explanation and has little to commend it.[44]

But if Luke's obvious concern with the Roman state's attitude
to Christianity is not motivated by apologetic considerations, how
is this bias to be accounted for? The answer would seem to be
suggested by those considerations which determined his description of the trial of Jesus. In our discussions of this episode,[45] we
had reason to reject the alleged apologetic concern of Luke in
favour of the view that his interest lay rather, firstly, in bringing
out the duplicity and hostility of the Jews and, secondly, in showing the Roman powers as involuntary agents in the divine plan.
The Jews are held up for blame: the Romans are neither praised
nor condemned, but, instead, they are simply presented as being
open to what the divine plans required of them and, in this way,
they make an indirect witness to Luke's claims on behalf of Jesus.
Luke's favourite psalms are thereby fulfilled: 'The Lord sends
forth from Zion your mighty sceptre; Rule in the midst of your
foes' (Psalm 110.2). And again: 'Ask of me and I will make the
nations your heritage, and the ends of the earth your possession'
(Psalm 2.8). In his description of the trial, Luke is concerned to
bring out the Jewish iniquity, not to reduce the part of the Roman
power. That is, as it were, a by-product of his main purpose which
is motivated, however, not by an anti-Jewish outlook, but by a
concern to make explicable the continuing rejection of the
Christian proclamation by the Jewish people.

Luke is not seen as favourable to the Roman powers. Rome does
give way to Jewish pressure, even though it is seen to be of evil
intent (23.13–25), Pilate is not presented in a favourable light
(13.1), and Rome's later destruction of Jerusalem is invested with
all the horror of a political event (23.28–31). In Acts, while it is
true that no Roman officials ever condemn Paul or the gospel that
he preaches, but rather that they show an impartiality which does
not accept the enemies' actual charges, nevertheless, as a whole,
they are totally uncomprehending as to the real nature of the
Christian proclamation. The centurion at the Cross may represent
the Gentiles, but by no stretch of the imagination can he be taken

to foreshadow the later response of the Roman state to Jesus, at
least as that response is portrayed by Luke (23.47). His positive
response is unique and is not repeated by any other Roman
official. Rather, Christianity remains an enigma to them and the
cupidity of Felix prolonged Paul's captivity in an attempt both to
procure monetary gain, and also the favour of the Jews (Acts
24.26, 27). Paul's arrival at Rome, any more than Jesus' condemnation to a cross, does not present Roman justice in a favourable
light.

The other episodes where the civil power is present make
dubious reading from an apologetic point of view. At Philippi,
Paul and Silas are beaten as a result of false accusations and,
while it is true that the magistrates apologize to them, they, nevertheless, ask them to leave their city (Acts 16.39). Christianity
presents a disturbance and threat to the peace of the state which
the Roman power is not able to cope with. At Thessalonica, it is
the Jews who offer false witness (Acts 17.6–7 cf. Luke 23.2) but,
though it is obviously false, the authorities are disturbed and,
once again, the apostles are compelled to leave (Acts 17.8–10).
Rome does not come down on their side, neither does she give
them any real protection. Gallio, it is true, implicitly rejects the
Jewish accusations by refusing to become an arbiter of such
matters (Acts 18.12–17), but here Luke's purpose seems to be to
present additional material regarding Jewish perversity rather
than to make a defence of Roman practices. Overall, these episodes
show very little evidence of anything in the nature of real apologetic. Christianity, it is true, is declared to be not guilty of deliberate
subversion and innocent of vicious practices, but Luke does not
hesitate to present it as a constant threat to the peace of the civil
power. It is seen as a danger and his officials seem scarcely more
able to cope with it than are Pilate or Festus. These episodes do
not prepare the ground for looking upon his final scenes in Rome
as preludes to a release granted by a judicious and unbiased
Roman government. Rather do they leave entirely open the possibilities regarding Paul's fate. Indeed, if the Emperor follows the
manner of his subordinates, expediency might well be expected
to be his maxim. There is nothing to suggest that he would resist
Jewish pressure if that were applied consistently. He might well
acquiesce even though he would do so without conviction.

Paul really comes to Rome as the result as much of Roman

prevarication and duplicity as of Jewish prejudice and hostility. If Rome is seen as doing nothing positive to bring about his appearance there, she certainly does not pursue a justice which is immune from Jewish pressure and unyielding to Jewish bigotry. Her officials may declare that Christianity is innocent of those things which are brought against her by the Jews but they do little to assert that it is harmless. The tribune, Lysias, realizes that Paul is no common agitator (Acts 21.37–40), but he still sees him as a disturber of the peace, a potential danger to the law he represents. Though he acknowledges that Paul has done nothing deserving death or imprisonment, he still commits him in custody before the governor (Acts 23.30), who keeps him prison for at least two years. When Festus also, in order to gain favour with the Jews, is prepared to go ahead with the trial, Paul is compelled to appeal to Caesar (Acts 25.11). Festus' later defence of his action before Agrippa and his witness to Paul's innocence do not alter the fact that he was prepared to put him on trial and that Luke records that Paul by no means had confidence in its final outcome (Acts 25.25). The whole account of Paul's appeal to Rome abounds in inconsistencies. Rome accepts Paul's innocence, yet she is not prepared to act on it but rather treats him as a threat to the peace and one who might well be sacrificed in order to procure security and establish Jewish favour. It is essentially an account of double standards and does little to substantiate Conzelmann's assertion that 'In the end it is confidence in the justice of the Emperor that forms the great climax of the narrative'.[46] The attitude of Luke–Acts to the state is far removed from that which sees the powers that be as ordained by God. The state is not as yet hostile, but it is fickle, its officers open to corruption and faced by Christianity with something that is beyond their comprehension.

But for Luke that does not really matter, for their very inability to comprehend witnesses to the fact that they are responding to the action of God which has been released in their midst through the exaltation of Jesus of Nazareth. Luke does not suggest that God's final action inaugurated by that event will win over the Roman state. What he does maintain is that the Roman state is compelled to co-operate in something greater than itself, that God uses it to achieve his purposes both in the crucifixion of Jesus and in the arrival of Paul at Rome. Paul's arrival at Rome witnesses not only to the fact that Jewish disbelief springs from disobedience rather than from a sound evaluation of the meaning of Jesus, but also to the fact that the powers of the state can be open to be used by God for his final work. Both the Jews and Romans co-operate to get Paul to Rome and thereby prove the lordship of Christ just as earlier they had co-operated to enable that status to be achieved through the crucifixion.

Luke therefore clearly sets the story of Jesus in the context of world history. Because the one who is laid in the manger is born at the time of the universal census, at the time when the whole world is on the move (2.1–3), he is the sign of the openness of that world to the irruption of God's saving event. Because, after John, 'all flesh' is to see the salvation of God (3.6), his appearing is marked, not only by its place in Jewish national history, but also in its relation to the history of the Roman world (3.1–2). In the beginnings of the story the final significance of the whole event is foreshadowed.

TO ALL NATIONS

The universal setting of Luke's work and his desire to show the worldwide outreach of the gospel is not open to doubt. What is more questionable, however, is the universalism that this is said to proclaim. Luke is indeed interested in the universal spread of the gospel, but this is not necessarily the same as his having a universal concern which is directed primarily towards the Gentiles, which envisages a continuing mission to them, and which is concerned with the ongoing growth of the Church and with their inclusion in its fold.[47] A number of factors compel caution here and would suggest that his interest in the Gentiles was primarily the outcome of his understanding of Jesus as God's final act for the Jewish people, that it was used to subserve his purpose of proving this rather than serving as an apology for the Gentile mission and a call to future action.[48]

In the first place, we have seen that Luke does not envisage an ongoing history in which the Church will continue to grow and the kingdom of God to be established thereby. Jesus is not the first chapter in a long story. The End has been separated from past events but it has not been given up as a near expectation, and the two volumes as a whole are written to strengthen belief in the sovereignty of Jesus which will be confirmed by the End. There is little idea of progress in this world. Paul comes to Rome as a prisoner—witness to the transcendent kingship of Christ rather than to a progressive establishment of his sway in this world. Israel as a whole rejects, and even amongst the Gentiles there is a large element of refusal (Acts 14.2–5; 17.33; 19.23–41). The Church is established and in places 'grows and prevails mightily' (Acts 19.17–20), but this is shown as a response to the proclamation of the Lord so that 'fear fell upon them all, and the name of the Lord Jesus was extolled'. It is recounted primarily as a witness to the sovereignty of the exalted Jesus rather than as a part of the climactic mission to the Gentiles. Luke has not turned away from the chosen people, and the incorporation of the Gentiles is not meant to make up for their rejection or to act as a substitute for a continuing concern with the Jews. The Jews are not abandoned and Gentiles do not take their place. There is in fact little interest in the Gentiles for their own sake. Their inclusion is the sign of the reality of the eschatological event in Jesus and acts as a foil to the rejection by the Jews, countering the damaging effect that such a rejection would otherwise have on Luke's claims. In other words, Luke's interest in the Gentiles does not seem to be primarily for their sake, but in order to illustrate or support some wider argument with which his writing is involved. His remoulding of the traditional eschatological beliefs enables him to show the mission to the Gentiles as the realization of Jewish expectations which counteracts any doubts that may arise from unfulfilled hopes. His recounting of the Gentile mission is entered upon in the service of his eschatology. As part of the scriptural expectations of the End-time, it is presented as a substantiation of Luke's claims.

His thought remained within the orbit of Jewish beliefs. Influenced by the Old Testament, he portrayed Jesus as the Christ of Israel, the one who fulfilled Old Testament hopes and brought God's eschatological promises to fruition. His interest in the course of the Gentile mission was occasioned by his concern with that. The Old Testament remained his guide, and he read Christianity in the light of his understanding of its oracles. It may indeed be that Luke himself was a Jew; more likely would it seem that he was a Gentile God-fearer, one who came to Christianity by way of a study of the Old Testament, one who saw a wider salvation realized only by incorporation into the sphere of the covenant people of God. It is this which he describes in Acts. His aim was not to encourage the Church in her missionary role, in Haenchen's words: 'to edify the churches and thereby contribute its part in spreading the word of God further and further, even to the ends of the world'.[49] Our understanding of Acts does not allow us to endorse Hahn's view that finds in the mission to the Gentiles the dominating theme of Luke–Acts.[50] It is indeed an important theme, but it is a secondary theme and one which performs a supporting role.

But does this view really do justice to Luke's Gospel as opposed to Acts? Jesus of course in Luke has no contact with Gentiles and it is not until after the exaltation that such a mission can begin. Nevertheless, does not the Gospel show such a width of concern as to suggest that Luke had the Gentiles in mind from the beginning, and in such a way that the mission to them was seen as the climax of his work? Does our view really give due weight to the humanitarian outlook which the Third Gospel manifests so clearly? In particular, how far does Luke's description of Jesus as the friend and champion of the sick, the poor, the penitent, the outcast, and of women suggest a prefigurement of the Gentile mission which in a sense controls and determines the description of his first volume?[51] On the whole, we must say that it has little bearing on it, but reflecting rather the rejection of Jesus by the official Israel, works within Old Testament ideas to see in the poor the ideal exponents of the attitude of humble dependence upon God and openness to his call. It refers rather to the Israel within Israel. It reflects a concern with divisions within Israel rather than an interest in a future Gentile mission.[52]

Equally, his introduction of the Samaritans is not meant in the first instance to focus attention upon the later universality of the gospel. Indeed, one of the most brutal rejections of Jesus is made by the Samaritans even though Luke is at pains to account for this by his scheme centring upon Jerusalem (9.52). Elsewhere the Samaritans are praised in the parable of the Good Samaritan (10.33) and in the story of the Ten Lepers (17.18–19). The former however, using the Samaritan only as a complete contrast to the Priest and the Levite, works entirely within accepted Jewish attitudes to Samaritans. The parable loses its point if the Samaritans as a whole are given a new status. In the miracle story, the Samaritan is used to emphasize the lack of response to Jesus on the part of the nine. He may indeed prefigure the inclusion of the Gentiles, but only as a contrast to the continuing rejection by the Jewish nation which remains the source of wonder which the incident evokes.

Hints of the incorporation of the Gentiles are of course found throughout Luke's Gospel but these nowhere suggest that the climax of the work of Christ is to be seen in such an incorporation or that it, rather than the concern with the Jewish nation, represents the fulfilment of Christ's work. The faith of the centurion is praised, but the grounds for Jesus' helping him is the Jewish assertion that he 'loves our nation'. Luke's rejection of the Jewish people here is less harsh than is Matthew's (13.28 cf. Matt. 8.12). In Luke's account of the parable of the Great Supper, the double invitation reflects the Gentile mission but it remains additional to that to the Jews rather than a substitute for it, while those who come are incorporated into the first group of those who respond (14.23). Those who were originally invited are firmly rejected (14.24), but, if it is right to see the later invitations as directed to Jews first and then to Gentiles, the Jews are not left without acceptance. The parable therefore rejects not the Jewish nation as a whole, but only those who refused the original invitation. It remains as a comment upon Jesus' rejection by the Jews as a whole and its climax is not to be found in the mission to the Gentiles. If the mission of the Seventy prefigures the later Gentile mission, it too means no more than this. It is given an eschatological context (10.1). Though it is set against the rejection of Jesus by some of those places in which his mightiest works were done (10.13–15), it also suggests that his disciples will meet rejection (10.10–12) and does not envisage more success than is encountered by the Twelve on their mission (9.1–6). Though it does draw lessons from the success of the Seventy, these do not centre upon the winning of the world, but upon the other-worldly realities to which the mission points.

This brings us to a consideration of the account of the rejection of Jesus at Nazareth (4.16–30) which, standing as it does at the very beginning of the ministry of the Christ, sums up Luke's understanding of the total accomplishment of that ministry as it embraces both the life of Jesus and the witness through the Holy Spirit. It is usual to find the point of this episode in its final verse: 'But passing through the midst of them he went away' (4.30), and to understand this as an expression of Luke's belief that the message of salvation was passing from rebellious Israel and was being given to the Gentiles. As King puts it: 'When a prophet is found unacceptable to his own, he is sent to others.' So what is primarily a rejection of Jesus by his own people becomes understood also as a rejection of his own people by him.[53]

But is this really what Luke intended? Did he mean Jesus virtually to will the rejection that he suffered? Does such an interpretation make sense of the references to Elijah and Elisha? Is Dupont right when he says: 'Il y avait bien des veuves et des lépreaux en Israel; mais les bienfaits de Dieu sont allés à des étrangers'?[54] These prophets are used to help solve the problem that Jesus performed no miracles in his own country. The wonders that other places had witnessed were not seen at home. In answer, appeal is made to the fact that Elijah went outside Israel to bestow his aid—widows in Israel found no answer in Him. Likewise, no lepers in Israel were healed by Elisha, but only Naaman the Syrian.

Yet the reference to these prophets cannot imply that Jesus' concern with those outside his own *patris*, and his lack of success there meant that he was turning aside from his own. Elijah and Elisha did not turn their backs upon their own people. They remained prophets to Israel, and this fact was not invalidated either by their success outside their own land or by their seeming lack of results among their own people.

They were God's instruments to Israel and what might be taken as evidence to contradict this role was, upon examination, in fact nothing of the kind. What was true for them was true also for Jesus. His rejection by his own people does not affect the validity of claims made on his behalf. His lack of success and that of his disciples with the people of Israel does not invalidate the fact that he is the Christ of God. Equally, the successes of his proclamation among the Gentiles does not mean that God's salvation has passed from her to them. Israel is still God's concern. 'No prophet is acceptable in his own country' (4.24). The truth of this statement is witnessed by Israel's history as a whole, as well as by her treatment of Jesus. Nevertheless, it does not mean that the prophet has turned his back upon his own people, or that his lack of success proved that he was not God's instrument to them.

'Today this scripture has been fulfilled in your hearing.' Jesus fulfils the prophet's expectations for Israel. The Jews rejected Jesus. 'But passing through the midst of them he went away.'[55] They could not destroy him or frustrate God's purposes for him. Their rejection of him did not stop him. He went his way, passing towards his ultimate glorification. This is the climax to which it points rather than to his mission to the Gentiles. Though it no doubt carries thoughts of this wider ministry, the significance lies, not in this, but in the progress of Jesus towards his exaltation. The climax of the story expresses, not the thought of the turning away of Jesus from his people, but the fact that rejection by them does not militate against him as the glorified one, and that lack of success in his own country does not mean that he is not God's final action to her.

At Antioch (Acts 13.46–7), Paul rejects the Jews there with the appeal to the Servant Song of Isaiah 49. Here, the mission to the Gentiles is almost given a climactic significance but that one should not really assign it such a place is shown by the fact that Luke also refers to this passage in Paul's speech before Agrippa (Acts 26.23) where Jesus is seen to proclaim light 'both to the people and to the Gentiles'. The proclamation of remission of sins to the Gentiles is a fundamental part of the events deriving from the exaltation of Jesus (Luke 24.47; Acts 1.8), but this is not to take the place of the call to Israel. Simeon recognizes Jesus as the 'light for revelation to the Gentiles' but this is itself to be involved in the 'glory of thy people Israel' (2.31–2). The climax is in the latter rather than the former and it is not replaced by the mission to the nations. The theme of Luke–Acts is the glorification of Jesus as Lord. As giving strength to that proclamation, the witness among the nations plays an important part, but it does not provide the climax of the work but gives a theme which, though constantly present, plays nevertheless a supporting role.

5

Men Waiting for Their Lord

Writing of Luke's handling of the six 'Amen' sayings in his Gospel O'Neill has said: 'We are witnessing the beginnings of pastoral theology'[1] for in them the evangelist has allowed his expression of God's saving action in Christ to pass into and determine the kind of response he hopes to elicit from his readers. It is pastoral theology because his interpretation arises out of concern for people in a particular situation, the needs of which have both shaped his theology and fashioned his appeal to his readers.

It is usually argued, and we have accepted this as the most likely possibility, that Luke's work was connected with problems arising from the failure of the parousia to happen, and the response he hopes to win from his readers is usually associated with this fact. But what exactly, in this situation, was the nature of the hoped-for response? More often than not, it is seen as one that is appropriate to the missionary situation of the church of which the reader is a member. He will be edified by the picture of the early Church and will be encouraged to take his part in its apostolic role, for, as Marshall puts it, it is likely that Luke 'regarded the essence of being a Christian as the activity of mission'.[2] If this is the main burden of Acts, Christians are enabled to share in the following of 'the way' by uniting to that Christian body which, built on the apostles and their preaching, links them to Jesus who, as a rabbi, the great teacher of parables and ethics, leads them towards their goal. Luke's gospel therefore becomes the first life of Jesus, and if, in the becoming, the *theologia crucis* has become lost in the *theologia gloriae*, this is made almost inevitable by his own particular understanding of the cross and of the nature of the Christian life.

However, if our reading of Luke, of his theology and of his

purpose in writing has so far been at all correct, the hopes he had for his readers must have been very different. He was, indeed, writing for a particular situation, and his theology as a whole merits the description pastoral. His work was occasioned by two problems, namely, that provided by the non-occurrence of the parousia, and that by the failure of the Jews to respond to Jesus. Both problems would have been brought to a head by the destruction of Jerusalem, and this would have increased one further difficulty, namely, the sheer incomprehensibility of Luke's claim that Jesus was indeed the Messiah of Old Testament expectations.

In such a situation, however, Luke did not abandon the eschatological expectations of the early Church. He reinterpreted them in such a way that hope in the End was not reduced but was rather increased. He made it a reality for men in spite of the delay and in spite of the seeming calamities of history. History since the ascension was not separated from eschatology, for it was made into the proof of God's eschatological act in Jesus, the witness that 'Jesus is Lord', the guarantee of the seal of that lordship which would be provided by the return and which was not to be long delayed.

Against this background, Luke's purpose was not to encourage a missionary outlook, for Christians were living in the last hour and the universal witness had already taken place. Little that was new could be added. The Church was in Rome; Paul had witnessed there; Jesus' sway was therefore being universally proclaimed; the Church was to wait expectantly for his Return. Again, Christians were not to look for the kingdom in this world. Their hope was in the other-worldly sphere of Christ, and their goal was beyond this world of space and time.

Jesus was God's final act. Luke's first aim was to encourage Christians to acknowledge this and to live in the faith that it gave. But they were persecuted by the Jews for this belief, and the support of Rome was tenuous, her attitude ambiguous. Christians were pulled down by the perplexities and uncertainties of their own making and by the hostility or indifference of others. In this situation, Luke's pastoral concern and his theology united to proclaim a message of hope tempered by warning. Christ Jesus was Lord, the revelation of his victory was sure and would be soon, but until that happened, and faced with the situation that had developed, Christians were under strain. It is only 'through many tribulations (that) we must enter the kingdom of God'.

Luke's theology presents the disciples as the eschatological community, possessing the promises of the covenant, living in unity, empowered by the Spirit, engaged in a universal witness, built upon the Twelve, created at Pentecost, and including the Gentiles in its embrace. His aim is to encourage his readers to acknowledge this, and to live in the power of that understanding.

They are therefore to live under the shadow of the kingdom, acknowledging its reality, empowered by its presence, and strengthened by its life. They are to live within its embrace—that is, they are to receive from it their means of living in the world, of waiting expectantly for its revelation and for that day when they will enter into it. Their source of life and the goal to which they move are grounded firmly in the existence of the other world.

This is the thrust to be seen in Luke's version of the Lord's Prayer (11.1-4). As a whole, Luke's version is directed to the coming of the kingdom of God and is therefore as eschatologically oriented as that found in Matthew. It is likely that he wrote the petition for the coming of the kingdom rather than that for the bestowal of the Spirit, for though the latter fits well into Luke's theology as a whole and parallels the Lucan form of the bread petition, it seems to have been introduced by a later interpreter in the light of the evangelist's inclusion of 11.13 and at a time when Luke's own eschatological urgency had been lost. But in any case, had Luke originally written it himself, he would have understood it against that background of a waiting for the return, for, as we have seen, in his view the Spirit proclaims not the delay of the coming kingdom but its guarantee.

Luke's own theology is represented in his form of the bread petition, *ton arton hēmōn ton epiousion didou hēmin to kath hēmeran*. Here, the present imperative and his use of *kath hēmeran* to qualify the request contrast strongly with the aorist imperatives of the other clauses. Nevertheless, though expressing a request for a continuing gift, they are not to be understood as non-eschatological substitutes for the original emphasis,[3] nor as shifting it from the future to a present manifestation of the kingdom.[4] Luke's eschatology is centred upon a present transcendent kingdom which awaits its future manifestation.[5] Because of Jesus, Christians can live in the confidence of its present reality and in the expectation of its coming revelation. Therefore in the present they need to be empowered by it, and their prayer is that even now they may go in its strength, in the knowledge that such a gift is both the first-fruit and the guarantee of its final revelation and of their incorporation into it. The petition is based upon confidence in the reality of the other world, of a certainty that its power exerts an influence in this world upon those who accept its reality and look for its final manifestation.

It is precisely this same eschatological emphasis which directs Luke's understanding of the Eucharist.[6] Through the 'breaking of bread' men's eyes are turned to the kingdom and are empowered by it as they anticipate on earth their participation of it in heaven. Luke's description of the Last Supper is dominated by Jesus' vow of abstinence (22.15, 16, 18) which, rather than anticipating a long wait between then and its realization,[7] through its connection with the suffering and its use of *apo tou nun* which links it to his proclamation before the high priest (22.69), looks forward to his own entry into the kingdom of God. Verse 17 suggests that Jesus himself was to share in the Passover, not with them, but in the kingdom and this thought is strengthened if *ouketi* is to be omitted from verse 16. The eschatological emphasis is developed by his convenanting a kingdom to the Twelve: 'As my Father appointed a kingdom for me, so do I appoint for you, that you may eat and drink at my table in my kingdom, and sit on thrones judging the twelve tribes of Israel' (22.29–30). The Lord's kingdom is about to become a reality as he enters into God's kingdom which he is to share and which by virtue of his exaltation is to be his also. The disciples will be associated in that rule, though as yet it is reserved to the future, even though their earthly authority over the eschatological community anticipates their rule in the kingdom. Their eating and drinking at his table at the Last Supper guarantees their future role.

Luke's emphasis at the Last Supper is therefore an eschatological one which centres around two points, namely, in the first place, the reality of Jesus' heavenly kingdom in the present, and, secondly, a confident expectation of a share for the disciples in that kingdom in the future. In their post-ascension meals they are overshadowed by the Lord's kingdom and anticipate their incorporation into it. For this reason Luke emphasizes the part of the bread and omits any association of the cup with the death of Christ.[8] The Last Supper and the meals which are to flow from it are not a looking back and the means by which men are incorporated into the death of Christ, but a looking forward whereby the participants anticipate the status which will eventually be theirs. The bread is not broken as a sign of the broken body, but its sharing is a sign of fellowship with the risen, exalted Lord. Jesus is present in the meal, empowering them with the life of the kingdom and with the promise of its fullness in the future (24.30–1, 35; Acts 1.4).

During his account of the course of the ministry, Luke brings out, more than does either Matthew or Mark, the significance of the meals with Jesus as anticipations of those in the kingdom. Men will claim a share in the kingdom by virtue of the fact that he ate and drank with them in the days of his ministry (13.26). But his eating with the Pharisees only proclaims their rejection of him and of what he represents. The witness—'Blessed is he who shall eat bread in the kingdom of God' (14.15)—is followed by the parable of the Great Banquet (14.15–24), which tells of the rejection of those who were invited originally and which in Luke, unlike Matthew 22.1–10, since it appears in the context of eating with Pharisees, makes a direct link between those meals and the kingdom. In contrast, Luke emphasizes the success of the meals with the publicans and sinners. He takes over Mark's account of the banquet at Levi's house (5.29–32 cf. Mark 2.15–17), but he adds a similar meal at 15.1–2 which becomes the setting for the parables of the Lost Sheep, the Lost Coin and the Prodigal Son. The point at which Zacchaeus is declared to have found salvation is when Jesus goes in to be his guest (19.7).

In Acts therefore the Eucharist is called the Breaking of Bread and has the character of a meal eaten with eschatological joy (Acts 2.42, 46; 20.7). This is unlikely to be a different kind of Eucharist, unknown to Paul and his followers,[9] nor does it seem likely that the description arises from the *disciplinum arcani*. In the New Testament the phrase is found only in Luke, and his use of it is determined by his own theological emphasis as this can be gathered from his description of Jesus' meals in general and of the Last Supper in particular. His thought rests upon the presence of Jesus, of the reality of the kingdom, of its casting its presence over the earthly lives of the disciples, and of the promise of their future participation in it. The Eucharist does not look back to the cross, and it contains no thought of incorporation into the death of

F

Jesus. It is rather a strengthening in the present and a guarantee
for the future.

Luke's aim is therefore to encourage his readers to respond with
that urgency which his understanding of the eschatological situation requires. Though they are opposed by enemies, threatened
by doubts, and weakened by apostasy (Luke 12.8–10), he tries to
restore them to a confidence and steadfastness by giving them a
message of hope which assumes that even now they are able to
live, not in the kingdom it is true, but within a situation where
the kingdom already shows its presence and its power. The initial
signs are a guarantee that it will soon be completely revealed by
the parousia, the nearness of which brings not only joy, but also
an urgent warning.

Luke therefore demands watchfulness. His conclusion to the
apocalyptic discourse underlines this need (21.34–6) and his
parables of chapter twelve, with Peter's question: 'Lord, are you
telling this parable for us or for all?' (12.41), set within the context
of the reality of the other world (12.4–7, 13–31), bring out the
necessity of vigilance in view of the impending imminence of the
End. 'You also must be ready; for the Son of man is coming at an
hour you do not expect' (12.40).

But times are hard, and the second great requirement that Luke
makes of his readers is steadfastness. The disciples ask Jesus,
'Increase our faith' (17.5), and, as the subsequent teaching shows,
this for Luke is seen primarily in a confidence in the unseen world
which finds its guarantee in the coming of the parousia, and in a
faithfulness to this in the face of various distresses. This faithfulness is to show itself in a wholehearted response which issues in a
renunciation of the things of this world and in a surrender to the
call of Christ. Luke has in no way watered down the complete
demands that he found before him in Mark's portrait of Jesus.
At 9.23, though he adds *kath hēmeran* to Mark's call to take up
the cross and follow Jesus, this is to be seen, not as a blunting of
the Marcan summons to an absolute surrender, but rather as a
complete application of the demand as Luke understands it.
This differs from Mark because Luke has no sense of the saving
significance of the cross of Jesus, and his call does not therefore
envisage a unity with Christ in his death. Rather the cross represents the complete way of surrender, of suffering, of self-
renunciation. It is the final outcome of the Lord's obedience to his

Father. Luke therefore sees no saving value in the death of the disciple, nor does he see a need to encourage a mystical relation between Lord and disciple through a metaphorical dying. What is required is rather a following of Jesus in the way of the cross, in the way of surrender and of obedience which the cross embodies. *Kath hēmeran* brings out the continuous summons to do this, the daily act that is required, but, since the same phrase appears in the Lord's Prayer (11.3), it represents too a daily discipline by means of which a daily sharing in the benefits of the reality of the kingdom can be achieved. Daily renunciation brings daily participation in the Bread of Heaven, in that glory which derives from the transcendent kingdom. The 'pilgrimage' nature of the demand is seen at 14.23 where Luke reads: 'Whoever does not bear his own Cross and come after me, cannot be my disciple'.[10]

Peter's confession of faith (9.20) leads into the challenge to take up the cross (9.23). The transfiguration (9.28–36) leads into the journey to Jerusalem which begins with the proclamation of the surrender required of the would-be disciple (9.57–60), and of the wholehearted, continuing steadfastness that must follow. 'No-one who puts his hand to the plough and looks back is fit for the kingdom of God' (9.62). The mission of the Seventy with its forward glance at the life of the post-Pentecostal Church, follows immediately. Later in the journey, the parable of the Great Supper (14.15–24) speaks of the widespread invitation to the kingdom's banquet. But the promise of the parable is immediately tempered by the demands which follow it and which, as Luke makes absolutely clear, are directed to the multitudes who accompanied Jesus and who prefigure those who are later drawn into the banquet from all sides. Utter dedication is required (14.26). The end is not contained in the beginning, for the initial response leads to greater demands, the foundations need a costly edifice to be built upon them, the declaration of war leads to an out-and-out, prolonged engagement of the enemy (14.28–32). Salt is excellent, but salt that can no longer perform the functions of salt is worse than useless (14.34).

It is in the context of the need for the utmost urgency in the extremes of an eschatological situation that Luke's attitude towards riches and poverty is best interpreted. This is not simple and it does not make for a correct exegesis of Luke's thought if its complexities are reduced and he is seen as simply Ebionite in his outlook. R. E. Brown would appear to oversimplify when he maintains that 'In the spiritual outlook of Luke's Gospel, the only proper use of wealth is to get rid of it, to give it to the poor'.[11] Rather, S. Brown is right[12] where he sees a more complex attitude in Luke's writings where there are both passages which require complete renunciation of earthly possessions, but also those which teach a right attitude to the continuing possession of wealth. These two groups cannot come together in a simple harmony. Nevertheless, it is unlikely that they should be taken as referring to successive stages of the Church's existence, either by suggesting as does S. Brown himself, that renunciation takes on divergent forms in the age of Jesus and in that of the Church—that confrontation with the earthly Jesus required abandonment of riches while inclusion in the early Church required a right use of them— or by maintaining, as does Conzelmann, that the ideal laid down by Luke was one for the initial period of the age of the Church and that it was not meant to be an actual proposition for the evangelist's own time.[13] The two approaches cannot be separated as easily as this, for they lie alongside each other in Luke's Gospel and confront the reader in his actual situation. Acts shows how they were worked out in the initial stages of the eschatological community, but the 'communism' of Acts is not without difficulties of interpretation and is in the first instance a vehicle for Luke's theology of the nature of the new community rather than a specific guide for his readers to follow.

But the fact is that there are passages in Luke's Gospel which present his contemporaries with a call to complete renunciation. Though some of these, such as the description of how the early disciples left all to follow the Master (5.11, 28), can be seen primarily as historical accounts of events in the life of Jesus, nevertheless, at other times the command to final surrender meets the reader with the urgency and compulsion of an absolute demand in the present. 'Whoever of you does not renounce all that he has cannot be my disciple' (14.33) is set in the context of Luke's own time. Luke 12.33 speaks to Luke's contemporaries when it says: 'Sell your possessions and give alms; provide yourselves with purses that do not grow old, with a treasure in the heavens that does not fail, where no thief approaches and no moth destroys. For where your treasure is, there will your heart be also.' These cannot easily be made to be directed to only one section of the eschatological community, whether it be a vertical division, so referring only to its early stages, or a horizontal one applying only to a certain section of the readers. The commands are there, spoken against a belief in the transitoriness of this life and in the reality of the other world.

On the other hand, Luke makes much of Jesus' friendship with tax-collectors; Levi, after his call—and, incidentally, after it has been said that he had left 'all' (5.28)—'made him a great feast in his house' (5.29); Zacchaeus is not required to give up everything (19.1-10); in the parable of the Pharisee and the Publican, it is the latter who is justified (18.9-14). In Acts, the situation is by no means one of complete abandonment of property. Cornelius is not required to give up his possessions (Acts 10.1), and Lydia retains her goods (Acts 16.14-15).[14]

The communism of Acts, which Luke describes in his own summaries (Acts 2.44-5; 4.32-7), is not one in which no property was held, but rather a sign of the unity of the people of God, of its compassion and concern.[15] The basis of Luke's description of the community of goods is not a dislike of property but the eschatological situation of the community. In this ideal era, where all the members of the community are together awaiting the revelation of the kingdom and are already empowered by the Spirit, derived from Christ's ascension and pointing to his parousia, there is a harmony and unity where no need is left unattended. Joseph's action is put forward as typical of this community, and the crime of Ananias and Sapphira is not their failure to get rid of property, but their lying and pretence which break up the harmony and endanger the real eschatological outlook of the fellowship.[16] The joy and fear which are present in these events are marks of the eschatological nature of the happenings (Acts 2.43, 46; 5.11, 41).

What then is one to say about Luke's teaching on riches? Can this double standard be reconciled? If the Evangelist were thinking in terms of a continuing situation, if he were laying down ethical standards for a community which was to continue, the bringing together of his two approaches would seem to be a near impossibility. It would then suggest an ideal incapable of realization, a reflection of his own prejudices and of his social outlook. It would be little more than an impractical guide in which he has increased Jesus' condemnation of wealth but which, out of the sheer necessity of encouraging the developing life of the Church, has, in fact, had to lower—indeed, to abandon—the ideals it puts forward.

An approach is provided, however, if we accept that Luke is not laying down a guide for a continuing and developing church life, but is addressing himself to a particular situation. He is faced by the dangers of a weakening faith, of a falling away from the enthusiasm of the initial profession of Christianity. His aim is to foster urgency, and he does this by encouraging his readers to see the reality of the other world and to expect its manifestation in the very near future. He must counteract their immersion in this world, and one of the things which encouraged this was a concern with possessions. Wealth has been shown to be ensnaring. He therefore presents the call to complete renunciation. He presents the ideal and brings out the inherent danger of riches. While too much may have been made in the past of Luke's social concern, it would be wrong to deny altogether the influence of this on his theological ideas. There is a humanitarianism in the Third Gospel which cannot be ignored. But by far the greater influence is to be found in the use of 'the poor' in the Old Testament whereby poverty is idealized and then is used as a term to embrace the whole righteous people of God. The poor are God's remnant, the ones who are open to his saving action, and, since Luke portrays Christians as the eschatological Israel, it is hardly surprising that he sees them as the true poor who recognize God's salvation, and that he looks upon riches as a snare preventing the openness to God's grace that is required.[17]

Near to each of the blocks of eschatological teaching which he gives in Chapters 12 and 17–18, Luke puts forward some material about riches which regards them as snares, immersing men in this life and turning their eyes away from the reality of the transcendent kingdom. In Chapter 12 the parable of the Rich Fool (12.13–21)—the one who 'lays up treasure for himself and is not rich toward God'—is followed by teaching on the relative value of the things of this world as compared with the things of the kingdom (12.22–32). Matthew allows a seeking after the things of this life, provided that the kingdom is the first object of concern (Mathew 6.33). Luke knows of no such concession. In the light of the parable that he has given, attention to riches is a delusion. He therefore issues the absolute command: 'Instead, seek his kingdom, and these things shall be yours as well' (12.31). The things of this life are not ignored, for God's providence will grant them. The principle on which he works is given some three verses later (12.34): 'For where your treasure is, there will your heart be also.'

To his other block of eschatological teaching (17.20—18.8) Luke adds, firstly, the parable of the Pharisee and the Publican (18.9–14) and the story of Jesus and the children (18.15–17) which talk of the need for absolute trust and humility before the presence of God's saving action, and then appends the story of the rich young ruler who is unable to face up to the surrender that such an outlook demands (18.18–30). Riches are not necessarily a bar to entering the kingdom (18.25–7), but they do present a stumbling-block to entry into that attitude of absolute surrender that is required. It is therefore 'easier for a camel to go through the eye of a needle than for a rich man to enter the kingdom of God'.

But Luke is nevertheless aware that not all his readers are poor, and his realism makes it certain that though he puts the ideal before them, they are unlikely to enter upon absolute poverty. His Gospel therefore contains a block of teaching which discusses and suggests the right use of riches. This is found in Chapter 16 and is based upon the parable of the Unjust Steward. Luke 16.1 makes a new beginning, so that the teaching is now addressed specifically to the disciples and through them, in accordance with Lucan usage, to the contemporaries of the Evangelist. Though the parable may have been more generally about resourcefulness and the need for decisive action in view of an impending crisis, since Luke appends verses 9–13 to it and therefore reads verse 9 in their terms, the interpretation has now become more specific and is concerned with the right use of money in the light of the coming parousia.[18] The steward, faced with money, is overwhelmed with *adikia*, that is, he adopts the characteristic attitudes of this age, lives according to its principles, and is immersed in its snares.[19] Nevertheless, even he, when faced with a desperate situation and still acting from the perspective of *adikia*, makes use of money and secures friends for himself. In contrast, the disciples must recognize the eschatological demands of God, to face the crisis of the situation they are in, and let it lead them out of *adikia* to use their possessions wisely and in such a way that they might please God and win friends for themselves in the heavenly places. This idea of winning friends may seem less than truly Christian, and less than Luke generally allows,[20] but for him wealth is a very real snare, it becomes almost an inevitable mark of God's disfavour, a guarantee of impending doom, so the only thing is to use it in order to gain an escape from this almost inevitable fate. As far as Luke is concerned, a rich man has the cards stacked heavily against him and his use of the woes (6.24-6) is not merely for rhetorical effect. Nevertheless, verse 9 enjoins use of riches, not their complete abandonment and rejection, for verses 10-13 talk of faithful stewardship of that which basically belongs to another. Faithful use of this leads to the gift of salvation which really is one's own. But the whole ends with a warning nevertheless: 'You cannot serve God and mammon' (16.13).

Chapter 16 also contains the parable of Dives and Lazarus (16.19-31). The tale which the parable appears to take over takes up the Lucan emphasis upon the perils of wealth and the coming reversal of fortunes. In this it links up with the attack on the Pharisees in verses 14-15 'for what is exalted among men is an abomination in the sight of God'. However, it is not just about this theme,[21] for it is separated from the earlier teaching about wealth by verses 16-18, which talk of the continuing validity of the Law and its abiding value in the saving purposes of God, in spite of the grace of the gift of the kingdom. The conclusion of the parable takes up this point, that Moses and the prophets rightly understood should have led men to repentance, but if they evoke no response, it is wholly unlikely that the resurrection of Jesus will bring about what they were unable to effect. The point of the parable is therefore found in the problem provided by the continuing Jewish rejection of Jesus. Nevertheless, the use of the tale by Luke does show his antipathy towards the rich, so that the rich man is seen as the one standing in need of repentance and as suitable to represent unfaithful Israel as a whole. It does not, however, condemn a misuse of wealth or the hardness of the rich man in his blindness to the needs of others. It rather points out the fact of wealth as making for pride and complacency, which issue in a rejection of God.

What we have then in Luke's teaching about riches is something directed to a specific situation rather than what could be termed more general ethical instruction. Coloured, it is true, by his social concern, it is nevertheless determined by his theology, which is designed to evoke a response of awareness in an eschatological situation where his readers are to see themselves as the final people of God awaiting the complete revelation of his kingdom. It is in this situation that Luke addresses his readers, but what is noteworthy about his work here is that it shows little overall interest in the growth and development of the individual's Christian life. This fact has been pointed out by Schuyler Brown,[22] who accounts for it by maintaining that 'Luke sees the salvation of the individual as indissolubly connected with the Church, since only through the latter's historical mediation is the Christian enrolled in the present phase of salvation history.' This explanation, however, is unlikely, for not only does it, in general, make Luke's work more the vehicle of salvation history than it is, but it would ascribe to the Evangelist an interest in ecclesiology which he does not have, and a 'catholic' attitude to the sacraments and ecclesiastical instruments which is absent from his work. The reason, rather, is that Luke's concern is more limited, more immediate. It is to produce a particular response at a specific point of time, and this entails linking the individual to that eschatological situation with which he should be faced and in which he should find himself. Luke's is not a handbook of long-term exhortation, nor is it a theology which convey's the whole nature of the Christian life. It is directed towards his overall purpose and this means a concentration in both his theology and its practical application. We have already seen that, though Luke is not unaware of the wider spiritual and ethical implications of the presence of the Spirit, this is not his concern, which is rather to see the Spirit as the mark and guarantee of the true eschatological nature of the community it calls into being, and to be the means of witnessing to the eschatological truth of the exaltation of Jesus. Likewise with his concern with the response of his readers. In this particular situation, what is required is not an ethical striving, but an attitude of complete faith in God. This accounts for the remarkably little amount of material in his Gospel which could be described as pure ethical instruction. It is not that he is indifferent to ethical demands. Indeed, he emphasizes these in his account of John the Baptist, where the preaching of repentance is addressed to the crowds in general (3.7–9) in contrast to Matthew's assertion that it was directed to the Pharisees and Sadducees (Matt. 3. 7–10). Luke includes teaching on practical conduct and social responsibility both to the crowds in general and to the tax-collectors and

soldiers in particular (3.10–14). But though John's setting is
eschatological,[23] and Conzelmann is over-simplifying when he says
that in Luke's picture 'the eschatological call to repentance is
transposed into timeless ethical exhortations',[24] nevertheless,
John appears as the last of the prophets, so that his preaching is
stamped with the ethical character of the prophetic outlook. It is
preparatory and points forward to the gospel which Jesus proclaims and which, in contrast, sets forward the gracious salvation
of God (4.18–19) which has only to be accepted.[25]

Luke is not setting out to elicit an ethical response, or to urge
the developing Christian life upon his readers. His Gospel
includes the parable of the Good Samaritan (10.25–37), but it is
probably a mistake to see the main point of this in its commendation of a particular way of life. Creed accepts it as a practical
illustration of a type of conduct which is enjoined by Jesus,[26]
while Jeremias sees it as a parable about 'boundless love'.[27] But
whatever may have been the application of the original, Luke's
own thought is probably more complex here.

The connection between the introduction and the parable is
somewhat artificial. Luke recognizes it as a doublet of Mark
12.28–31 which he omits from his Holy Week controversies.
Nevertheless, he has revised it so that the lawyer himself states
what is required to inherit eternal life. But the further question of
the Lawyer: 'And who is my neighbour?' (10.29) is not really
answered in the parable itself, which, strictly speaking, should
have had the Samaritan as a victim. Instead, it becomes a story
about one who acted as a neighbour, who knew what the answer
to the question was even if the Jew, who should have known,
did not.[28] Luke is plainly interested primarily in the fact that he
was a Samaritan. But, more than this, the episode is set in a
context which has a direct bearing upon the interpretation of the
parable. Jesus has just begun his journey to Jerusalem, the
Seventy have been sent out to prepare his way and have returned
full of joy, having tasted success but also having met with a certain
degree of rejection (10.10–15). Jesus rejoices at the success, but
in such a way, however, that the failures are acknowledged even
though they are used to give depth to the success (10.21–22). It
is joy in the grace of God which is uppermost. 'Blessed are the
eyes which see what you see. For I tell you that many prophets
and kings desired to see what you see, and did not see it, and to

hear what you hear, and did not hear it' (10.25). At this point a lawyer who would himself say that he 'saw' stands up and as the representative of the opposition, those who stand in contrast to the disciples, 'tests' Jesus. He himself rightly represents the outcome of the Old Testament faith which knows what is required. He is able to answer his own question: 'What shall I do to inherit eternal life?' and does not need Jesus to tell him. He knows, but that for him is not enough. 'But he, desiring to justify himself, said to Jesus, And who is my neighbour?' This was his fatal error, and what was his, was that of Jewry as a whole, namely, the desire to justify itself instead of being open to see and accept the gracious act of God. His mistake was that of the Pharisee of another parable (18.9–14) and that was why the Tax-collector went down 'justified rather than the other'. So Luke tells a story about a Samaritan, one who in the situation with which he was confronted, could put forward no claims, expect no reward, assume no status. But he it was, rather than the representatives of Israel, who fulfilled the Law. So the parable becomes one about grace, about acceptance, and also about self-justification which comes to nothing. The Samaritan rather than the lawyer, the priest, or the Levite stands with the disciples and merits the description 'blessed'. So Luke closes the section with the story about Martha and Mary. 'Martha, Martha, you are anxious and troubled about many things; one thing is needful. Mary has chosen the good portion, which shall not be taken away from her' (10.41–2).

There is in Luke nothing which resembles the higher righteousness of Matthew's Sermon on the Mount, whether this be seen as a gift or as an ideal. Indeed, much of the content of the Sermon on the Mount is absent from the Third Gospel. This, of itself, may not be significant, for Matthew may have searched out this kind of teaching or may himself have been responsible for it on the basis of a constructive use of the Old Testament, inspired by the idea of contrast between the Law of Moses and that of Jesus. But its absence from Luke at least shows that the Third Evangelist did not think in terms of a new law and that his interest in the Old Testament, though of overriding importance, was not in seeing it primarily as containing ethical requirements which have now to be discussed in the light of the coming of Jesus. But we cannot necessarily assume that Matthew was adding to what he found in his sources. Luke might well have been subtracting, and we can-

note rule out the possibility that he knew the whole contents of the
Sermon either from Matthew himself or from that Gospel's
sources. Both the introduction to the sermons given by the two
Evangelists and their form of the Beatitudes are consistent with
the use of a common source.[29]

But there is no equivalent in Luke of the more directly ethical
parts of Matthew's sermon. He does not have the sections on
murder, adultery, oaths, or retaliation. This again, of course, may
mean only that the contrast between the laws of Moses and of
Jesus that these sections imply was not acceptable to him. His
Jesus was much more favourably disposed to the Law. Again, the
Matthaean background of controversy with the synagogue may
account for that evangelist's sections on almsgiving, prayer, and
fasting which are also missing from Luke. But Luke was certainly
not favourably disposed to the Jewish religious attitude which
resulted in their rejection of Jesus and, if he was interested in the
developing lives of his readers, there seems little reason for his not
including these sections or at least something like them.

But Luke's handling of his parallels to Matthew's paraenetic
sections suggests that the Christian life was not one of his main
concerns. Matthew 6.19–21 contains an exhortation to lay up
treasures not on earth but in heaven. A real parallel to this is found
in Luke 12.33–4 and both Luke and Matthew end with the
identical injunction: 'For where your treasure is, there will your
heart be also.' Nevertheless, both the form and the setting of the
teaching suggest very different outlooks in the two Evangelists.
Matthew's passage appears in a setting of very definite ethical
instruction. Luke's, on the other hand, as we have seen, occurs in
a chapter which has a direct forward thrust which looks ahead to
the parousia of Jesus (12.8, 40). No longer are men to 'seek first
his kingdom and his righteousness' (Matt. 6.3). Luke has, 'Instead,
seek his kingdom' (12.31). The demand is unconditional, the
contrast is absolute. The call is to complete surrender. It is an
abandoning of this world and a turning to that which is to come,
an attitude of renunciation rather than the cultivation of an outlook which maintains a balance between this world and the next.
Luke's readers are already out of this world as they look forward
to what is to follow.

The eschatological nature of the situation that Luke is addressing
is apparent at another point at which he varies from Matthew,

namely in his reporting of Jesus' command for settlements to be made between adversaries without going to law (12.57–9, Matt. 6.25–6). In Matthew, this is found as part of the rules for life within the new community. In Luke, however, it appears at the end of chapter 12, against the background of the imminent Return of Christ. This should encourage an attitude of watchfulness, but the multitudes (verse 54 as opposed to 12.22, 'he said to the disciples') cannot read the signs of the times (verses 54–6). Instead, they act as if no urgency were required. They even engage in disputes, as though such things were important. But their imprisonment by law is taken up into the last judgement, it passes over into it and, because of their lack of discernment: 'I tell you, you will never get out until you have paid the last copper' (12.59).

Luke's different emphasis is nowhere more clearly revealed than in his teaching on prayer. Though he does enjoin prayer for 'those who abuse you' (6.28), and encourages prayer to 'the Lord of the harvest to send out labourers into the harvest' (10.2), the way that he handles his material as a whole shows that general teaching on prayer, and more especially the part it plays in the continuing development of the Christian life and character, is not really his main concern. In his account of the healing of the possessed boy, immediately following the transfiguration (9.37–45, cf. Mark 9.14–29, Matt. 17.14–21), he omits Mark's reference to prayer, for he is not concerned to give general teaching on the subject.

Luke's thought on prayer is directed towards a particular situation, to an encouraging of steadfastness in that situation, and is set against a quickening expectation of the coming of the End. Its basis is the exaltation of Jesus, its hope is the return, and its subject is the strengthening of steadfastness in circumstances which tend to weaken faith in both these events.

Luke's version of the Lord's Prayer arises out of his eschatological beliefs. In Matthew, the prayer is a pattern prayer, an example of how to pray—'Pray then like this' (Matt. 6.9)—a model for all their praying.[30] It is a prayer grounded in the confidence that 'your Father knows what you need before you ask him' (Matt. 6.8); its effectiveness is conditioned by the disciples' forgiveness of others (Matt. 6.14); it has its roots in the daily life of the Christian community and is seen as part of the devotions of the Christian disciple. In Luke, the situation is entirely different. Jesus is asked to teach the disciples to pray, but what he gives them is not a pattern but the actual form and content of their prayer. 'When you pray, say' (11.2). This is the prayer they must utter. Luke directs attention towards a particular prayer for a particular situation. It is a prayer which seeks the coming of the parousia, which asks that, in the light of this, the disciples might live within the shadow of the kingdom, and that, while they wait, they might be faithful.[31]

To the prayer, Luke appends the parable of the Friend at Midnight, which advocates perseverance in the use of the prayer to the extent of importunity and promises that God's response is sure (11.5–8). To this is added some more teaching about prayer (11.9–13) which Luke has in common with Matthew 7.7–11. In the First Evangelist, it appears as part of the Sermon on the Mount; in Luke, the context gives it a more specific use, for it serves as a further comment upon the Lord's Prayer and is concerned with the request that that prayer makes specific. It is therefore eschatologically oriented and promises, not 'good things' as in Matthew which, whatever the Jewish background, here seems to mean primarily the things of this life,[32] but the gift of the Holy Spirit which marks inclusion within the eschatological community and guarantees the certainty of the End. Prayer is used to establish the witness of Christians at a time when persecutions occurred and apostasy threatened. The request is for faithfulness (17.5; 18.8).

This thought is taken up in Luke's other parable on the subject —that of the Importunate Widow (18.1–8). Whatever the original meaning of this parable,[33] as it now stands it is directed towards constancy, faith and steadfastness, towards the strengthening of hope in a situation which causes despair, towards a confidence in God and a certainty of vindication at the parousia. Faith means constant prayer for the coming of the parousia and issues in watchfulness and perseverance as it waits for that event.

This parable is followed by that of the Pharisee and the Publican (18.9–14), but though this discusses the prayer of each man, it does so, not out of an interest in prayer as such, but because of the attitudes towards God which the two prayers represent. The vindication which is promised (verse 14) is that which will occur at the parousia. Those who will enter the kingdom (18.17) are the ones who accept for themselves the status of children; those who in the age to come will receive eternal life (18.30) are those who in this life have accepted deprivation in order to follow Jesus.

Luke's final teaching on prayer is found in his descriptions of the Last Supper and of Gethsemane where it is seen to be closely connected with the Evangelist's thought about *peirasmos*, so that it becomes a commentary upon the last petition of the Lucan form of the Lord's Prayer. *Peirasmos* is used both of Jesus and of the disciples. They are told to pray *mē eiselthein eis peirasmon* (22.40, 46); Jesus addresses them as those who have continued *met emou en tois peirasmois mou* (22.28), and this is seen as virtually the reason for covenanting a kingdom to them (22.29); Satan is said to have entered into Judas (22.3); the passion means that he will have some hold over the disciples, though the prayer of Jesus results in the recovery of Peter's faith (22.32); and the way to the cross is represented as the hour of the 'power of darkness' (22.53).

Temptation is the moment when battle is entered between Satan on the one hand, and Jesus and his followers on the other. The first engagement was, of course, the initial temptation of Jesus after the baptism (4.1–13). The Spirit leads Jesus into the wilderness and then for forty days he is tempted by the devil. In Luke, the temptation extends over the whole period and it is presented as a fact to be recorded rather than as the actual purpose of the sojourn in the wilderness. It is not represented as a victory, no angels minister to the triumphant Jesus at its conclusion, and the devil departs only in order to emerge at a fitting moment. The whole episode is sombre, a shadow of things to come, and is represented as a serious attack upon Jesus by the adversary.

The conclusion of the episode points forward to Gethsemane and the passion, which becomes the 'opportune time' (4.13). Yet Satan is not absent throughout the ministry of Jesus.[34] The disciples are those who 'have continued with me in my trials' (22.28) and since the perfect tense refers to the life of Jesus and to its climax in the passion which is now beginning, rather than to the post-ascension period, this must mean that *peirasmoi* were present during Jesus' ministry. It may refer to the testing by a lawyer at Luke 10.25; more likely it refers to the battles with Satan represented by the healing of the Bent Woman—the one whom 'Satan bound for eighteen years' (13.16)—and by the mission of the Seventy, 'I saw Satan fall like lightning from heaven' (10.18). These episodes are put forward as occasions when trials of strength are taking place between Jesus and the Satan, and the more traditional temptations at the beginning of the ministry and at the passion are to be seen within the total context of these.

Now, at the passion, the decisive eschatological battle is to take place. Jesus is about to overcome the adversary, and his ascension will witness to this in terms of Psalm 110.1. Nevertheless, Satan will have some victory over the disciples. Jesus prays for Peter, that in spite of his defection his faith should not fail, and, through him, for the others, that their fall will not be complete. At Gethsemane, Jesus who is in agony is strengthened by an angel and fortified by prayer. He is ready for his final act of obedience; the disciples are to have their swords for the eschatological battle and they are told to pray that they may not enter into temptation (22.40, 46). With this, they must rise and be on the alert. Luke does not include Mark's 'they all forsook him and fled' (Mark 14.50) out of respect for the apostles, but 22.32 admits that they did fail. The *peirasmoi* caused them to fall, and it is only the resurrection of Jesus which restores them. Though Luke's account of Peter's denial deals more gently with the apostle by separating it from the witness of Jesus and so playing down the Marcan contrast and making the difference between faith and unfaith less severe, nevertheless, even Peter's fall is real, though temporary, since the look of the Lord (22.61) is a sign both of compassion and of promise of faith restored, and Luke 24.34 makes the appearance to Simon the basis of the restoration of the faith of the others.

Temptation, then, for Luke is real, and its effect is not softened by any compensations. As Shuyler Brown maintains,[35] in Luke *peirasmos* is wholly pejorative and is not given the positive value of a test whereby character is developed. It is rather being engaged by Satan, when the full power of the enemy is released. In Luke's parable of the Sower, those on the rock are they who 'in the time of temptation fall away' (8.13). This is his equivalent of Mark's 'tribulation or persecution on account of the word' (Mark 4.17). But it remains a part of the eschatological testing, since the initial temptation of Jesus was an episode determined by the Spirit (4.1–2), *peirasmos* characterized his passion, and the temptations which the disciples are to pray to avoid are those which are part of the events of the last age. Prayer is for the avoidance of the full blast of the battle, for a share in the power of the kingdom, and for its final manifestation.

So for Luke, the object of the disciples' prayer is, firstly, for the coming of Jesus, for the revelation of his glory, the manifestation of his power, and, secondly, for safety while they wait, for faithfulness to the Lord, for protection from the ravaging of Satan. His interest in prayer is thus a limited one, but is wholly in accordance with his overall concern. This is all the more noteworthy because it seems to conflict, firstly, with his interest in the part that prayer plays in the life of Jesus and which makes him introduce it at crucial moments in the Lord's life, and, secondly, with his frequent mention of it in the Acts of the Apostles. Ott has remarked upon this change of emphasis, noting that, in the Gospel, it is stressed in relation to perseverance, but that in Acts it is found in relation to mission and conversion. Brown sees it in Acts primarily in relation to the life of the Church, but Marshall notes that it is found also in connection with individuals.[36] We are told of the prayers of Stephen (Acts 7.59), of Cornelius (Acts 10.4), of Peter (Acts 10.9). The life of the Church is one of prayer (Acts 2.42) and the content of the model Apostolic Prayer is for faithfulness and effective witness (Acts 4.24–30). The servants of God are chosen after prayer (Acts 13.2–3) and it is with prayer that missionaries are sent out.

Why then is Luke's actual teaching of prayer more limited than the example he gives of its practice both in the life of Jesus and in that of the early Church? In the main this is because, though his two volumes are descriptive and so indirectly have an influence upon the lives of his own generation, his work is not set forth as an ideal which is to be imitated by others, but as an account of the past in order to bring men to a particular decision in the present. He is not out to edify the Church by equipping it for a continuing role, but, by giving a description of its origins, to recall the Christian community to the true nature of its being and to bring about a particular aim in a definite situation, to reawaken faith, encourage constancy, and restore hope. Prayer sustained Jesus in his situation and enabled him to attain the goal of the ascension. Prayer deepened the life of the early Church and enabled it to engage in the universal witness as the guarantee of the truth of the proclamation. Prayer will strengthen his contemporaries as they wait as the eschatological community for the parousia. Prayer will enable them to be steadfast as it turns their eyes towards the other world and assures them of its reality.

Finally, in connection with Luke's seeming lack of material relating to the general development of the Christian life, should be mentioned the fact that he does not appear to encourage his readers to engage in missionary activity, nor does he have material which sees their lives as witnesses to the world in which they are set. Witness in Luke seems to have a clearly, if narrowly, defined meaning. The main task of the witnesses is connected with their seeing the risen Jesus and so of being enabled to affirm the truth of the resurrection (Acts 2.32; 3.15; 4.33; 5.32; 10.41; 13.31). This is supremely the work of the apostles, but Stephen is called a witness (Acts 22.20), mainly one suspects because of his vision of the exalted Lord. Though the initial narrative of Paul's vision contains nothing about his seeing Jesus, his own claims before the people (Acts 22.1–21) and before Agrippa (Acts 26.2–23) bring out this fact in order that he may be constituted a true witness —in chapter 22 of the fact that at his conversion he had seen and heard the Just One, and in chapter 26, somewhat more surprisingly, not only of this, but of the appearances which were to follow (Acts 26.16). As Haenchen remarks at this point: 'Paul is depicted as a constant recipient of heavenly visions'[37] and it is these which provide both the source and content of his witness.

The speeches at the ascension, however, make the witness wider than to the Resurrection alone. In Luke 24.45–8, the essence of the witness is to be found in the fact that Jesus fulfilled scriptural expectations in his suffering, resurrection, and in the universal proclamation of forgiveness in his name, and that this fulfilment is proof of his messianic status, which is guaranteed by the resurrection. The disciples are the interpreters of these things, which are themselves the real witnesses to Jesus. The Lord's command is not one to engage in missionary activity so much as to understand the nature and significance of that activity once it comes about. Missionary activity must be theirs (24.49) but their task is more than that; it is to give the significance and to draw out the meaning of the outgoing, universal community, as it is established by the outpouring of the Spirit.

Acts 1.8 seems to suggest a more active missionary role, but in Acts the apostles do not themselves really engage in missionary activities and they certainly do not go to the ends of the world. In view of the narrow requirements of a witness, that is, to be one who has seen the risen Lord, this is unlikely to refer to the ongoing mission of the Church as a whole, and therefore it seems that the apostolic witness is not necessarily thought of in terms of an active participation in the actual outgoing mission of the Church. Rather the universal spread of the word of God means that the apostolic witness is within a world-wide setting. Luke starts from the fact of the universal proclamation and, in the light of Luke 24.45–8, sees this in terms of its witnessing to the truth of the claims about Jesus. The Twelve are the interpreters whose very existence both as the sign of the eschatological nature of the community, and as the summoners of that community to recognize its own significance, gives meaning to what Luke is to record of the universal witness, of its centre in Jerusalem and of its inclusion of the Gentiles. The witness of the Twelve is their existence which proclaims the eschatological nature of the community.

Luke's Gospel alone contains two missionary journeys, those of the Twelve (9.1–6) and the Seventy (10.1–20). That of the Twelve is taken over more or less from Mark (6.7–12), but the journey does not prefigure either their activity after Pentecost or the life of the Church as a whole, for the Lord's saying about the taking of a sword (22.35–8) contrasts the later times with that of the initial journey. They are therefore not portrayed as examples to later missionaries. Their original journey was unique. They were a sign, as in Mark, of the arrival of the eschatological time and, in contrast to Matthew (10.1–42), Luke does not regard Jesus' instructions to them as being of value to later missionaries in the Church.

Luke places more emphasis in this connection upon the Mission of the Seventy (10.1–20). Here, again, however, it is probably an oversimplification to say with Ellis that 'For him, the Mission of the Seventy is the continuing task of the Church'.[38] Its relation to the situation of Luke's own time is not to prefigure what is still to go on, but to point out the significance of what has happened. The story has an eschatological message and setting. They go only 'where he himself was about to come' (10.1), and their message is one of the reality of the kingdom, irrespective of men's acceptance or rejection of it. Much of the material is paralleled in Matthew, including the description of the message as a proclamation of the kingdom (Matt. 10.7), but in Luke there is nothing resembling Matthew's long-term warnings about coming sufferings (Matt. 10.17–33). Luke has much of this in his eschatological discourses (12.2–12; 21.12–19) where it refers to persecutions rather than to suffering in the cause of missionary endeavour.

Luke 12.11–12 and 21.12–19 speak, not of a conversion of their adversaries, but of steadfastness under persecution. Luke does not suggest that, at such times, the accusers will be won over. This happens neither in the case of Stephen (Acts 7.57–60), of the apostles before the Sanhedrin (Acts 4.13–22; 5.21–42), nor of Paul (e.g. 19.21–41; 23.1–11). Luke's interest is much more in the significance of the journey, which he finds in its witness to the defeat of Satan (10.18–20) and, if he sees this mission as prefiguring that later one to the Gentiles, it is this point which should be carried over so that the wider mission also is seen as evidence of the reality of the kingdom and as the prelude to the coming of the Lord (10.1).

Luke has nothing resembling Matthew's use of the similes of salt and light which are in the First Gospel applied to the lives of Christians in relation to their witness before the world (Matt. 5.13–16). Luke's double use of the lamp imagery is made to refer only to the need of single-mindedness and integrity on the part of the disciples (8.16; 11.33), while the salt image is used in the interests of encouraging constancy and steadfastness (14.34–5). While this usage follows that of Mark (4.21; 9.50), it nevertheless adds strength to the contention that the Third Evangelist is not writing in order either to encourage an active missionary commitment on the part of his readers or even to uphold them in their duty of witnessing before the world.

Luke's aim is rather to help his readers to be aware of the full nature of the eschatological situation that they are in, to respond to it by seeing themselves as members of the eschatological Israel, the heirs of promise, the covenantal people of God awaiting the final manifestation of what has already been achieved. They are one with those whom he describes as the foundation members of that community in its early days in Jerusalem (Acts 2.44–7).

It is this understanding which governs Luke's presentation of the Beatitudes (6.20–6) and of the Sermon on the Plain which depends upon them (6.17–49). Until the Sermon, Luke has been following the order of his Marcan source with a fair degree of accuracy. He has, indeed, changed the place of the rejection at Nazareth (4.16–30, cf. Mark 6.1–6), in order to set it out as the prologue to the ministry, but the only other major alteration in this part of the Gospel is to be found in his call of Simon and that of James and John (5.1–11). In Mark, these calls appear as the first act of the ministry (Mark 1.16–20), but Luke transfers them to the conclusion of the early days in Capernaum. Jesus is already known to Simon for he has already healed his mother-in-law, but there is as yet no special relationship with him, and, when Jesus is not to be found, it is not 'Simon and those with him' who search him out (Mark 1.36) but the people in general (4.42). Luke's change in order allows him to pass immediately from the Nazareth episode to the Capernaum ministry which, in the light of the sermon (4.23), must be seen as its immediate sequel. But it also means that the call to become fishers of men (5.10) does not come until after the nature of the Lord has been revealed and recognized. The call is the direct result of the manifestation of the glory of Jesus and of his true significance in the miracle of the fishes, for in that he is shown as the eschatological Lord (5.8). Now therefore, the disciples are being built up into a real group who follow and accept his lordship in contrast to the Pharisees and the teachers of the Law who attack him (5.21, 30, 33; 6.2, 7). Jesus calls tax-collectors and sinners to his table which prefigures the eschatological banquet (5.29), he is the bridegroom bringing the new wine which many will reject (5.39), the Son of Man who is Lord of the sabbath (6.5, 9). He wins many disciples, but the representatives of official Israel, of the nation which is God's chosen people, are already refusing to respond and preparing to do away with him (6.11).

At this point, Luke introduces the appointing of the Twelve. He omits the Marcan account of the withdrawal to the sea (Mark 3.7–12), for this is used by him to introduce the Sermon on the Plain (6.17–19). Like Mark, he makes the choice take place in the hills, but for him it occurs only after Jesus has spent a night alone in prayer, and he makes it clear that the Twelve, though distinct and glorified with the name of apostles, are chosen from a larger group of disciples who are to remain with him and who will accompany him on his journey (9.18, 23; 19.37–40). Because he is aware of the larger group which accompanies Jesus, and because he knows that at least their representatives, the Seventy, were sent out on a missionary journey, he omits Mark's statement of the reason for the choice of the Twelve, 'that they might be with him, and be sent out to preach, and to have authority to cast out demons' (Mark 3.14). In Luke, this is not what makes the Twelve distinctive, which is to be found rather in their eschatological

significance of declaring the nature of the new community as that
of eschatological Israel. Luke knows that their missionary,
authoritative functions were shared by others and that this has
been made necessary by the passing of time and so he allows fully
for the presence of others in this task. But the Twelve are the
statement of the function of the Christian community as that of
the Israel of God, renewed and refashioned in the last days, and
their presence is the perpetual call to that community to be aware
of its true nature.

Jesus therefore comes down from the mountains with the 'great
crowd of disciples' and with the Twelve and now addresses them
all in the sight and hearing of the people. In Matthew also the
sermon is addressed to the whole group of disciples (for the
Twelve have not yet been separately named) in the presence of the
crowd (Matt. 5.1; 7.28), and this suggests that both Evangelists
are to be traced to a common source at this point. Luke's Beatitudes are distinctive but they are entirely at one with the development of his narrative as it has led up to this stage. They put
forward a truth to those who are presented as the eschatological
Israel and they become the foundation charter of the new community.

Both Matthew and Luke open their sermons with a set of
Beatitudes, but the differences are such that C. H. Dodd states:
'It may at any rate be said that if either evangelist be supposed to
depend on the other, or both upon some hypothetical source,
something much more radical than a mere "editing" of borrowed
material is to be taken into account.'[39] It is not our purpose here
to enquire into sources, but, in view of the frequent tendency to
see the Lucan shorter forms as evidence of a more primitive en-
vironment, it must be said that, as they stand, they fit completely
into Luke's theology as a whole, into the place they occupy in
the development of the overall Gospel plan, and that there is no
reason to suppose that they could not have assumed the shape
they now have as a result of Luke's own selection, editing, and
theological presuppositions.

As they now stand, Luke's Beatitudes are a statement of the
kind of people who have responded to Jesus, expressing their
position as the heirs of Old Testament piety, announcing their
vocation as the eschatological Israel, and promising their future
reward in the kingdom of God. The direct form of address in the

second person plural fulfils the double function, not only of making promises to specific groups of people, but also of bringing the total *laos* to a recognition of its true meaning and significance. The poor, the hungry, the mourners, and the excluded are promised blessings, but the whole group is reminded that it is the poor, the hungry, the mourners, and the excluded; its members are the inheritors of the kingdom. The basis is not their own action or any merit of theirs, but the initiative and grace of God.

For Luke's Beatitudes are essentially a proclamation of the saving activity of God, a promise that, in Jesus, God's eschatological redemption has drawn near. They take up the thought of Isaiah 61 as that expresses the initial announcement of the meaning of Jesus' ministry and they make explicit the hopes contained in the Magnificat (1.46–55). In the sermon, the emphasis is upon the fact that the poor, and the others, though blessed already, will receive the fullness of those blessings in the future which is less timeless and more explicit than the corresponding forward look in Matthew. Luke's thought may revolve around the idea of *peripeteia*,[40] but it is to be realized only in the future entry into the kingdom of God. Verse 23 becomes a comment upon the whole series: 'Rejoice in that day and leap for joy, for behold your reward is great in heaven.' Luke turns his readers' eyes to a future fulfilment, guaranteed by the event of Christ, to be accomplished outside time and beyond history.

In keeping with this, the Beatitudes put forward no ethical ideal which can be achieved or towards which a man can strive. Matthew presents a type of character which has divine approval even if it be regarded as a divine gift. He offers virtues which a Christian should practise and which become the conditions of entry into the kingdom.[41] Sometimes, indeed, Luke's version is interpreted in these terms. So R. E. Brown can talk of the ideal of Luke's Beatitudes and can suggest that they are put forward as states to be imitated.[42] But as we have seen, Luke did not demand poverty of all his readers, and he did not exclude all rich men from the kingdom. He certainly did not expect all his readers to become poor, hungry, mourners, and persecuted. He puts forward characteristics of the Christian community, and this, together with a social prejudice which he does indeed have, causes him to shape the Beatitudes as they are. But he does not stop at their social implications but in accordance with the Old Testament outlook sees these as the makings of the ideal remnant, the kind of people who can respond to God, the ones who are open to God's grace. This is the primary influence upon him at this point, and it causes him to take a further step, which is to see the whole Christian community as the recipients of God's promises to the poor and the weak. These are the ones who were expected to constitute eschatological Israel, and so Luke summons the community to see itself as that—as the poor, the hungry, the mourners and the oppressed, in other words, as the community of the End-time. The beatitude is not a command or an ideal; it is a statement of the eschatological nature of the Christian community, a recalling of their response to God, and a promise of his future completion of his initial grace. It summons Christians to be men waiting for their Lord.

6

Luke the Evangelist

W. C. van Unnik has recently described Luke–Acts as a 'Storm centre in contemporary scholarship' and the book of essays[1] which, under this title, his own introduces shows quite clearly how Luke's work is being approached from a number of ways which are representative of very different points of view. Undoubtedly, the most widespread and influential approach to Luke–Acts at the moment is that which sees the author primarily as an interpreter of the event of Jesus in terms of salvation history and, in connection with this judgement, it is worth recalling R. R. Williams's quotation from a private letter of C. H. Dodd, who gives it as his opinion that 'I suspect that we shall have to give Acts over, so to speak, to Conzelmann'.[2]

It is against this background that these chapters have been written and they represent a conviction that much recent work on Luke has been led astray by its own deep-rooted suspicions about the validity of the historical approach of Luke–Acts. Though these interpreters are right to see that Luke's historical treatment was determined by his theological presuppositions, nevertheless, their own understanding of that theology is coloured by a false dichotomy between history and eschatology which fails to allow that history can be employed in the service of an eschatological understanding of God's act in Christ by using the past to recall men to a decision in the present. This means that the presence of eschatological material in Luke–Acts is often virtually ignored because of the assumption that an interest in history, or a use of it in the service of a theology of Jesus Christ, inevitably excludes a living belief in the return of Jesus as Lord as an event which directly impinges upon the faith and expectations of the writer and his companions.

Our first task therefore was to see that Luke wrote against the background of the return of Jesus, which he expected to happen in the lifetime of some at least of his contemporaries. Once this was established, it meant that a fresh look had to be taken at the purpose of the two-volume work, for it could no longer be seen as a radical reinterpretation of the earlier outlook, and one which, by proclaiming long-term attitudes to the nature of Christian belief, turned man's eyes towards the world by encouraging a positive outlook to its history and institutions. If we have been right, Luke did not expect the world to continue and he did not envisage the ongoing life of the Christian Church as an instrument of God's saving purposes. Jesus was not the centre, but the climax of God's salvation history; his ascension brought that history to a conclusion; what has happened since then has been the outcome of that event, the necessary witness to it. This has now been accomplished, and Luke and his readers await the final witness, the complete revelation of the lordship of Jesus which the parousia will bring.

Luke's aim therefore was to re-establish that faith in the lordship of Jesus which his readers had once shared, but which was now in danger of being lost because of the problems that such a belief faced. These were mainly threefold, namely, the failure of the parousia to take place as expected, the lack of response on the part of the Jews, and the very nature of the life of Jesus and, above all, of his crucifixion. The first, Luke answered by pointing out the necessity of the delay and by reasserting the belief in the immediacy of the return; the second, he faced by describing the sheer rebellious nature of the disobedience which the Jewish rejection entailed; the third, he countered by showing that the life of Jesus was of one piece with the whole saving work of God of which it was the climax.

In all this, Luke's aim was primarily to bring about a response to Jesus in the present, a response which meant the looking for his revelation in the near future, a living even now in power derived from the transcendent kingdom, and a turning aside from the world which was running fast towards its end. He was within the main stream of the early understanding of the significance of the events centred around Jesus. His Jesus was no hero of the past, but the Lord of the present; he was not the founder of a religion, but the fulfilment of God's saving action; what he called into being was not a continuing Church, but an eschatological community which existed to wait for his final appearing. For Luke, the universality of the witness is not some stage leading into a programme of future action, but an event that has been realized, as it has been made necessary, by the claims made on behalf of Jesus. Without it, Jesus could not have been put forward as God's eschatological act, for without it Luke could not have claimed that scriptural expectations of the last days had been fulfilled.

But Luke's interest in the Gentiles does not form the climax of his work. It arises rather from the fact that the Gentile witness proves the truth of his claims on behalf of Jesus, and that this emphasis is needed to counteract the fact of the continuing Jewish rejection of the kerygma. Luke has not dismissed the Jews, and the Gentiles have not taken their place. The Jews who accept are the true Israelites, and the Gentiles are incorporated into them. Luke's Christianity never strays far from its Jewish origins, for he sees it as the fulfilment of the initial covenant; he regards it as the seal of that covenant rather than as its substitute. For Jesus himself takes his place firmly in Jewish history as the outcome of God's promise begun through Abraham, as the successor of the saving figures under the old dispensation. Jesus on earth is one with them; Jesus in heaven is still controlled by their expectations and hopes.

Luke, then, is a highly articulate and consistent theological writer. But his theology is used in the service of his pastoral and evangelistic skill, for it is as a pastor, as a preacher, that he must be judged. He was writing a message for a particular situation, and it is in terms of that situation, rather than in terms of the various estimates of later generations, that his success must be estimated. If we have been right, his work was no early attempt at demythologizing, neither was it a fresh interpretation having the nature of a long-term vision of the programme and possibilities before the Christian Church. Luke was indeed a humane man, concerned with the outcast and the neglected, but this is to be seen primarily in terms of the fact that the despised Gentile had been brought within the orbit of God's saving activity through Christ. This was the point from which Luke started—the wonder at the incorporation of the nations into God's saving work in his people Israel. Add to this the amazement caused by the rejection of that action by the vast majority of the Jewish nation, and the basis for Luke's theology is laid. His theology was pastoral, and it was practical. Its brief was the wonder of God's saving concern, its source was the Old Testament. Luke the theologian must be seen only in the service of Luke the evangelist, and Luke the historian can be understood only as the servant of both.[3]

Throughout these chapters our purpose has been to try to understand what Luke was saying through his chosen vehicle of historical writing. No attempt has been made to assess the actual historical value of his work. This is still not our purpose, but, nevertheless, certain conclusions which are relevant to this do emerge.

In the first place, the real historical problems of Luke's work should not be underestimated.[4] That he may have shown a good understanding of matters of Roman law, politics and administration, in no way alters the basic fact that his picture of the early Church cannot easily be squared with that gleaned from the Pauline letters.[5] The Council of Acts 15 remains enigmatic; if Peter had already had the full experience of the Cornelius episode, it remains very hard indeed to understand the Antioch incident of Galatians 2.11–14: the Paul of Acts seems other than the Paul of Romans, Galatians, and Corinthians. Haenchen rightly sees that the problem here is caused, not by lack of sources or an inadequate appreciation of the historical situation, but by the subordination by Luke of his history to his theology. This is the fundamental factor—and it does not concern Luke's competence, but his purpose. And if we have been right, his purpose was more dominated by theology, and his history was used more positively as its tool, than even Haenchen allows. The Lucan picture of unity, of harmony, of unimpeded progress, and of the Jewishness of what emerged, was caused, not by practical historical problems which faced the new community, but by his theological belief that this community was the eschatological people of God, the heirs of God's promises, and the fulfilment of Old Testament expectations. This controlled his descriptions in Acts in exactly the same manner as we have seen that it controlled his Gospel. There, the life of Jesus, his 'historical' progress to Jerusalem, his resurrection appearances, and his ascension, are all the outcome of theological presuppositions which determine also the nature of the infancy narratives. In his second volume, too, the history is written 'from faith to faith' to express the conviction that what has emerged is really what it ought to be, that it is determined by the purposes of

God. Luke knows what the community is; his work describes its emergence as his vision of this dictates it.

For in this, Luke stands firmly in the line of the Former Prophets of the Old Testament and of its other historians. It is here that his true matrix is to be found, so that his writing can only be understood when the full influence of the Old Testament ideas and beliefs is allowed. In the Old Testament, we have, in Gärtner's words, 'a religious view of history which, practically speaking, is unique'.[6] The past is recounted in order to elicit a particular response in the present, and it is the nature of the response which it is hoped to establish which determines how the history is described. The past is seen as the basis for the present, and it is the present which determines the interest in the past. History is seen through the eyes of what must have been, as the expression of a faith that is.[7] All Israel must have come out at the Exodus, for all Israel is represented as the possessor of God's covenantal activity. The Settlement becomes a conquest because Yahweh was giving her the land. Jerusalem had to be saved because it was Yahweh's city, but, when she fell, it was because of Yahweh's action to punish her transgression. Even contradictory statements about such things as the Temple treasures represent what 'must' have been, as historical events are seen to be moulded by the theological convictions of the writers.[8] The significance —and indeed the understanding—of what must have happened in the past, remains open to the ever new reinterpretation of the present which is the dominant factor in the historical descriptions it calls forth.

Luke is the heir of this tradition of history writing, and he makes full and creative use of it in his two volumes. If we have been right in our understanding of his work, his history was used in the service of his theology and is to be seen as a description in concrete terms of what his faith proclaims. History becomes the servant of his theology, which is itself well within the eschatological approach of early Christianity. It is as kerygma rather than as history that his work must in the first place be judged.

But this raises once again the essential Jewishness of Luke's background. We have seen that his interest in the Jewish nation remained and that the Gentile mission was neither his overriding concern, nor did it form the climax of his work. The background to his work was provided by the Old Testament, which also

determined the way he looked at the saving work of God in Christ
Jesus. But are we to go further than this and suggest that Luke
himself was a Jew and that his work was directed, at least in the
first instance, not primarily to Gentiles, but to Jewish Christians?[9]
To go so far on either of these points would probably be a mistake.
Luke's background is certainly Jewish, but the nature of this is
best provided for, not by an ethnic Jewishness but by a religious
one, that is, by the influence of the Old Testament through becoming the heir of its promises. We have seen that Luke's theology
is best understood if he is accepted as having come to Jesus by
way of the Old Testament. But equally, his theological use of
that book is of such a kind that makes it likely that he came into
the Jewish faith rather than that he was born into it. Luke's
embrace of the Jewish religion is almost completely without
tensions. The only point at which he shows a dissatisfaction with
it or a shrinking from its demands is on the question of circumcision which, for him, is that part of the Law which is superseded
by Christ, but which even then is not abrogated for the Jew.
Christ represents a freedom from the requirement of circumcision
rather than a negation of it or a denial of its value. Luke reveals an
intellectual conversion to Judaism which accepts its promises,
which he sees fulfilled in Jesus. He was a student of the Old
Testament, but he was himself numbered among the Gentiles,
and it is this which determines his interest in the poor, the outcast, the Samaritan, and, ultimately, in the Gentiles themselves.
Luke's Jewishness must be emphasized, but it is the Jewishness
of one who has come into Judaism by conviction.

Further than this we cannot go with any degree of certainty.
Yet we can conjecture that Luke was not a proselyte, but a God-
fearer. Dibelius has shown the central importance of Cornelius in
Acts. The care with which, in the Gospel, he narrates the story of
the centurion's servant (7.1-10) is also obvious. The faith of both
men is apparent. Cornelius, a God-fearer, is one who has great
concern for 'the people' (Acts 10.2); the unnamed centurion of
the Gospel is described as 'one who loves our nation, and he built
us our synagogue' (7.5). Certainly, in the attitude of these two
men there is something which seems to come close to a self-
portrait of Luke himself. If he were a God-fearer, it would give a
ready key to his theology, to its Jewishness, and the influence of
the Old Testament upon it; to its love of the Jewish nation and its

belief in her priority; to its respect for the Law; but also to its joy at the gift of the full incorporation of the Gentiles into the eschatological people of God without the harsh requirement of circumcision. In Jesus, Luke found complete freedom, complete joy, in the full and gracious activity of God.

But what of Luke and Paul? How does our understanding of Luke–Acts affect our attitude to the question whether its author could have been the companion of the Apostle to the Gentiles? There is no room for certainty here, and perhaps little for more than the probable, but, overall, it does give some support for the contention that the two men could have known and worked alongside each other, that Luke knew Paul in the flesh and was an actual disciple of his.

Against such a possibility there are two main problems, namely, that provided by the nature of Luke's theology, and that by his picture of Paul. To take the latter first: Luke's Paul does seem hard to square with the Paul of the epistles. While the fact that the purely 'historical' picture of Paul that Acts gives by making him a notable preacher and worker of miracles seems to contradict Paul's own estimate of himself,[10] this is not of great importance, for it could just reflect the different impressions made by Paul upon his opponents and his followers, and Luke's picture is in any case governed by his desire to parallel Peter and Paul and to present both as inspired by Jesus the *archēgos*.

More important are the problems presented by the 'theological' picture of Paul which emerges, in particular by the account in Acts of his relations with the Jerusalem church, and his attitude to the Jewish religion. With regard to Paul and Jerusalem, the picture which Luke paints must be seen as part of that wider harmony which he gives to the early Church as an essential ingredient of his belief in it as the eschatological community, centred upon Jerusalem, united in faith, all-embracing in its scope, and the possessor of the eschatological Spirit. This picture arises out of his theological conviction, and it is this which causes him both to make Paul the willing instrument of the Jerusalem church, and to limit the term 'apostle' to the original Twelve.[11] Paul is—according to Luke's understanding, if not according to that of later generations—in no way belittled by this treatment, but is rather extolled as the supreme witness of the lordship of Jesus which Luke's theology makes it possible to assert. The

Twelve in Jerusalem acknowledge the call of Paul; he is truly the witness to the resurrection; he shares in the knowledge of the risen Christ. His knowledge is not mediated by Jerusalem, but is recognized by them. He is the unifier of the eschatological community.

But all this stems from a second point, which is Luke's picture of Paul's relations with the Jewish people. Paul in Acts, as we have seen, is not an exponent of successive stages of *Heilsgeschichte*. Bornkamm is right to disagree with those who maintain that Paul gave up his work with the Jews.[12] But neither does Luke represent Paul's work among Jews and Gentiles as successive stages of his concern. The two are much more closely run together, and Luke does not see the Jews as merely a preliminary stage in the mission, but is rather concerned with bringing out the sheer perversity of the Jews in rejecting the gospel. Luke's Paul is therefore much less a figure of the *Heilsgeschichte* than is often maintained. He has not turned his back on the Jews, but maintains their priority. But this would be true of the Paul of the epistles also. Although Munck underplays Paul's disputes, he is nevertheless right to emphasize Paul's continuing concern with the Jewish nation and to allow for their place in the covenantal people of God.[13] While this appears clearly in Romans 9—11, it underlies the earlier chapters of that epistle also, where there remains a tension between the priority of Israel and the universality of God's concern, where Paul's understanding of history and of the historical matrix of Christianity causes him to shrink from the logical conclusions to which his argument would seem to be leading and which would deny the remaining value of God's particularity in the past, and its resulting special relationship with his people Israel.

But what of Paul's attitude to the Law? Even if it be agreed that Paul was more torn apart than is often suggested, and even if full allowance is made for 1 Corinthians 9.19–23 and 7.17–24, could his attitude have been as positive as Acts maintains? Could he conceivably be thought of, by one who knew him, as having made the concessions of the Apostolic Council and also as having promulgated them in the interests of the unity of the eschatological people of God?[14] Could he have been thought, by a companion of his, to have gone on to the circumcision of Timothy (Acts 16.3) and to have entered upon his final vow at Jerusalem (Acts 21.26)?

If Haenchen is right in seeing this latter event as connected with Paul's handing over of the Collection, then it would be in keeping with the principles of 1 Corinthians 9.20. The same point could apply to the circumcision of Timothy which, in view of the ambiguity surrounding the possible circumcision of Titus (Gal. 2.3), cannot simply be dismissed as an historical impossibility, or, more important from our point of view, as having been ascribed to Paul by one who knew him.[15] Our question is not so much one of historical accuracy as whether the picture of Paul in Acts —allowing fully for the fact that history is used in the service of theology and that Luke's theology does cause him to portray as events of history things which did not necessarily happen— whether this picture could conceivably have been by one who knew Paul. Paul was not completely adverse to pragmatic considerations where the effectiveness of his missionary work was concerned, and he had not, as Vielhauer allows, entirely cut his links with the Jewish nation.[16]

In the final resort, what will determine the possibility or otherwise of the Evangelist's link with Paul, is our estimate of the theology that his two volumes express. Luke uses the history of Paul, as he uses the history of Jesus and that of the early Church, in the service of his theology, for Luke's Paul certainly preaches the theology of Luke. His picture of Paul is just consistent with one painted by a companion of the apostle if, and only if, his theology as a whole, in the service of which it is used, does not militate against such a relationship. In deciding upon this, it is important to remember that, at least in our understanding of him, if Luke were a companion of Paul, he was, nevertheless, a God-fearer first, one who came to Christianity by way of a deliberate turning to a Judaism in which he lived without the personal tensions of a kind which had shaped the thinking of the Apostle to the Gentiles.

And, if we have been right, Luke was at least no defaulter from the outlook of early Christianity but lived within its eschatological framework. Jesus was the fulfilment of what had gone before, the final act of God for men. The world is passing away and the End is coming soon. Now is therefore, for Luke as well as for Paul, the 'acceptable time', now 'is our salvation nearer than when we believed'. Luke's whole work could be seen as a commentary upon these ideas which Paul expresses here. Already the kingdom

thrusts its shadow over the lives of men, for it is established already
in the other world. The Spirit is the *aparchē* (Rom. 8.23), the
arrabōn (2 Cor. 1.22), of the kingdom of God. What is required
of men is an urgent decision for Jesus as Lord in the present.
All this is very close to Pauline theology, and could well bear the
marks of one who had been a close companion of that apostle.

It is true that, in Luke, there is not that condemnation of what
has gone before that Paul expresses. Jesus fulfils the Law and
perfects that to which it pointed and which it partly realized
(Acts 13.39). Again, if this shows a positive attitude to the Jewish
religion—and this, if our interpretation of Stephen's speech is
correct, reveals itself throughout the two volumes—the Areopagus
speech shows a favour to Gentile religiosity which contrasts
strongly with Romans 1.[17] Yet, as we have seen, Paul can take a
more positive attitude to the Jewish faith, and he is not a complete stranger to the Wisdom tradition in Israel. On the other
hand, however, Luke does maintain all too clearly that rejection
of Jesus condemns the religion that such a rejection favours, and
proclaims a harsh judgement on such an attitude. Ignorance is an
excuse only of the past. So the Areopagus speech ends with a stern
appeal: 'The times of ignorance God overlooked, but now he
commands all men everywhere to repent, because he has fixed a
day on which he will judge the world in righteousness by a man
whom he has appointed' (Acts 17.30-1). The speeches to the Jews
contain similar urgent warnings (Acts 2.40; 3.26; 7.51-3;
13.40-1). Luke's theology suggests that men should be led to
Jesus, but it makes very little allowance or excuse for those who
are not moved to accept. The Areopagus speech and that of
Stephen are here of one piece, and in their facing of a situation
where rejection takes place, are not out of keeping with the attitude of Paul.

Where Luke does differ from Paul is in his treatment of the
cross, but at this point he seems to depart from early thought as a
whole for here, at any rate, Paul is building upon the kerygma that
he has received.[18] Here Luke is at his most distinctive, but this
was inevitable so long as his interest was centred upon the exalted
Lord who brings men into salvation as a present act. For Luke's
Christology is dominated by the concepts of the Old Testament
which made him treat Jesus as an individual figure and which
allowed for no element of mysticism. Yet, within the limits

allowed by the Old Testament, he comes as far as he can in emphasizing the present activity of the ascended Lord and in giving a positive value to the cross. Nevertheless, on this he cannot share Paul's emphasis and approach and, that he should not do so, is not necessarily surprising for, in the first place, the authority of the Old Testament was for him supreme and he shared nothing of the love-hate relationship which seemed to characterize Paul's outlook. But, in the second place, his own personality was of such a different kind from that of Paul that he could not completely take over the sense of freedom and release which the apostle found through the cross. His life was no re-production of that of Paul and his theology is therefore different since, for him, the risen Jesus spoke to needs which were of another kind. Kümmel makes the point that 'we cannot know to what extent Paul was understood by his contemporaries in his specific theology',[19] and when we remember how far Paul's own person-ality was responsible for that distinctiveness, then we can see how it would have appeared in a different light to another man. But in rejecting Paul's solution at this point, Luke was rejecting, not merely Paul, but the whole tradition which stood behind him, in favour of a theology fashioned by the pastoral needs of his readers and founded upon a close study of the Old Testament.

In all this therefore, Vielhauer's solution is too simple, when he says that 'the author of Acts is pre-Pauline in his Christology, and post-Pauline in his natural theology, conception of the Law, and eschatology'.[20] Such an approach underplays the individuality of Luke and of his theology, and, because he differs from Paul, this does not necessarily demand that he should be placed at a distance from the Apostle to the Gentiles any more than his differences from Mark demand a belief in a Proto-Luke.

But there are indications, on the other hand, that Luke could, indeed, have learned much from Paul. We have already seen that his eschatological outlook comes close to that of the apostle, but there are other points of contact. Luke may not have talked of justification by faith alone, yet his Gospel contains the parables of the Pharisee and Publican (18.9–14), of the Prodigal Son (15.11–32), of the Good Samaritan (10.25–37), and emphasizes the neces-sity of taking the lowest place (14.7–11). All these push the Pauline doctrine back firmly into the life of Jesus. No other Gospel con-tains more about the free, unmerited grace of God, of the wonder of the inclusion of the outcast. No other Gospel exercises more thought about the seeming rejection of Israel; no other Gospel puts more emphasis upon Jesus as the climax of Israel's history.[21] At all these points, Luke could well show the influence of Paul and, even if his answers show the stamp of an approach which was his own, the questions which caused them may well owe their urgency to the Apostle's influence.

Had Luke written much later than Paul, it seems almost certain that he would have made the apostle more like his own letters and have given him a more anti-Jewish outlook. Unless his purpose were that favoured by the disciples of Baur, or unless his thought were dominated by ideas of a *religio licita*, Luke's writings and his Paul would have been much more on the lines of O'Neill's interpretation. But Luke was not so hostile to the Jews, his Paul does not break away from the Jewish nation, his Christology is his own. Luke's work seems to be more on the lines of one who was close enough to the Apostle to respect, admire, and follow him, but to do so with an independence which, though not uninfluenced by the other's answers, propounds its own solutions born out of a confidence of a grass-root knowledge of what he is proclaiming. Certainly here is impossible, but caution must be employed before concluding that what we have in Luke–Acts would have been impossible for a companion, who was also an admirer, of the apostle Paul.

For it is as the work of a pastoral theologian of the first order that Luke–Acts must be received. Luke was the interpreter of the early Christian tradition, but what he presented was other than that revised version of Christianity with which he has sometimes been accredited, for he stands firmly within the main stream of the early eschatological tradition. He was not the first reductionist in the interests of clarity and relevance, but was a stranger to much that the liberal tradition has seen in him.

But does this mean that his work, while it should be accepted much more readily by the existentialist interpreter, nevertheless, has little to say to the Christian who is involved in history, for, if we have been right, Luke was proved wrong in his expectation of an early End? What does Luke add to the total biblical interpretation of the event of Jesus, if it is not a missionary outlook, a positive view of the world, or a near-catholic understanding of the Church and its life? His value lies in the fact that, without abandoning the eschatological outlook of early Christianity, he was able to see the significance of continuing history, that it could be used as an indirect witness to the lordship of Jesus which was, nevertheless, reserved for its fullness to the sphere of the transcendent. In this he was not completely new,[22] and he could well have learned the beginnings of his approach from Paul, but it was his genius to link that history to the life of Jesus, which was its prelude and reason, in a continuity which also allowed for discontinuity, and to see that, in spite of the perplexities that history contains, it can through the eyes of faith be seen as pointing to the lordship of the Christ. Since he did not expect the world to continue, he did not give an answer that could be ours completely, but he does point the way to an approach which can use salvation history as the means of coming to a real existential encounter with the living Lord and which also sees that that encounter has some significance for the continuing life of the disciple in the world.

Notes

INTRODUCTION

1. C. K. Barrett, *Luke the Historian in Recent Study* (London 1961), p. 22.
2. A. von Harnack, *Luke the Physician* (London 1907), p. 147.
3. 'C'est le plus beau livre qu'il y ait. Le plaisir que l'auteur dut avoir à l'écrire ne sera jamais suffisamment compris.' Ernest Renan, *Les Évangiles*, Œuvres complètes de Ernest Renan, tome v, p. 205.
4. W. Manson, *The Gospel of Luke* (London 1930), pp. xxiv, xxvii.
5. M. Dibelius, *Studies in the Acts of the Apostles* (London 1956). The volume is the E.T. of a collection of essays originally written between 1923 and his death in 1947.
6. Op. cit., p. 185.
7. H. J. Cadbury, *The Making of Luke–Acts*, 2nd edn (London 1950), 1st edn 1930.
8. J. M. Creed, *The Gospel According to St Luke*, 2nd edn (London 1950), 1st edn 1930.
9. Creed, *Luke*, pp. 165–6. Cf. *From Tradition to Gospel* (London 1934), original German 1919, pp. 17–18.
10. Op. cit., p. lxxi.
11. Op. cit., p. 301.
12. 'Interpreting Luke–Acts in a Period of Existentialist Theology', in *Studies in Luke–Acts*, ed. L. E. Keck and J. L. Martyn, London 1968.
13. Philipp Vielhauer, 'On the "Paulinism" of Acts' in *Studies in Luke–Acts* (original German 1950), pp. 33–50.
14. Ernst Käsemann, *Essays on New Testament Themes* (London 1964), pp. 28–9, 136–48; *New Testament Questions of Today* (London 1969), pp. 21–2, 236–51. (Original German publications in 1952, 1954, 1957 and 1963).
15. Hans Conzelmann, *The Theology of St Luke*, London 1960 (original German, 1953).
16. Ernst Haenchen, *The Acts of the Apostles*, Oxford 1971 (original German 1956). In his discussion of Haenchen's commentary, Rohde, *Rediscovering the Teaching of the Evangelists* (London 1968), pp. 196–7, asks whether it really is to be included within a discussion of redactional-critical treatments of Luke's work or whether

it remains rather within the presuppositions and outlook of the Form-critical treatment of Dibelius. Rohde admits that no complete division can be made between the two, but he is critical of Haenchen for not always giving due weight to Luke's theology. Though Haenchen sees Luke as having a distinctive theology which appears through much of the work, he does not seem to have made full allowance for it in his handling of the individual episodes, while in the movement of the book as a whole, he has seen the main driving force, not in Luke's theology as such, but in the historical and practical needs of the evangelist's day.

17. Helmut Flender, *St Luke, Theologian of Redemptive History* (London 1967), p. 3.

18. Op. cit., pp. 49, 117.

19. e.g. Hans-Werner Bartsch, *Wachet aber zu jeder Zeit*, Hamburg-Bergstedt, 1963; Bo Reicke, *The Gospel of Luke*, London 1965; I. H. Marshall, *Luke, Historian and Theologian*, London 1970. In spite of its English title and of the difficulties in interpreting the work as a whole, Flender's book, cited in note 17, should probably be included here. See also Kaestli, *L'Eschatologie dans L'Œuvre de Luc*, Geneva 1969, which, though seeing Luke as working within the framework of salvation history, is, nevertheless, critical of the more rigid expositions of his theology in its terms.

20. Vielhauer, op. cit., p. 45.

21. R. Bultmann, *Theology of the New Testament* (London 1955), vol. 2, p. 117.

22. Ulrich Wilckens, *Die Missionsreden der Apostelgeschichte*, Neukirchen 1961; 'Interpreting Luke–Acts in a Period of Existentialist Theology' in *Studies in Luke–Acts*, London 1968; 'The Understanding of Revelation within Primitive Christianity', in *Revelation as History*, London 1969.

23. Oscar Cullman, *Salvation in History*, London 1967.

24. *Interpreting Luke–Acts in a Period of Existentialist Theology*, p. 77.

25. Op. cit., p. 237. See also the point of view of Grässer, *Das Problem der Parusieverzögerung in den synoptischen Evangelien und in der Apostelgeschichte*, Berlin 1957.

26. Op. cit., p. 237. cf. Kaestli, op. cit., p. 97, 'Il ressorte nettement que, la fièvre apocalyptique qui marquait la tradition antérieure est systématiquement atténuée ou effacée par le troisième évangéliste.'

27. The position which is taken here comes very close to that embraced by R. H. Hiers, 'The Problem of the Delay of the Parousia in Luke–Acts', *NTS* (1974), pp. 145–55. 'On the one hand, he undertakes to show that Jesus had not mistakenly believed or proclaimed that the parousia was near. On the other hand, Luke holds before his own contemporaries—who might still have included a few survivors of the earliest community—the hopes (and warning) that

the kingdom of God and/or Son of man might come soon' (p. 146).
I should want to substitute 'immediate' for 'near' in the first sentence,
and the word 'will' for 'might' in the second. I am less convinced than
Hiers that Luke was concerned to safeguard the supernatural
character of Jesus. Changes which seem to play down the immediacy
of Jesus' expectation would seem to derive rather from Luke's
understanding of the significance of the ascension.

CHAPTER 1

1. I. H. Marshall, *Luke*, p. 18, describes Luke as an evangelist;
   C. K. Barrett, *LH*, p. 67, sees his two volumes as preaching.
   S. G. Wilson, *The Gentiles and the Gentile Mission in Luke–Acts*,
   Cambridge 1973, thinks that the balance in Acts between accurate
   reporting and mistaken inference, between the following of sources
   and his freedom with them, between historical concern and theological interpretation, is best explained by seeing practical, pastoral
   considerations as the main determining factor in Luke's work.
2. Rohde, *Rediscovering*, p. 177, criticizes Conzelmann for the certainty with which he assumes that the eschatological expectation
   was fundamental to early Christianity, whilst Van Unnik, 'Luke–
   Acts a Storm Center in Contemporary Scholarship' *SLA*, p. 28
   asks whether 'the delay of the parousia really wrought that havoc
   that it is sometimes supposed to have done?' I owe my own caution
   here to John Fenton, who rightly once criticized my use of the
   phrase 'the crisis caused by the delay of the parousia'. E. Ellis,
   Eschatology in Luke (Philadelphia 1972), pp. 16–20, thinks that the
   problem was not the delay of the parousia but a false apocalyptic
   speculation. This was itself, however, occasioned by the non-
   appearance of the parousia and seems to have been widely influential. Luke's obvious concern with this point makes it likely that
   those to whom he wrote were genuinely troubled.
3. Page references are to the English edition of H. Conzelmann,
   The Theology of St Luke, London 1960.
4. Cf. H. Flender, *St Luke, Theologian of Redemptive History* (London
   1960), pp. 5–6: 'Thus as we see it, Luke has planned his Gospel
   on more levels than Conzelmann has allowed us to see.'
5. Vincent Taylor, *Behind the Third Gospel*, 1926. Recently, Caird,
   Saint Luke (Pelican Gospel Commentaries 1963), pp. 227–9.
6. In contrast to the presuppositions of Vincent Taylor.
7. C. P. M. Jones, 'The Epistle to the Hebrews and the Lucan
   Writings' in Nineham, ed., *Studies in the Gospels* (Oxford 1955),
   p. 135.
8. This speaks against Kaestli's argument in *L'Eschatologie dans
   L'Œuvre de Luc* (Geneva 1969), p. 55 that Luke here moves the
   emphasis from the parousia to the appearance before the Son of
   man at the resurrection of the dead. Though the idea is appropriate
   to Luke's thought as a whole and is apparent at his account of the

death of Stephen, it is not his intention to speak here of the deaths of individual Christians but of the parousia of the Son of man.

9. As Ellis says, *The Gospel of Luke* (London 1966), p. 246, the context seems to require a chronological significance which seems to make 'mankind' or 'believers' impossible. 'Jesus' generation' though possibly original, seems hardly in its strict sense to have been Luke's meaning. Ellis's own suggestion of 'last generation' which includes several life-spans seems of the nature of special pleading and is criticized by Wilson, 'Lucan Eschatology', *NTS* xvi, 1970, who thinks that Luke may have stretched the phrase to include contemporaries of Jesus who were still alive. But this makes the phrase less positive than Luke himself intends, and is in danger of making a virtue out of necessity. The place of this section in the discourse between verses 25–9 and 34–6 makes it unlikely that verse 32 refers to the signs of the parousia rather than to the parousia itself (Moore, *The Parousia in the New Testament*, Leiden 1966).

10. Conzelmann, *Theology*, p. 114.

11. W. G. Kümmel, *Promise and Fulfilment* (London 1957), p. 97.

12. Ibid., pp. 32–5.

13. J. Jeremias, *New Testament Theology*, vol. i (London 1971), p. 101.

14. See the discussion in Kummel, *Promise*, pp. 32–5.

15. N. Perrin, *Rediscovering the Teaching of Jesus* (London 1967), p. 74.

16. W. G. Kümmel, *Promise*, p. 34.

17. Johannes Weiss, *Jesus' Proclamation of the Kingdom of God* (London 1970), pp. 77–8 notes that in Luke 17.21 'Jesus asserts something which generally he does not presuppose elsewhere; the *Basileia* is already here in some invisible form.' Weiss is right to see the present reality, however, as 'the altogether supranatural and superhistorical establishment of the power of God over Satan to whom for a while the world has been subjected'.

18. A. R. C. Leaney, 'The Days of the Son of Man' in *The Gospel according to St Luke* (London 1958), pp. 68–72.

19. See the discussion of this section by C. E. B. Cranfield, 'The Parable of the Unjust Judge and the Eschatology of Luke–Acts', in *SJT*, vol. 16 (1963), pp. 297–301. Cranfield's article provides a valuable corrective to too easy an acceptance of Conzelmann's general thesis. The close connection of this section with 17.22–37, however, makes it most likely a reference to an actual parousia at a time which is not far off, and the article's attempt to see the *Naherwartung* in terms of the possibility of its occurrence at any moment or as an epilogue to the decisive events in the life, death, and resurrection of Jesus seems to be at variance with Luke's understanding. The thought of the parable demands a real vindication both in time and soon. As Conzelmann notes (pp. 123–4), the section 'provides a commentary on the petition "thy Kingdom come"' and, as we shall see below, this refers to the actual event of the parousia.

20. J. Jeremias, *The Parables of Jesus* (London 1954), pp. 84, 116. But, *pace* Jeremias, Luke does not write about 'persistent and humble prayer'. The passage is centred upon the judge and his vindicating act. Luke sees prayer almost entirely in relation to avoiding the *peirasmos* of Satan and to summoning the parousia. (See pp. 161ff.) The Lucan introduction, like the conclusion, refers to the parousia; the use of 'the Lord' and of 'faith' points back to 17.5 and reveals the hand of Luke. 18.8b is of a unity with the rest of the Lucan interpretation.

21. Cranfield, op. cit., p. 299, contra Jeremias, op. cit., p. 116.

22. Conzelmann, *Theology*, p. 104.

23. Wilson, 'Eschatology', p. 338.

24. Ellis, *Luke*, p. 141.

25. Creed, *Luke*, p. lxxxi.

26. Perrin, *Rediscovering*, p. 17.

27. G. W. H. Lampe, 'Luke' in *Peake's Commentary*, rev. ed., London 1962, notes that it is in keeping with Luke's view that 'the supreme object of prayer is the gift of the Spirit'. Nevertheless, it seems likely that Luke wrote the petition for the coming of the kingdom and that he included a phrase made necessary by its use in the early Church, without however necessarily making its theology his own. See further pp. 161ff.

28. Jeremias, *Parables*, pp. 90–1.

29. Luke's version at 11.20 turns attention away from Jesus' ministry to the God who stands behind it. Jesus is not empowered by the Spirit but is the instrument of God. His adversaries test him and see him as the instrument of Satan but he points them away from himself to God. The miracles become the sign that God is working through him. There is therefore no section here about blasphemy against the Holy Spirit (Matt. 12.31–32) which links this to the person of Jesus. This means that, though Luke uses *ephthasen eph' humas* which carries the meaning 'The kingdom of God has come upon you' (Kummel, op. cit., p. 107), the kingdom, so far from being seen as a 'present reality in the ministry of Jesus' (Ellis, *Luke*, p. 161), is given a transcendent reference. What happens on earth witnesses to something in the other world. This is the sphere of the kingdom, not merely as a present reign or rule of God (G. E. Ladd, *Jesus and the Kingdom*, London 1966), but as a real victory over the living forces of Satan, for, though this is, as yet, invisible, it is nevertheless, for Luke, concrete and spatial.

30. Luke 16.16 presents peculiar difficulties of interpretation, but though few confident conclusions can be drawn, consideration of it is vital because, as Kummel points out (op. cit., p. 121), it is a definite statement (perhaps, indeed, the most definite) of the present existence of the kingdom. Difficulties arise, however, in assessing just how it believes this present existence is realized. G. Schrenk (*TDNT*, vol. 1 (Michigan 1964), pp. 609–13) maintains that *biazetai* is middle active and though he admits that the verb

is nearly always used *in malam partem*, he believes that its use of *eis* here means that it must be translated, not as 'to exert force against', but as 'forcefully to press into'. He therefore sees the verse as a joyful allusion arising out of Luke's missionary bias and universal expectations. But this hardly gives *biazetai* a bad sense. Rather, the verse sees the kingdom as in some way under siege. This is brought out clearly by F. W. Danker (*JBL*, lxxvii (1958), pp. 231–43), who concludes: 'All indications point to usage of the word *biazetai in malam partem*. The kingdom is a victim of attempted forced entrance.' It is possible therefore that the opponents are the rulers in the spiritual world, for this would fit Luke's understanding of conflict in the supernatural realm and of the kingdom as a present reality only in the transcendent. However, it makes *pas* a little hard to explain, for its more natural meaning is one of 'all men'. But Luke nowhere else talks in this way of men entering or attacking the kingdom as a present happening. Entry remains a future action (6.20; 9.27; 13.29; 14.15; 19.11; Acts 14.22). At 18.17, those who will enter the kingdom are those who receive it as a child. The rich ruler is told to sell his possessions that he might have treasure in heaven (18.22), even though, when he refuses, Jesus does talk about entering the kingdom as though it could be a present possession. More likely, however, the actual entry is reserved for the future (18.24) for the promise to the disciples clearly finds its climax in the future (18.30). In 16.16–17, the purpose of the saying is to state that the gospel of the kingdom has not done away with the Law. Perhaps *biazetai* is used against those who think that it has. But it is 'the gospel of the kingdom' rather than the actual kingdom itself which men are besieging. It is the proclamation of Jesus and his followers which is under attack. The kingdom itself remains transcendent. On this verse, Conzelmann notes (*Luke*, p. 112), 'The coming of Jesus does not mean the kingdom is near, but that the time for the preaching of the kingdom has come.'

31.   C. K. Barrett, 'Stephen and the Son of Man' in 'Apophoreta', Haenchen Festschrift, *BZNW* 30 (Berlin, 1964), pp. 36–7.
32.   *NTS* 1 (1954–5), p. 9.
33.   Bartsch, *Wachet aber zu jeder Zeit* (Hamburg-Bergstedt 1963), p. 112.
34.   Käsemann, *Essays on New Testament Themes* (London 1964), p. 28.
35.   J. M. Robinson, *The Problem of History in Mark* (London 1957), pp. 66–7.
36.   G. von Rad, *Old Testament Theology*, vol. 1 (Edinburgh 1962), p. 346.
37.   Wilson ('Eschatology', p. 347) suggests: 'It seems quite probable, purely on the basis of his eschatology, that Luke wrote Acts a considerable time after the Gospel, and that in the interim period his views developed and changed.' He says that we should be wary of expecting the same teaching in both volumes. This, however, still

sees Acts primarily as a continuation of a historical narrative begun
in the Gospel rather than, as I believe it is, a supplementary volume
giving confirmation of the thesis which the Gospel puts forward.
The aim of Acts is not to justify a future expectation (which however, as Wilson admits, it does not suggest to be wrong), but to
vindicate a confidence in the present status of Jesus based upon a
past event. Luke's eschatological presuppositions are the same
throughout his two volumes.

38. See Wilson's discussion of this in 'The Ascension; a Critique and
    an Interpretation', *ZNW*, 59 (1968), pp. 227–9.

39. E. Franklin, 'The Ascension and the Eschatology of Luke–Acts',
    SJT 23 (1970), pp. 191–200.

40. J. A. T. Robinson, *Jesus and his Coming* (London 1957), pp. 43–51,
    suggests that in Mark 14.62 Jesus speaks, not of a future coming,
    but only of his immediate vindication. Whatever Jesus himself
    meant, it seems certain that Luke's alterations make it clear that he
    understood Mark to expect a return which was regarded as a climax
    of the glorification of Jesus, and it was this which he avoided by
    his alterations and omissions.

41. It is not important for our purpose whether Luke obtained a basis
    for his account of the Ascension from earlier traditions or whether
    he himself introduced it as a historical event as a result of his own
    reflections on the Christian belief in Christ's exaltation. In the
    absence of other early historical references, and in view of Luke's
    use of history both in his narrative in general and of the ascension
    in particular, it seems to me likely that he himself was responsible
    for understanding it as an actual event in time and space. What is
    more important for our purpose, however, and what can more
    easily be assessed, is the actual use and purpose he gave to the event,
    and the distinctive theological outlook he centred around it.

42. See the discussion by A. M. Ramsey, 'What was the Ascension?'
    in *Historicity and Chronology in the New Testament* (London 1965),
    pp. 135–44.

43. C. F. Evans, *Resurrection and the New Testament* (London 1970),
    p. 96.

44. D. E. Nineham, *Saint Mark* (London 1963), pp. 447–8.

45. Evans, *Resurrection*, p. 112.

46. J. A. T. Robinson, *Coming*, pp. 134–6.

47. See the discussion in J. G. Davies, *He Ascended into Heaven*
    (London 1958), pp. 54–5.

48. Barrett, 'Stephen', p. 37.

49. At Acts 22.14, Ananias does say that Paul, at his conversion, not
    merely heard a voice, but also saw the Righteous One. This, how-
    ever, is not really a contradiction of Luke's general outlook, but
    is made necessary by his insistence that a witness has to be one who
    has seen the Risen Jesus (Marshall, *Luke*, pp. 41–4). Since, at this
    point, he is primarily concerned to vindicate both the missionary

work of Paul and his activity among the Gentiles, he is concerned to establish the full qualifications of the Apostle and the correctness of his missionary direction. Cf. Acts 9.17.

50. Davies, *Ascended*, p. 54 accuses Luke of inconsistency here, but he is right to see that this is occasioned by his theological interest and concern.

51. This lack of mention of the ascension elsewhere in Acts might seem strange in view of the importance that it assumes for Luke and of his frequent pointing to it in the Gospel (see my article referred to in n. 39). In the Gospel, it (rather than the parousia) is presented as the event to which the life pointed forward and in which it found its climax. In Acts, however, the ascension represents the value judgement on Jesus which the book as a whole justifies. The whole book is seen as depending upon it and witnessing to it even though it is always seen as the moment of entry into that present glory of Christ which it is the real concern of the book to proclaim. It is not found in the speeches as a separate event—other than in the Pentecost speech where the presence of the Spirit is seen as its guarantee—because it is itself the value judgement rather than the grounds upon which a value judgement about Jesus is to be based and which is instead provided supremely by the resurrection. Luke historicizes a value judgement. This may be seen as a further pointer confirming our suggestion that the understanding of the ascension as a separate event in time and place comes *de novo* from Luke himself.

52. A. R. C. Leaney, *The Gospel according to St Luke* (London 1958), p. 296; Ellis, *Luke*, p. 279.

53. Barrett, *LH*, p. 56.

54. Davies, *Ascension*, p. 42.

55. See the discussion by P. A. van Stempvoort, 'The Interpretation of the Ascension in Luke and Acts', *NTS*, v (1958), pp. 30–42. For the discussion which follows, I am greatly indebted to this article and also to the discussion in Barrett, *LH*, pp. 55–8, though my interpretation differs from theirs in so far as it does not see Acts 1 as the beginning of the continuing history of the ongoing Christian community. Evans, op. cit., p. 101, n. 103, criticizes van Stempvoort on the grounds that the double understanding of the ascension, which he believes Luke to have, implies a 'very considerable disjunction in Luke's mind between his first and second volumes'. This criticism may have weight against van Stempvoort's historical approach, but it is met when it is seen that each description is the vehicle of a theological value judgement, and that together they form an integrated assessment of the significance of the earthly events that Luke records.

56. W. G. Kümmel, *Introduction to the New Testament* (London 1966), p. 110, *contra* P. Menoud, 'Remarques sur les textes de l'ascension dans Luc–Actes', *BZNW*, 21 (1954), 148–56.

57. *Contra* van Stempvoort, op. cit., p. 33.

58. *Contra* A. N. Wilder, 'Variant Traditions of the Resurrection in Acts', *JBL*, 62 (1943), p. 311.

59. As Haenchen writes, *The Acts of the Apostles* (Oxford 1971), p. 141, the length of time was probably denoted by the 'sacred' number of 40 days. Wilson, 'Ascension', p. 271, suggests that it refers to an undefined period and that it is determined by the Pentecostal setting of the outpouring of the Spirit. In any case, what was important for Luke was simply to underline the fact that Jesus was seen after his resurrection. The length of time was not important; the theological enlightenment of the apostles was.

60. This point is brought out clearly by Wilson.

61. *Op. cit.*, p. 39. It will be clear that I am unable to follow van Stempvoort in his understanding of the significance of Luke's second interpretation of the ascension, pp. 41–2. I find its importance rather in the way it uses the past history of Christian expansion to support its contention that Jesus is Lord, and to arouse the hope that this will soon be clearly seen in the coming of the parousia. Acts 1, *pace* van Stempvoort, is not concerned with the problems of 'realized eschatology'.

62. Ellis, *Luke*, p. 13. He says this even though he recognizes that in Acts 'kingdom of God' is used only of a future event. Luke might regard the Spirit as 'the anticipation of the End in the present' (Cullmann, *Christ and Time* (London 1951), p. 73), but this is not the same thing as saying that it brings the kingdom in the present. This can only be if the kingdom is working within history and, as we have seen, this is not an idea that is favoured by Luke. The 'anticipation' is a guarantee of the future kingdom rather than a partial realization of its presence. The Spirit does not bring an embodiment of the kingdom but power derived from it and a pledge of its reality and present existence.

63. Acts 3.6, 16.

64. Haenchen, op. cit, p. 720, maintains that Luke 'practically eliminates the Roman community by his silence' in order that Paul may be presented as the one who indicates the proclamation in that city and so come to a fitting climax of his activity. But, if this were so, Luke would surely have omitted 28.15 altogether and would have noted Paul's success with more flourish than he does. See pp. 116ff.

65. V. C. van Unnik, 'The "Book of Acts" the Confirmation of the Gospel', *NT*, iv (1960), pp. 26–59. See also his introductory essay in *SLA*, p. 29 where he questions the usual understanding of the relation between the two volumes of Luke's work. An approach which also sees the second volume as confirmation of the first is found in J. Dupont, 'Le salut des Gentils et le livre des Actes', *NTS* 6 (1959–60), pp. 132–55.

66. Van Unnik himself says as much when (*SLA*, p. 29) he asks whether 'church history' or 'history of Christian missions' are true descriptions of Luke's purpose in Acts. 'We must not go by our impressions but by the indications the writer himself gives. In the great com-

mission (Acts 1.8) the disciples are not merely sent out but are called "witnesses".' See pp. 165ff.

67. R. Bultmann, *History and Eschatology* (Edinburgh 1957), p. 35.
68. D. S. Russell, *The Method and Message of Jewish Apocalyptic* (London 1964), p. 220.
69. Von Rad, op. cit., vol. 2, p. 118.
70. Conzelmann, *Theology*, p. 36.
71. U. Wilckens, 'The Understanding of Revelation within the History of Primitive Christianity', in *Revelation as History* (London 1969), p. 95.
72. Conzelmann, it is true, is guarded on this point and does not deny the present activity of Jesus and the present relationship between him and the Christian. He takes full account of the Lucan use of 'the name' and says, 'We can go so far as to say that to speak of the efficacy of the name is the specifically Lucan way of describing the presence of Christ' (*Theology*, p. 128). Nevertheless, alongside this, and providing the real grounds for a lasting link between the Christian and the saving work of Christ is the transmission of the message by the Church which removes the Christian's remoteness, both from the life of Jesus and from the parousia. He therefore holds that 'in the Church we stand in a mediated relationship to the saving events—mediated by the whole course of redemptive history—and at the same time in an immediate relationship to them, created by the Spirit in whom we can invoke God and the name of Christ' (p. 208). Wilckens, however, leaves aside this direct relationship (*Revelation*, pp. 94-8). For him, the 'name' of Jesus is 'what the apostolic witness said about Jesus'. By this we are incorporated into the time of salvation. Wilckens holds that Luke could not have answered: 'How could the act of God in past time become an act of salvation?' May this not be because Luke would not have shared the presuppositions upon which the question is based? For Luke, the moment of salvation is the present.
73. Von Rad, op. cit., vol. 1, p. 183.
74. Käsemann, *New Testament Questions of Today* (London 1969), p. 22.
75. Marshall, *Luke*, p. 84.
76. R. Bultmann, 'History and Eschatology in the New Testament' *NTS* 1 (1954-5), p. 15.

CHAPTER 2

1. On this see the discussion in J. C. O'Neill, *The Theology of Acts*, 2nd edn (London 1970), pp. 172-85; Kümmel, *Introduction to the New Testament* (London 1966), pp. 113-6.
2. C. F. D. Moule, 'The Christology of Acts' in *Studies in Luke-Acts*, pp. 160-1. Cf. G. D. Kilpatrick, *Jesus in the Gospels and the Early Church* (Drawbridge Memorial Lecture 1971), pp. 3-7. Whereas

Moule is interested in Luke's use of 'Lord' to show that he was concerned with what actually happened, Kilpatrick talks more of traditions about Jesus in their earlier and later forms.

3. Acts 2.32–6.
4. This suggests that Luke was writing to people who already shared his beliefs about Jesus, and that he was arguing from past events to obtain a particular response from them in the present in order that they might make a realistic acknowledgement of that lordship.
5. F. Hahn, *The Titles of Jesus in Christology* (London 1969), pp. 81–5.
6. Haenchen, *Acts*, p. 187.
7. O'Neill in the first edition (1961) of the work cited in note 1, pp. 124–6.
8. W. Foerster, *TDNT*, vol. III, p. 1089, suggests that in Acts it implies divine dignity. This, however, is to underestimate the importance for Luke of Psalm 110.1. A. W. Wainwright, *The Trinity in the New Testament* (London 1962), pp. 81–6, is extremely cautious and dissents from O'Neill's opinion (*SJT* viii, 1955, pp. 155–74) that the title ascribed divinity to Jesus. In the first edition of *The Theology of Acts*, p. 131, O'Neill reverses his position to say: 'At this stage there are no indications that there was any confusion between the two Lords or any attempt to claim divinity for Jesus because he was called Lord.' Cullmann, *The Christology of the New Testament* (London 1959), p. 237, is guarded about the significance of the *Kyrios* title in Luke–Acts.
9. Though S. Mowinckel, *The Psalms in Israel's Worship* (Oxford 1962), vol. I, pp. 57–61 can talk of the 'divinity' of the king in Israel, this description is so hedged around with qualifications as to suggest that it has lost its full meaning. 'In spite of all "divinity" the king is a human being, and there is an enormous distance between man and the real God. . . . That the king in Israel should have been regarded as identical with Jahweh, or in the cult have played Yahweh's part is thus wholly improbable.' See the less extravagant understanding of Ps. 110.1 in A. Weiser, *The Psalms* (London 1962), p. 694.
10. U. Wilckens, *Die Missionsreden der Apostelgeschichte* (Neukirchen 1961), p. 178; R. P. C. Hanson, *The Acts* (Oxford 1967), p.39.
11. See pp. 132ff.
12. O'Neill, *Theology*, 1st edn, pp. 119–29. He emphasizes that Luke uses the title in order to set out the argument that Jesus fulfils O.T. messianic expectations; it is concerned with 'a disputed category of Messiahship'. It is not necessary, however, to assume that this reflects a later usage or that it is occasioned by Jewish messianic speculation which did not systematize until after A.D. 70. Luke's usage is not a question of discussion with outsiders but rather of doubts within the Christian community itself, especially in a community which had been nurtured on the O.T. The career of Jesus was a stumbling-block, and doubts about his messianic status were raised. The problem shows itself in all the gospels,

where the necessity of the suffering is treated and it becomes acute where, for other reasons, the community's belief is threatened.

13. Conzelmann, *Theology*, p. 171.

14. Bo Reicke, *The Gospel of Luke* (London 1965), p. 60: 'It is clearly seen that Luke, more than any other Evangelist, makes constant reference in this last act (i.e. the story of the passion) to the fact that in the suffering, death, and resurrection of Jesus the Old Testament is fulfilled.'

15. J. A. T. Robinson, 'The Most Primitive Christology of All', *JTS* n.s. vii, 1956, pp. 177–88. See the discussion of this in O'Neill, op. cit., pp. 124–9, and in Moule, op. cit., pp. 167–9.

16. O'Neill, *Theology*, pp. 125–7.

17. For Luke, the cross is not an isolated incident, but rather the climax of the whole series of sufferings and the prelude to the exaltation.

18. See the discussion in Kümmel, *Introduction*, pp. 99–100 on the reasons for Luke's emphasis upon the theme of a journey. Marshall, *Luke*, pp. 148–53, points out that the idea of a journey is already present in Mark but that Luke has considerably expanded it and emphasized its importance. 'What is new in this section is the stress on Jerusalem as the ultimate goal of Jesus, the place where he must suffer.' Nevertheless, in spite of this, he maintains that 'the rejection and suffering of Jesus at Jerusalem is not the controlling factor' and suggests, rather one feels as a counsel of despair, that 'the theme is the broader one of suffering'. Bo Reicke, 'Instruction and Discussion in the Travel Narrative', *Studia Evangelica* (1959), pp. 206–16, sees conflict and edification as predominant but, again, perhaps does not give enough weight to the Lucan emphasis upon progression towards a goal.

19. Conzelmann, *Theology*, pp. 64–5. But his linking of the journey to its goal in Jerusalem is significant (p. 64), even though we cannot accept this as progress to a climax which is pictured as a non-eschatological event.

20. H. E. Tödt, *The Son of Man in the Synoptic Tradition* (London 1965), pp. 105–8. He comments 'This view reveals a direct christological interest' and says, 'It is of primary importance that the attention is no longer solely directed towards the future parousia of the Son of man as is done in the other sayings concerning the Son of man's coming, but is complementarily directed to an historical event which must happen first.'

21. See Moule, *Christology*, pp. 169–70.

22. H. J. Cadbury, 'The Titles of Jesus in Acts', in the *Beginnings of Christianity*, part 1, 'The Acts of the Apostles', vol. v, pp. 366–9 warns against too easy an assumption that the Suffering Servant of Deutero-Isaiah is specifically in mind here, and the same point is made by M. D. Hooker, *Jesus and the Servant* (London 1959), pp. 109–10. Acts 3.13 does, however, have other pointers to the Servant Songs, and the wide Lucan use of the Servant figure

suggests that it is this which is in mind here. But Luke points also
to the suffering of other O.T. figures and his use of *pais* with a
Davidic connection in the Apostolic Prayer suggests that he isolated
the *Ebed Yahweh* much less than modern critics are wont to do,
that he did not take over the technical implication of the term
in so far as this included vicarious sufferings, but that he saw him as
representing and, in a sense, focusing a pattern that is common to
the figures of the Old Covenant. He must not be isolated in Luke's
thought, neither must reference to him be understood as a taking
over of the total Isaianic portrait.

23.   R. N. Longenecker, *The Christology of Early Jewish Christianity*
(London 1970), p. 106.

24.   G. D. Kilpatrick, *JTS* xliii (1942), pp. 34-6. Rejecting the translation 'righteous' because he believes that it could not have a part in
Luke which is at all comparable with *huios theou* in Mark, he maintains that 'innocent' on the other hand 'accords more satisfactorily
with the theme of the Lucan passion story and with the general
purpose of the Gospel'.

25.   Moule, *Christology*, p. 177.

26.   G. D. Kilpatrick, 'Acts 7.52, *Eleusis*', *JTS* xlvi (1945), pp. 136-45.

27.   See pp. 134ff.

28.   C. H. Dodd points out, *The Interpretation of the Fourth Gospel*
(Cambridge 1953), pp. 256-7, how the Servant idea has an influence in John which is not limited to a concern with the vicarious
suffering of Jesus. He sees its influence in forming the Evangelist's
idea on the mission of Jesus which is directed both to Israel and to
the world. Like the Servant, Jesus will care for his own (10.3, 9).
It is possible too that 'we should also find in the Servant passages
of Second Isaiah a clue to the mysterious idea of the "exaltation"
of the Son of Man'. In this we see a point of contact between Luke
John even if, unlike John, the Third Evangelist does not centre
this Servant usage on the death of Jesus. The Servant idea does,
however, help him to explain the significance of the death as he
understands it.

29.   So F. F. Bruce *The Acts of the Apostles* (London 1952), p. 66;
Marshall, *Luke*, p. 87; A. J. B. Higgins, 'The Preface to Luke and
the Kerygma in Acts', in *Apostolic History and the Gospel*, ed.
W. W. Gasque and R. P. Martin, London 1970. On the other hand,
Lampe, *Acts*, p. 886, says that *ērxato* at Acts 1.1 is 'not emphatic
and is little more than an extended form of the past tense'. J. H. E.
Hull, *The Holy Spirit in the Acts of the Apostles* (London 1968),
pp. 179-80 suggests that it emphasizes that what Jesus did was a
beginning rather being a pointer to his continuing work. Haenchen,
Acts, pp. 97-8, maintains that it cannot describe Jesus' continuing
activity through the Spirit in the apostles because 'Jesus is dwelling
in heaven which must receive him until the parousia'. Van Unnik,
Confirmation, p. 31, makes the same point and says that 'it is rather
mysterious how the very long story of Paul's captivity in Jerusalem,

Caesarea and his voyage to Rome which altogether occupies the quarter of the whole can be explained in that way'. While this approach does carry some weight, and it is true that Jesus is not directly seen as continuing his activity through the Spirit, nevertheless, he is less absent than Haenchen suggests (see p. 195, n.72), and he is active in the events of Paul's captivity, to which Van Unnick appeals (Acts 21.13-4; 23.11). In a real sense Acts can be seen to reflect Jesus' continuing work. However, the emphasis of Luke–Acts is primarily upon how God's eschatological work has been achieved through Jesus, and the results of his exaltation. The Spirit is made possible by him. Jesus is the focus, but not necessarily the whole of God's eschatological activity. In this case, *erxato* emphasizes the fact that the work begun in Jesus' career has been completed in the universal spread of the gospel.

30. Marshall, op. cit., p. 170.
31. C. K. Barrett, 'Stephen', pp. 36-7.
32. The shorter text rather than the longer text is the true vehicle of Luke's theology. The omission of the sacrificial death of Christ leaves the emphasis upon the presence of the risen Christ and the looking forward to the realization of the eschatological act of God. Luke's account is addressed to his contemporaries. See the excellent discussion of A. Vööbus, 'A new Approach to the Problem of the Shorter and Longer Text in Luke'. *NTS* 75 (1968-9), pp. 457-63.
33. This is much more Pauline than Lucan (Lampe, *Acts*, p. 919) and since it appears in a speech which is designed to be Luke's testimony to Paul (Dibelius, *Studies*, pp. 155-8), it cannot be used to point out, as does R. R. Williams, *The Acts of the Apostles*, London 1953, that 'Acts which is sometimes said to have only a weak doctrine of the atonement treats the cross as the means whereby the Church has been purchased for God'. There is no indication that Luke has made this outlook his own.
34. G. W. H. Lampe, *Reconciliation in Christ* (London 1956), p. 42.
35. E. G. Selwyn, *The First Epistle of St Peter* (London 1952), p. 94; Hooker, op. cit., p. 125.
36. Creed's statement, *Luke*, p. lxxii, that 'there is indeed no *theologia crucis* beyond the affirmation that the Christ must suffer, since so the prophetic Scriptures had foretold' is only a half-truth. Cf. also Barrett's opinion, *LH*, p. 59, where he says that the speeches treat the death 'negatively, as an unfortunate event which nevertheless, in view of the resurrection, need not be an obstacle to faith'. The suffering of Christ, reaching its climax in the cross, plays an important part in Luke. It is the only means by which glory can follow and, while it is true that the glory always shines through the sufferings, it does not allow them to be side-stepped. Luke's description of the agony of Gethsemane (22.39-44) is most realistic, and the sufferings of Paul are full and complete. There can be no glory without suffering (disciples are enjoined to take up the cross daily) and the cross alone enables the exaltation to be achieved.

37. Cullmann, *Christology*, p. 30, distinguishes between calling Jesus A prophet and THE prophet, i.e. the one of eschatological expectation. At Luke 7.16 Jesus is not called the prophet of the End-time, though at Acts 3.22 and 7.37 the Deuteronomic expectation is applied to him; but this does not necessarily mean more than that he is conceived of in prophetic terms. Cf. Moule, *Christology*, p. 162. Marshall on the other hand, *Luke*, pp. 125–8, thinks that 4.18 refers the expectation of the eschatological prophet to Jesus. Ellis, *Luke*, p. 143 thinks that the voice at the transfiguration indicates an understanding of Jesus in terms of the eschatological prophet (9.35).

38. Ellis, *Luke*, pp. 119–20. Lampe on the other hand, *Luke*, p. 830, sees the response as in accord with Luke's presentation of Jesus.

39. This comparison is strengthened if C. F. Evans is right in seeing the central section of Luke's Gospel as modelled on Deuteronomy. 'The Central Section of St Luke's Gospel' in *Studies in the Gospels*, pp. 37–53.

40. See the important article by Jervell, 'The Law in Luke–Acts', *HTR* (1971), pp. 21–36, which, contrary to Conzelmann, op. cit., pp. 146–8, maintains that Luke asserted the permanent validity of the Law and avoided the tradition that Jesus criticized it. Jesus does not supersede it or even deepen it but is himself under it. See Bo Reicke, *Gospel*, pp. 57–8 for a presentation which emphasizes Luke's interest in the continuity between the old and new covenants. I would prefer to see Luke as not thinking in terms of a new covenant at all, but rather to accept that he describes Jesus as the fulfilment of the one covenant initiated at the time of Abraham.

41. J. A. T. Robinson, 'Elijah, John, and Jesus', in *Twelve New Testament Studies* (London 1962), pp. 28–52 shows that Luke's thought on Elijah cannot be reduced to a simple pattern. He believes that, though Luke omits the incident when Jesus points to John as Elijah, this is because he has already made the identification (1.17). Luke himself identifies John as the forerunner and Jesus as the Christ, but his work allows an Elijah Christology of Jesus to be recovered. More likely it is Luke himself who brings out the Elijah traits in Jesus, and the fact that he can present Jesus in terms of Elijah in the main body of the Gospel and still retain the Elijah picture of John in the infancy narratives suggests that he is thinking primarily of the prophetic character of both rather than of a second, eschatological Elijah. This would have some bearing also on his use of the prophet designation of Jesus. Cf. Wilson, *Eschatology*, p. 333: 'For Luke Elijah was a model of the godly man, and he wants to use him typologically of both John and Jesus. For this reason Luke avoids directly identifying Elijah with either John or Jesus.'

42. Luke's concern with the Old Testament and the fundamental part this played in forming his ideas is brought out clearly by Bo Reicke, in his section on 'The drama of redemption', *Gospel*, pp. 46–74.

43. Paul Schubert, 'The Structure and Significance of Luke 24', in *Neutestamentliche Studien für R. Bultmann*, Berlin 1957.

44. This would make it likely that Luke's primary concern was not with outsiders but with those who had already embraced Christianity.

45. Eduard Schweizer, *Jesus* (London 1971), p. 140. The whole section pp. 137–46 is worth lengthy consideration. Note especially p. 144; 'The earthly life of Jesus is never seen without the resurrection; and above all we have already noted that Luke always understands the Jesus event in the categories of a message that must be heard if one is to share in it. In other words, he never succeeded in carrying out the programme formulated in theologically misleading terms in Luke 1.1–4, namely having his work taken seriously as the work of a historian, like the competing projects of his contemporaries. He was too good a witness to Jesus to let that happen.'

46. See G. W. H. Lampe, 'The Reasonableness of Typology' in Lampe and Woollcombe, *Essays in Typology*, London 1957.

47. Cullmann, *Christology*, pp. 45–7.

48. Floyd V. Filson, *The Gospel according to St Matthew* (London 1960), p. 29; K. Stendahl, 'Matthew', in *Peake's Commentary*, rev. ed. p. 798.

49. Schweizer, op. cit., p. 139.

50. H. F. D. Sparks, 'The Semitisms of St Luke's Gospel', *JTS* xliv (1943), p. 134.

51. Evans, *Central Section*, p. 37.

52. Van Stempvoort, op. cit., p. 35.

53. H. F. D. Sparks, 'The Semitisms of Acts', *JTS* n.s. 1, pp. 16–28.

54. See further chapters 3 and 4.

55. See the discussion of this speech in C. S. C. Williams, *The Acts of the Apostles* (London 1957), pp. 78–9.

56. Max Wilcox, *The Semitisms of Acts* (Oxford 1965), ch. vi, pp. 157–79.

57. Martin Rese, *Alttestamentliche Motive in der Christologie des Lukas*, Bonn 1965.

58. Leaney, *Luke*, p. 53.

59. Wilcox, op. cit., pp. 47–8, points out that *en tais eschatais hēmerais* reflects, if not a source of some kind, at least informed interpretation. But he admits that the variant, even if not from the author's own hand, supports an eschatological interpretation which was clearly acknowledged by Luke himself. There seems little to suggest (*pace* C. H. Dodd, *According to the Scriptures* (London 1952), p. 48) that the inclusion of Joel 2.28–32 reflects early usage. The use Luke makes of the speech as a whole and his eschatological understanding of the Spirit suggest that both the quotation and the alterations are the result of his own choosing.

60. Haenchen, *Acts*, p. 226, notes how strongly Acts 4.24 is linked to the Septuagint.

61. Ibid., p. 91.

62. Ibid., p. 92: Conzelmann, *Theology*, pp. 173–84: U. Wilckens, *Die Missionsreden der Apostelgeschichte*, pp. 139–42.
63. Conzelmann, *Theology*, p. 175. This point of view is criticized by I. H. Marshall, 'The Resurrection in the Acts of the Apostles', in *Apostolic History and the Gospel*, pp. 101–3. He maintains that there was a near universal belief in the early Church that God raised Christ, that there is is not a particularly strong tendency towards subordinationism in Luke, and that the only new factor is the active use of *anistēmi* with God as the subject (Acts 2.24, 32; 13.34, 37; 17.31). Though Marshall has countered Wilckens's arguments, he has not really allowed for the overall subordinationist outlook of Luke's total work.

CHAPTER 3

1. Conzelmann sometimes portrays Luke as maintaining a firm link between Christianity and its source in Israel: 'The continual reminder that the Church is grounded in redemptive history prevents the connection with Israel from being forgotten' (*Theology*, p. 145). In practice, however, he reduces this to a question of historical origins rather than one of real unity or even of lasting continuity. The period of Israel is over before Jesus begins his ministry and the period of the Church represents a conscious growing away from its source in Israel. The Church is Israel only in so far as she has taken over her place in the scheme of redemptive history (pp. 145–8, 162–7). Though Haenchen, *Acts*, p. 102, makes full allowance for Luke's attempts to throw a bridge between Jews and Christians, this is only in order to demonstrate 'the implicit unity which confirms the continuity of the history of salvation in the divine will'.
2. For criticisms of Conzelmann's view which divides salvation history into separate periods see Wilson, *Eschatology*, pp. 331–6; Paul Minear, 'Luke's use of the Birth Stories' in *Studies in Luke–Acts*, pp. 111–30; Flender, *St Luke*, pp. 122–5.
3. O'Neill, *Theology*, p. 71.
4. Conzelmann, *Theology*, pp. 16n. 3, 18n. 1, 172.
5. H. H. Oliver, 'The Lucan Birth Stories', *NTS* 10 (1963–4), pp. 202–26 argues that the birth narratives are integral to the Evangelist's theological purpose in Luke–Acts as a whole. However, his belief that Luke later in the Gospel was able to suppress the close relationship between John and Jesus because this had already been established in the birth-stories seems to destroy Conzelmann's view which Oliver is at pains to uphold and to make his own interpretation of the picture of John in Luke 1—2, in terms of Conzelmann's understanding derived from the body of the Gospel, dubious in the extreme. In his understanding of the eschatological implications of the Spirit's activity in the early chapters, he also seems really to be at odds with Conzelmann. W. Barnes Tatum,

'The Epoch of Israel: Luke 1—11 and the Theological Plan of Luke–Acts', *NTS* 13 (1966–7), pp. 184–95, develops an understanding of Luke's outlook on the Spirit in these chapters which sees it as an effort 'to characterize that period in salvation-history before the ministry of Jesus as the epoch of Israel'. But in this he fails to give due emphasis to Luke's appreciation of the eschatological function of the Spirit. It is more than just the spirit of prophecy. He also fails to show the unity through fulfilment to which these early chapters point. See the discerning treatment of these chapters by Minear in the work cited in n. 2.

6. D. R. Jones, *JTS* xix (1968), pp. 19–50.
7. Ellis, *Luke*, p. 74.
8. Lampe, *Luke*, p. 826 thinks that the judgement will affect Mary herself as well as Israel as a whole. Leaney, op. cit., pp. 21–4, sees Luke as taking Mary to represent Israel.
9. See the article of N. A. Dahl, 'The Story of Abraham in Luke–Acts', *Studies in Luke–Acts*, pp. 139–58.
10. His thought here could be something like that expressed by Paul in Romans 9. Like Paul, he has also a hope of a return after the stumbling (2.34). Leaney, *Luke*, p. 100.
11. R. E. Clements, *Prophecy and Covenant* (London 1965), pp. 62–6.
12. Oliver, op. cit., p. 217.
13. Of Conzelmann's use of 16.16, Minear says (op. cit., p. 122): 'It must be said that rarely has a scholar placed so much weight on so dubious an interpretation of so difficult a logion.'
14. This understanding is in keeping with the interpretation of the Apostolic Council that is offered below.
15. Wilson suggests, *Eschatology*, p. 335, that Luke 3.18 presents John as preaching the kingdom. It is true that *evangelizomai* which is used here is used by Jesus in his programmatic statement at Nazareth (4.18). This, however, is not the same as preaching the kingdom, which in Luke is transcendental and which can only be proclaimed in the Christian dispensation. The verb has a wider reference in Luke and the actual object must be referred from the context.
16. The 'Conzelmann pattern' which Wilckens finds in the speeches of Acts, *Missionsreden*, pp. 101ff, appears somewhat over-subtle.
17. See pp. 58ff.
18. R. H. Lightfoot, *The Gospel Message of St Mark* (Oxford 1950), pp. 60–9.
19. Kümmel, *Introduction*, p. 105, says that the details of 19.43f correspond with descriptions of Titus' march upon Jerusalem and therefore are shaped *ex eventu*, even though Jesus' prophecy of judgement upon Jerusalem must be regarded as historical. *Contra*, G. B. Caird, *Saint Luke* (London 1963), p. 217.
20. Creed, *Luke*, p. 187, following Weiss, allows that the verse suggests that the Jews will acknowledge Jesus when he returns. On the other hand, Ellis notes, *Luke*, p. 191, that 'it must be left an open question

204 NOTES TO CHAPTER 3 (PAGES 91–2)

whether the prophecy anticipates that Jerusalem will "see" Jesus in a future conversion or in a recognition of his Lordship, too late in the final judgement'. However, in view of its O.T. background (Psalm 118.26), the cry can hardly be anything other than one of welcome. Jerusalem fulfils her eschatological role for which her history has prepared her. This verse does not even deny some future to her Temple and perhaps G. W. H. Lampe is too strong when in *St Luke and the Church of Jerusalem* (London 1969), p. 15, he suggests that Luke saw the Temple supplanted by Jesus and the Spirit. It is just possible that Luke takes the quotation from Amos 9.11 (LXX) to refer to the restoration of a temple in Jerusalem, A. Cole, *The New Temple* (London 1950), pp. 48ff. This is rejected by R. S. McKelvey, *The New Temple* (Oxford 1969), p. 90, who understands the reference as being to the restoration of the Davidic kingdom. This, according to Lampe (*Luke*, p. 909) is reinterpreted as the new universal people of God. He allows that 'tabernacle' ought possibly to be more strictly interpreted, but maintains that, in this case, it refers to the resurrection of the body of the son David. Haenchen, op. cit., p. 448, denies any reference to the restored Davidic kingdom or even to the true Israel. For him it refers to 'the Jesus event that will cause the Gentiles to seek the Lord'.

21. M. Simon, *St Stephen and the Hellenists* (London 1958), pp. 24–6. O'Neill, *Theology*, p. 74, criticizes this on the grounds that if Luke omitted it at the trial for this reason, why should he have included it at the trial of Stephen? But this point is not valid if it is accepted that Stephen's speech is a defence against such a charge. Luke defends Christians against such accusations because he himself is favourable towards the Temple. He therefore doesn't want any hint at all that Jesus might have been critical of it. Mark, as far as Luke was concerned, was too hostile to the Temple.

22. M. Simon, 'Retour du Christ et Reconstruction de Temple' in *Recherches d'Histoire Judéo-Chrétienne* (Paris 1962), p. 10, points out the certainty of the expectation of the renewal of the Temple in Jewish hopes.

23. It is not enough to suggest with Brandon, *The Trial of Jesus of Nazareth* (London 1968), p. 142, that Luke is simply abbreviating.

24. Assessment of the significance of 22.67–8 varies greatly. Conzelmann, op. cit., p. 85, sees it as dissociating Jesus from the messianic title; Creed, op. cit., p. 278, suggests that it shrugs off the question and turns it aside; Ellis, op. cit., p. 261, that it qualifies an acceptance of the title. I do not think that Luke is here motivated by apologetic considerations.

25. Creed, *Luke*, p. 279, accepts that the verse implies assent but nevertheless suggests that the use of the personal pronoun expresses a certain protest against the question. This seems unlikely in view of the use at 1.35. Rather, the personal pronoun signifies that the Jews really should have acknowledged—and intellectually at least did

acknowledge—the true status of Jesus. It underlines their sheer perversity in rejecting him.

26. G. D. Kilpatrick, 'A Theme of the Lucan Passion Story and Luke 23.47', *JTS* xliii (1942), pp. 34–6.

27. Brandon, op. cit., p. 147, notes that Luke presents Pilate as trying to strike a bargain with the Jews. He was willing to have Jesus flogged even though he believed him to be innocent. 'He depicts the governor as endeavouring to placate the accusers of an innocent man by substituting a flagellation for death. This charge prepares the way for the amazing paradox of a Roman governor's sentencing to death one whom he had publicly proclaimed to be guiltless.'

28. Conzelmann, op. cit., pp. 89–90.

29. Cf. pp. 139ff.

30. For interpretations which see Luke as emphasizing the renewal of Israel and the extension of the covenant through her, see the articles of J. Jervell, especially 'Das gespaltene Israel und die Heidenwöller' in *ST* 19 (1965), pp. 68–96, 'Paulus—der Lehrer Israels' in *NT* 2 (1968), pp. 164–90, 'The Law in Luke–Acts' in *HTR* 64 (Jan. 1971), pp. 21–36. See also N. A. Dahl, 'The Story of Abraham in Luke–Acts' in *Studies in Luke–Acts*; 'A People for His Name' in *NTS* 4 (1957–8), pp. 319–26, J. Dupont, *Laos ex ethnōn* in *NTS* 3 (1955–6), pp. 323–7.

31. E. Schweizer, *Church Order in the New Testament* (London 1961), p. 69. Cf. Haenchen, op. cit., pp. 163–4. C. K. Barrett, *The Signs of an Apostle* (London 1970), pp. 47–54, sees that it is 'Luke's anxiety to represent the Church in its mission to the world as the outcome of, and continuous with, Jesus and his mission to Israel' which makes him think of apostleship as exclusive to the Twelve and causes him to emphasize their place as companions of Jesus during his ministry. The eschatological significance of the Twelve is recognized by K. H. Rengstorf, 'The Election of Matthias', in *Current Issues in New Testament Interpretation*, ed. W. Klassen and G. F. Snyder (London 1962), pp. 178–92, though he tends to see Luke as finding this primarily in its authentication of a continuing concern with Israel. C. K. Barrett, *New Testament Essays* (London 1972), pp. 78–9, accepts the eschatological nature of the episode, but thinks that Luke did not take this over with his source but saw its significance rather as a link between Jesus and the Church.

32. Though it is important to note that it is the action of one of their number which makes the Cornelius episode possible and who later interprets its significance to the new community. See pp. 122ff.

33. H. E. W. Turner, *Why Bishops?*, London 1955, describes the Twelve as 'the right markers of the New Israel'. Luke would have seen them as the fulfilment of the Old Israel as well.

34. See Chapter 5.

35. Against Conzelmann, op. cit., p. 95.

36. Luke places the gift of the Spirit in a setting which has universal implications but this is not the primary significance of the event for

him, which is found rather in its renewal of Israel, and it does not represent the beginning of the universal mission. W. L. Knox, *The Acts of the Apostles* (Cambridge 1948), p. 83, maintains that Luke actually restricted the universal significance contained in the original narrative. It is only after the eschatological renewal of Israel that the mission can begin.

37. Luke 2.25; Acts 8.2; 22.12.

38. This seems to suggest very strongly the re-making of the united Davidic kingdom.

39. J. G. Davies, 'Pentecost and Glossolalia', *JTS* n.s. 3 (1952), pp. 228–31.

40. Knox, op. cit., p. 86; J. D. G. Dunn, *Baptism in the Holy Spirit* (London 1970), pp. 48–9.

41. Haenchen, *Acts*, sees the tongues of fire and the renewal of speech as pointers to a Sinai tradition but he adds: 'If Luke however was —as we may assume—acquainted with this or a similar tradition, he did not adopt it mechanically, for he says nothing of a new law, and the Spirit is represented as an individual gift to each Christian.'

42. For this reason one must be careful of sharing Dunn's conclusion that for Luke 'Pentecost was the beginning of the new covenant in the experience of the disciples', op. cit., p. 49.

43. For the background of this outlook in the Old Testament, see R. Martin-Achard, *A Light to the Nations* (Edinburgh 1962).

44. C. H. Dodd, *The Apostolic Preaching and its Developments* (London 1950), pp. 21–3.

45. Yet in the light of the infancy narratives and of his account of the rejection of Jesus at Nazareth, it seems unlikely that Luke could possibly have expected Jerusalem as a whole to respond to the proclamation of the exaltation of Jesus. Divisions appear inevitable and are apparent in the varied responses to the outpouring to the Spirit at Pentecost.

46. This is the strength of O'Neill's interpretation of Acts. 'His theology must be looked for primarily in the movement of his history,' *Theology*, p. 71. See the appreciation of this approach by Conzelmann, 'Luke's Place in the Development of Early Christianity' in *Studies in Luke–Act*, p. 309. Nevertheless, one may wonder whether O'Neill really does approach Stephen's speech in accordance with his own canon of interpretation—whether he makes due allowance for the particular place it occupies in Acts, and whether he isn't perhaps too anxious to find agreement between it and the overall static theology of Acts which is then interpreted in the light of his understanding of the speech.

47. The point of importance here is that Christians still use the Temple after Stephen's speech.

48. Israel must become what she is, 'the people of God', but there is no suggestion that her status has been taken from her and given to another.

49. Haenchen, on the other hand, sees the two promises as com-

plementary statements about the one event (op. cit., p. 208).
50. So the pattern in the life of Jesus is repeated.
51. Haenchen, *Acts*, p. 289.
52. A. J. F. Klijn, 'Stephen's Speech', *NTS* 4 (1957–8), pp. 25–31, 'summarizing, we may say that the meaning of Stephen's speech is to show the Jews not belonging to his group as having been always disobedient to the law of God' (p. 28). Lampe, *Jerusalem*, pp. 9–10: 'From the beginning, as Stephen's speech is meant to show, there have been two "successions" in Israel.'
53. O. Cullmann, 'The Significance of the Qumran Texts for Research into the Beginnings of Christianity' in *The Scrolls and the New Testament*, ed. K. Stendahl (London 1957), p. 28.
54. M. Simon, 'Saint Stephen and the Jerusalem Temple', *JEH* 11 (1951), p. 127.
55. M. Simon, *St Stephen and the Hellenists in the Primitive Church* (London 1958), pp. 24–6.
56. O'Neill, *Theology*, pp. 76–7.
57. B. Gärtner, *The Areopagus Speech and Natural Revelation*, Uppsala, 1955, writes that the speech adopts a 'wholly adverse attitude' to Temple and sacrificial services. For him the speech shows 'the uselessness and the vanity in the Gentiles' conception of God and their worship of God' (pp. 169, 206, 211–12). Yet Luke presents Paul as having a much more conciliatory attitude towards his hearers. Vielhauer, 'On the Paulinism of Acts' in *Studies in Luke–Acts*, p. 35, notes that 'the tone of the demand is not of accusation but rather of enlightenment'. Haenchen, op. cit., p. 520, says that Paul calls them 'very religious' in a good sense and it is not necessary to see this as mere rhetoric. Cf. Lampe, *Acts*, p. 913. Haenchen also points out (p. 285) that the LXX does not employ *cheiropoiētos* only of idols.
58. W. Manson, *The Epistle to the Hebrews* (London 1951), p. 34.
59. R. E. Clements, *God and Temple* (Oxford 1965), pp. 88–99, 'Deuteronomy had broken with a mythological understanding of Israel's cult and had replaced mythology with theology'.
60. Ibid., pp. 90–2.
61. H. W. Hertzberg, *1 and 2 Samuel* (London 1964), p. 287.
62. N. A. Dahl, 'The Story of Abraham in Luke–Acts' in *Studies in Luke–Acts*, pp. 143–8. He finds the speech centred in a plan of promise and fulfilment. The promise is the Lucan alteration of Gen. 15.14 to read: 'And afterwards they shall come out and worship me in this place' (Acts 7.7); its fulfilment is not the Temple, as the Jews believe, but Jesus, the embodiment of the house of David. This does not condemn the Temple, but rather the Jewish attitude to it.
63. See the interpretation of Psalm 78 by Artur Weiser, *The Psalms* (London 1962), pp. 538–43.
64. This point is made by Dahl, op. cit., p. 146.
65. Haenchen, *Acts*, p. 116.

66. Marshall, *Luke*, p. 75, though recognizing that the pictures of Paul as found in Acts and the Epistles cannot be harmonized in detail, nevertheless maintains that 'this does not mean that the two pictures are irreconcilable, and we believe that the two can in fact be harmonized in general terms'.

67. P. Vielhauer, 'On the Paulinism of Acts', op. cit., pp. 33–50; E. Haenchen, 'Luke and Paul', op. cit., pp. 112–16; G. Bornkamm, 'The Missionary Stance of Paul in 1 Corinthians 9 and Acts', in *Studies in Luke–Acts*. pp. 194–207, is somewhat more sympathetic to the Acts portrait, though in *Paul*, London 1971, he uses Luke's picture with extreme caution, maintaining that the difficulties in treating Acts as the historical basis for the life of Paul 'compel us to abandon the widespread practice of uncritically combining Acts and the letters and to use great restraint in drawing upon the former' (p. xxi). Cf. John Knox, *Chapters in a Life of Paul*, London 1954.

68. Walther Schmithals, *Paul and James*, London 1965, especially pp. 43–62. 'In spite of Acts, Paul did not engage in a mission to the Jews, however inconvenient that may have been thought to be.'

69. Bornkamm, *SLA*, p. 200, writes: 'There is not the slightest reason to contest in a wholesale manner the picture, drawn by Acts (admitting that it is heavily schematized) which shows Paul (a) as a rule using the synagogues as a basis of operations for his mission and (b) seeking to remain within the realm of the synagogue until a final conflict rendered that impossible.'

70. F. Hahn, *Mission in the New Testament* (London 1965), pp. 81–2.

71. Schmithals, op. cit., p. 57.

72. Bornkamm's belief (*SLA*, p. 201) that Luke views Paul's work amongst Jews and Gentiles as successive stages in his various local ministries needs some qualification.

73. Even the word 'climax' has to be used with extreme caution and in such a way as not to suggest that the Gentile mission was for Luke the ultimate goal of Christianity to which the Jewish mission was merely preparatory.

74. These occur at Antioch (13.46–7), at Corinth (18.6), and at Rome (28.25–8). Only 18.6, however, has the character of a rejection of the Jews by Paul, though even this is limited by the account of the belief of the ruler of the synagogue. Acts 13 and 28 speak of a condemnation of the Jews, but in such a way as to explain the divisions among them and the fact that they refuse to hear rather than to make a break with them. At 13.11 and 28.26–7 the disobedience of the Jews is explained so that it does not become an argument against the kerygma.

75. Haenchen, *Acts*, p. 116.

76. Bornkamm, *SLA*, p. 201.

77. Haenchen, *Acts*, p. 101. Schmithals, op. cit., p. 59, rejects this approach by maintaining that the 'Jews' lack of faith cannot have distressed Luke as a real theological problem'. This, however, is

precisely what caused Luke concern, for it arose as soon as the early history of the Church was considered and indeed, as soon as the Jews' attitude to Jesus was seen to be completed by their rejection of the early kerygma. While Schmithals may be right to suggest that Luke's solution could not have been acceptable to later times, it is wholly in accord with the theology of one who might have known the apostle Paul.

78. Vielhauer, op. cit., pp. 41–2. Haenchen's objection (*Acts*, p. 412) that such a view 'imputes to Luke a venture into problems which were foreign to him' is possible only because he plays down the theological interest of Luke in his actual handling of the various scenes.

79. B. S. Easton, *The Purpose of Acts* (London 1936), pp. 9–10, though we cannot share his view that this is described by Luke for the purpose of presenting Christianity as a *religio licita*. Easton's emphasis upon the Jewishness of Luke's presentation of early Christianity is wholly to be welcomed and has in general been too little appreciated. 'According to him Christianity is no new and independent religion, about which the government was still to make up its mind. Christianity is nothing more or less than Judaism and as such has been explicitly recognized by Rome as a *religio licita*' (p. 10).

80. Notice the terms in which Paul's first preaching is reported at Acts 9.22.

81. Vielhauer, op. cit., p. 41.

82. Lampe, *Jerusalem*, p. 27.

83. O'Neill, *Theology*, p. 83.

84. In Jerusalem, Paul may have been refused, but the reason is not that Jerusalem has entirely rejected the gospel, for Acts 21.20 points to a thriving church in which many thousands believe. O'Neill, *Theology*, pp. 108–9, argues that Acts 21.20 means for Luke a working arrangement in which a minority of Jewish Christians retains the rights of observing the Mosaic law. Yet 21.21 implies that it is only the Jews among the Gentiles whom Paul is turning away from the Law and Luke does not understand the Jerusalem church as an outmoded minority.

CHAPTER 4

1. Op. cit., pp. 4–6.

2. This seems to be the significance of Acts 20.25, 36–8, 21.11–14.

3. Easton (*The Purpose of Acts* (London 1936), p. 10) and Haenchen (*Acts*, p. 726) see the Lucan use of *akōlutōs* as serving his desire to show, and thus to encourage, the toleration of Rome towards the preaching of Christianity. In view of Luke's overall attitude to the Roman authorities (see pp. 134ff) I find this hard to accept. Rather, Luke's concern is with the free proclamation of the gospel in Rome in accordance with the promise of the risen Christ in Acts 23.11.

4. E. Haenchen, 'The Book of Acts as Source Material for the History of Early Christianity', in *SLA*, p. 278.
5. Lampe, *Jerusalem*, p. 5.
6. Ibid., p. 5.
7. O'Neill, *Theology*, pp. 67–70.
8. Ibid., p. 70.
9. See pp. 179ff. The reasons for Luke's interest in Paul seems likely to stem from his being a companion of the apostle.
10. F. Hahn, *Mission in the New Testament* (London 1965), pp. 130–1.
11. Ibid., pp. 71–5.
12. Jacques Dupont, 'Le Salut des Gentils et la Signification Théologique du Livre des Actes', *NTS* 6 (1959–60), pp. 132–55.
13. Haenchen, *Acts*, p. 448, though see the criticisms of O'Neill, *Theology*, 2nd ed., pp. 122–3. He argues that a free rendering of the Hebrew of Amos 9.12 would have made James's point and that Luke or his source altered the last part of verse to conform to the LXX. But in any case it means that the sentiments now expressed are those of Luke and shows that he himself found an interpretation based on the Hebrew text unacceptable.
14. N. Q. King, 'The "Universalism" of the Third Gospel', in *Studia Evangelica*, 1959, p. 205.
15. This is why the Gentile mission does not begin immediately. The nations must be incorporated into an Israel that has herself been renewed.
16. J. Jeremias, *Jesus' Promise to the Nations* (London 1958), pp. 55–61 shows how the Old Testament expected an 'eschatological pilgrimage of the Gentiles to the Mountain of God'. He does not, however, seem to deal sufficiently with the change in outlook from that of an ingathering to an outgoing mission to them. It is this change which concerns Luke.
17. M. Dibelius, 'The Conversion of Cornelius' in *Studies in the Acts of the Apostles* (London 1956), pp. 109–22.
18. Ibid., pp. 111–12.
19. Ibid., pp. 110–11.
20. E. Haenchen, 'The Book of Acts as Source Material for the History of Early Christianity' in *SLA*, p. 266: 'Whoever can say that cancels out the preeminence of Israel whether he knows it or not; if God preferred one people such as Israel, he would be partial.' 'Luke has no inkling of the extent to which he thereby eliminates the continuity of the story of salvation between Jews and Christians.'
21. See above, n. 13. N. A. Dahl, 'A People for his Name', *NTS* 4 (1957–8), pp. 319–27, though he allows that Acts 15.14 has roots in early Jewish Christianity, nevertheless accepts that it expresses 'good Lucan theology' in that the evangelist sees the conversion of the Gentiles as a fulfilment of God's promises to Israel. It is difficult, however, to accept Dahl's further belief that for Luke the Jewish mission is a failure and that it now goes to the Gentiles who are thereby heirs of Israel's hope. He admits that Luke does not

see the Gentile church as 'Israel' and that he continues to use *laos* of Israel herself. This usage, and his belief in the fulfilment of the scriptural hopes, suggests that Luke has not yet 'written off' Israel or replaced her in God's purposes.

22. E. Schweizer, *Church Order in the New Testament* (London 1961), pp. 63–71, argues further than Dahl to suggest that Luke tells how the Church develops into a *tertium genus*, to be distinguished from both Jews and Gentiles. He allows, however, that the nations are added to Israel and that the early Catholic point of view which denied the name of 'Israel' to the Jews is not yet reached. This suggests that Luke did not therefore envisage such a separation between Jews and Christians as Schweizer himself suggests.

23. O'Neill, *Theology*, p. 101.

24. H. J. Schoeps, *Paul* (London 1961), pp. 66–7.

25. This is not to suggest that Matthew understood the Sermon on the Mount in this way but rather that Luke, if he knew Matthew or the first Evangelist's source, could have been aware of the possibility of such an interpretation.

26. Vielhauer, op. cit., pp. 41–2. Haenchen's comment (*Acts*, p. 412, n. 4) that such an interpretation imputes to Luke a 'venture into problems which were foreign to him' does not allow for Luke's obvious interest in the Law and the Temple and the part they played in the Jewish religion and its fulfilment in Christianity.

27. Marshall, *Luke*, p. 191, sees Acts 15.10 as the summary expression of Luke's attitude to the Law. 'The break in principle has been made when the Gentiles are no longer required to keep it and we must judge that the words of Peter represent the ultimate principle accepted by Luke.' Luke and Paul are thus, contrary to Vielhauer, seen to have essentially the same attitude to the Law. This evaluation seems to me to ignore the infancy narratives of Luke's Gospel, the significance of the Apostolic Decrees as Luke understood them, and the report of James and the elders to Paul in Acts 21.20–5. (On this last incident there seems to be little to support O'Neill's view (op. cit., pp. 108–9) that the Jewish-Christian group was a minority clinging to minority rights, for James's report is one of triumph rather than of apology and justification is given for an attitude to Gentile rather than to Jewish Christians. In Luke it is the disobedient Jews rather than the Christians who fail to keep the Law (Acts 7.53).)

28. See pp. 178–9.

29. Hanson *Acts*, p. 163.

30. John Knox, *Chapters in a Life of Paul* (London 1954), p. 39.

31. This verse, which links the visits to Jerusalem and Rome, suggests that Luke understands Paul's final visit to Jerusalem in terms of its enabling him to go to Rome rather than as a final turning aside from the Jews. It thus ties up with Acts 22.17–21 which sees Paul's earlier work among the Gentiles as issuing from his Jewish piety.

It is the disobedience of the Jews rather than their rejection by
Paul (and so by Jesus) which is here the concern of Luke.

32. On the Lucan modification of Galatians 2.13 so that disagreement
on a matter of principle is turned into a personal quarrel, see
Schmithals, *Paul and James* (London 1965), p. 71.

33. Conzelmann, *Theology*, pp. 209–13.

34. Ibid., pp. 95–6.

35. *TDNT* vi, p. 412. Ellis, *Eschatology in Luke*, pp. 11–15, gives more
weight to the eschatological significance of the Spirit and to the new
community, but he is unlikely to be right in seeing an identification
of the disciples with Jesus. The kingdom remains more transcendent
than he allows.

36. This seems to apply particularly to attempts to use Acts to justify
a Spirit-gift through Confirmation. Any ecclesiastical practice has
been submerged under Luke's narrowly-defined interest in the
Spirit.

37. Marshall points out (*Luke*, p. 91) that 'Luke does not stress the
relation of the Spirit to Jesus Himself as much as is popularly
thought'. Elsewhere, Luke introduces a reference to the Spirit in
10.21 where Jesus acknowledges his eschatological role.

38. Cf. Schweizer, *Church Order*, p. 35, who makes this point about
Luke's description of the Spirit's activity, though he, of course,
does so in terms of the Spirit's enabling an extended mission.

39. R. P. C. Hanson, *The Acts* (Oxford 1967), p. 31.

40. See the outstanding treatment from this point of view by B. S.
Easton, *The Purpose of Acts* (London 1936).

41. O'Neill, *Theology*, p. 177, says: 'The book of Acts, together with
Luke's Gospel, is probably the only work in the New Testament which
was specifically addressed to unbelievers'. See the modification of this
point of view in Kümmel, *Introduction*, pp. 114–15. C. F. D. Moule,
'The Intention of the Evangelists' in *The Phenomenon of the New Testament* (London 1967), pp. 100–14, thinks that Luke's Gospel was
intended to be read primarily by the outsider.

42. Op. cit., pp. 31–5.

43. Haenchen, *Acts*, pp. 731–2.

44. C. K. Barrett, *LH*, p. 63: 'No Roman official would ever have
filtered out so much of what to him would be theological and
ecclesiastical rubbish in order to reach so tiny a grain of relevant
apology.'

45. See pp. 87f.

46. *Theology*, p. 144.

47. This understanding is well expressed in Haenchen's interpretation
of the period after Pentecost as that of the universal embrace of
'the Word of God' (*Acts*, p. 98) and by Van Unnik's belief that the
book of Acts is best regarded as 'the confirmation of the Gospel'.
(See his article, 'Confirmation'.)

48. Dupont, 'Salut des Gentiles', rightly sees Luke's interest in the
Gentile mission as determined by his understanding of the Old

Testament promises of hope for the future. This influence, however, also suggests that Luke sees the Gentile mission as sup-
plementing the promises to Israel rather than seeing it as a substitute
for a continuing interest in the Jewish people. For Luke, the
Gentile mission is not the ultimate goal of God's saving act, neither
is his concern with the Jews merely to be regarded as a preliminary
stage in the history of God's saving deeds.

49. E. Haenchen, 'The Book of Acts as Source Material for the History
of Early Christianity', in *SLA*, p. 278. Cf. Lampe, *Jerusalem*,
p. 27; O'Neill, *Theology* (2nd ed.), p. 185.

50. Hahn, *Mission*, p. 136. Equally however, it must dissociate itself
from Wilson's view that the 'most striking characteristic of Luke–
Acts is precisely the lack of a consistent theology of the Gentiles',
Gentiles, p. 239. Wilson's careful study shows that Luke's concern
with the Gentiles is far less clearly defined than is usually supposed,
but our view would seem to allow for the complicated nature of his
approach and to embrace the various strands within a unified
theological outlook.

51. On this, see N. Q. King, 'The "Universalism" of the Third Gospel'.

52. For this, see pp. 168ff.

53. Ellis, *Luke*, p. 96.

54. Dupont, 'Salut des Gentiles', p. 143.

55. The R.V. translation, 'He went his way', is almost certainly a more
accurate rendering of the meaning which Luke assigned to *eporeueto*
at this point. Luke's use of the same verb at 9.51, the beginning of
his account of the journey to Jerusalem, and at 13.33, the reply to
Herod which stresses the inevitability of Jesus' progress to that
city, suggests that it is the thought of progress to a goal to be found
in Jerusalem which is uppermost in Luke's mind here. Cf. J. M.
Creed, *Luke*, p. 69.

CHAPTER 5

1. J. C. O'Neill, 'The Six Amen Sayings in Luke', *JTS* n.s. x (April
1959), p. 9.

2. Marshall, *Luke*, p. 200.

3. R. E. Brown, *New Testament Essays* (London 1965), p. 239.

4. Ellis, *Luke*, p. 163.

5. See pp. 21ff.

6. G. Wainwright, *Eucharist and Eschatology* (London 1971), pp.
37–41, discusses the eschatological orientation of Luke's account
of the Last Supper and, though accepting that these do not entirely
exhaust its eschatological expectations, nevertheless suggests that
the post-resurrection meals of Jesus with his disciples, and thus the
eucharists which flow from them, are the primary fulfilment of the
eschatological hopes then expressed. Any support that can be gained
from the New Testament for the view that the Eucharist is the

H

meal of the kingdom is to be found mainly in the Lucan writings. He accepts that Acts consistently refers *basileia* to the eschatological kingdom, but thinks that 22.16, if it were so understood, 'would speak for the only time in the New Testament of the fulfilment of an Old Testament type in "the kingdom" rather than in the ministry of Jesus or in the Church'. This latter point however is countered by the fact that, though Luke is talking of the Passover, it is not just the O.T. Passover, but that celebrated by Jesus before his exodus which is in mind. It is precisely the eschatological expectations of the Passover with which Luke is concerned and it is these which he carries over into the hopes of Jesus. The post-resurrection meals cannot be its fulfilment for no paschal symbolism is given to them and, in any case, in Luke's view they take place before the actual exaltation of Jesus. They help to explain the significance of the 'breaking of bread', but they do not exhaust the hopes for the future banquet. Luke 22 looks forward to the eschatological realization of God's redemptive act.

7. Ellis, *Luke*, pp. 252–3; Conzelmann, *Theology*, p. 115.
8. See Leaney's defence of the shorter text, *Luke*, pp. 72–5. 'It is not a covenant which the Lord inaugurates but a kingdom.'
9. See the discussion of the views of Lietzmann and of Cullman by A. J. B. Higgins, *The Lord's Supper in the New Testament* (London 1952), pp. 56–63.
10. This needs to be remembered when it is said that Luke does not have a *theologia crucis*. The cross plays a decisive part in Luke, and the journey to Jerusalem becomes a pilgrimage to it. But it is always seen as the culmination of the sufferings and is not in itself the redemptive event. Equally, the disciple is called to suffer and, though the suffering again is not redemptive, it is only through a patient endurance that glory is achieved. The pattern, by suffering to glory, is fundamental for Luke; because it was decisive for Jesus, it is imperative for those who follow him.
11. R. Brown, op. cit., p. 269.
12. S. Brown, *Apostasy and Perseverance in the Theology of Luke*, Rome 1969.
13. Conzelmann, *Theology*, p. 233.
14. The piety of Barnabas requires him to sell a field, not to dispose of all his goods. Acts 4.36–7.
15. Haenchen, *Acts*, pp. 232–5.
16. Ibid., pp. 239–41.
17. H. Ringgren, *The Faith of the Psalmists* (London 1963), pp. 40ff.
18. J. Jeremias, *The Parables of Jesus* (London 1954), pp. 33–6, 126–8.
19. Ellis, *Luke*, p. 201.
20. Luke would not be a stranger to the idea of justification by grace through faith alone.
21. Jeremias, *Parables*, pp. 128–30, though he makes the second point of the parable to be concerned with Jesus' refusal of a demand for a sign to prove that there is an after-life. But Dives' request is in

order to stop judgement rather than to produce knowledge. It is the question of the Jews' failure to repent which concerns Luke here, though the actual inclusion of the parable at this point may be because it refers to riches and so links up to the theme of much of chapter 16.

22. Op. cit., pp. 114–31.
23. Lampe, *Luke*, pp. 826–7.
24. Conzelmann, *Theology*, p. 24.
25. Luke's Sermon on the Plain (6.17–49) is essentially a charter for the community rather than ethical instruction for individuals. It is concerned with the unity of the eschatological group.
26. *Luke*, p. 150.
27. *Parables*, pp. 140–2.
28. This point would not be valid if Jeremias is right in thinking that Jesus is making use of an actual incident.
29. Both Matthew and Luke make Jesus address the disciples in the presence of the crowds (Matt. 5.1; 7.28, 29; Luke, 6.17, 19–20; 7.1).
30. E. Lohmeyer, *The Lord's Prayer* (London 1965), p. 71.
31. This view is contrary to that of D. Hill, *The Gospel of Matthew* (London 1972), p. 135, who accepts that 'the Matthaean form emphasizes the eschatological outlook while the Lucan is concerned with daily life', but who, nevertheless, maintains that Matthew's version is an elaboration of a simpler form of prayer, taught by Jesus, and more truly preserved in Luke. Jeremias, on the other hand, feels that the wording though not the form of Matthew is likely to be more original than that of Luke (*The Prayers of Jesus* (London 1967), p. 93).
32. Hill, op. cit., pp. 148–9.
33. See the discussion by C. E. B. Cranfield, 'The Parable of the Unjust Judge and the Eschatology of Luke–Acts', *SJT* 16 (Sept. 1963), pp. 297–301.
34. Conzelmann, *Theology*, p. 28, maintains that Jesus' ministry is a Satan-free period until 22.3 when Satan enters into Judas. For a ciriticism of this point of view see Marshall, op. cit., p. 87. Nevertheless, Conzelmann is right in seeing a real change of emphasis at 22.3, which marks the time when the real decisive engagement with Satan is begun.
35. This is a central thesis of the work cited in note 12.
36. See the discussion in Marshall, *Luke*, pp. 203–4.
37. *Acts*, p. 686.
38. *Luke*, p. 153.
39. C. H. Dodd, *More New Testament Studies* (Manchester 1968), pp. 8–9.
40. Ibid., p. 6.
41. Bornkamm, Barth, and Held, *Tradition and Interpretation in Matthew* (London 1963), pp. 16, 60.
42. Op. cit., pp. 269–70.

CHAPTER 6

1. *Studies in Luke–Acts*, ed. L. E. Keck and J. L. Martyn, London, 1968.
2. R. R. Williams, 'Church History in Acts; is it Reliable?' in D. E. Nineham *et al.*, *Historicity and Chronology in the New Testament*, p. 150.
3. C. K. Barrett, *New Testament Essays* (London 1972), pp. 86–7 emphasizes the pastoral concern of Luke, though at the expense of Luke the theologian. He seems to suggest that theologically at any rate Luke was something of a failure. Luke understood neither the theological questions of the early Church nor even those of his own time. This, however, would severely reduce his effectiveness as a pastor. Rather, I would feel that he was a competent theologian who used his ability in this field in the service of his contemporaries. R. H. Lightfoot, *The Gospel Message of Mark* (Oxford 1950), p. 14, holds together the pastoral and theological intentions of the Evangelist when he writes: 'One great aim which I suggest we should keep before us in these lectures is to seek to look at this Gospel through the eyes of its first readers. What did the Evangelist wish them to learn? What are his assumptions and his outlook? What is his purpose, and what means does he use to accomplish it?' Perhaps the reason why Luke is not fully appreciated as a theologian is simply the fact that he wrote his second volume and it is less easy to see real theological assumptions reflected in a story of the early Church than it is in a re-telling of the story of Jesus. Why should the history of the early Church also elicit a theological response? So Conzelmann is not able completely to do justice to the second volume in his treatment of Luke as a theologian, and though Haenchen gives due weight to Luke the theologian in the introduction to his commentary, this outlook does not really seem to permeate the commentary itself. Perhaps we should learn more from the Old Testament and from recent discussions of the aims and methods of the O.T. 'historians'.
4. F. G. Downing, *The Church and Jesus* (London 1968), pp. 1–44. See, too, the more specific discussions in Barrett, *Essays*, pp. 101–15 and Haenchen, art. in *SLA*, pp. 258–78. The discussion by R. R. Williams, op. cit., sees it as 'a possible interpretation of the past'. I would like to emphasize the word 'interpretation' more than he does. It seems to me that Marshall, *Luke*, pp. 21–52 does not give due weight to the number of historical problems in Acts.
5. A. N. Sherwin-White, *Roman Society and Roman Law in the New Testament*, Oxford 1963. Luke's accuracy in matters of Roman Law and provincial administration does not necessarily make him an accurate historian of the early Church. What it does is to show his ability and concern for detail (in spite of his occasional lapses). It suggests that any inaccuracies in his history arise, not from inability, carelessness, or misuse of sources, but from a belief which subordinates the historical quest to a theological understanding of

it as the result of God's workings. He, from a greater distance and in the light of his theological beliefs, can see its pattern, coherence and significance, and it is this which is his overriding concern.

6. B. Gärtner, *The Areopagus Speech and Natural Revelation* (Uppsala-Lund 1955), p. 9.

7. G. Von Rad, *Old Testament Theology*, vol. 1 (Edinburgh 1962), pp. 107–8, describes the picture of her history which Israel's faith constructed as 'confessional and personally involved in the events to the point of fervour. . . . Historical investigation searches for a critically assured minimum—the kerygmatic picture tends towards a theological maximum.'

8. A point made by Professor P. R. Ackroyd in a lecture, 'The Temple Vessels; a Continuity Theme', given to the Durham University Lightfoot Society.

9. See the discussion in Bo Reicke, *Gospel*, pp. 21–3, 58–9, 63–6; Ellis, *Luke*, pp. 52–3, 28–9; G. H. P. Thompson, *The Gospel according to Luke* (Oxford 1972), pp. 12–13.

10. Haenchen, *Acts*, pp. 113–4.

11. For a discussion of the 'exceptions' in Acts 14, see Barrett, *Essays*, pp. 80–2.

12. G. Bornkamm, 'The Missionary Stance of Paul in 1 Corinthians 9 and in Acts', in *SLA*, pp. 194–207.

13. J. Munck, *Paul and the Salvation of Mankind*, London 1959.

14. Though see the arguments of J. C. Hurd, *The Origin of 1 Corinthians*, London 1965, especially Chapter 7.

15. See the discussion of these points in Bornkamm's essay cited in n. 12.

16. Vielhauer, op. cit., p. 38.

17. Ibid., p. 34–7.

18. F. Hahn, *The Titles of Jesus in Christology* (London 1969), pp. 175–9. It is likely that the phrase 'according to the Scriptures' refers to the death of Christ rather than to its expiatory character, but there is little for the argument of M. D. Hooker, *Jesus and the Servant* (London 1959), pp. 117–20, that the expiatory justification could be a Pauline addition, because this understanding of the death of Christ is missing from the speeches of Acts. These, even if not Luke's own, are used by him as vehicles of his theology and show his hand. They are therefore very insecure bases for Dr Hooker's conclusions.

19. *Introduction*, p. 129.

20. *SLA*, p. 48.

21. C. K. Barrett, *Essays*, p. 83, admits that Luke has more of a *theologia crucis* than is sometimes allowed, but says: 'But the depths of his own christocentric theology he himself had not seen and understood, as Paul had seen and understood them.' While this is right, it seems to me something of a harsh judgement when he speaks of Luke's 'superficiality' (p. 86).

22. See for instance J. M. Robinson, *The Problem of History in Mark*, London 1957.

Select Bibliography

Barrett, C. K., *Luke the Historian in Recent Study*. London, 1961. (=*LH*)
— 'Stephen and the Son of Man' in *Apophoreta: Festschrift für E. Haenchen* (Berlin, 1964), pp. 32ff. (= 'Stephen')
— *The Signs of an Apostle*. London, 1970.
— *New Testament Essays*. London, 1972. (= Essays)
Bartsch, H. W., *Wachet aber zu jeder Zeit*. Hamburg–Bergstedt, 1963.
Bornkamm, G. *et al.*, *Tradition and Interpretation in Matthew*. London, 1963.
Bornkamm, G., 'The Missionary Stance of Paul in I Corinthians 9 and Acts' in *SLA*, pp. 194ff.
— *Paul*. London, 1971.
Brandon, S. G. F., *The Trial of Jesus of Nazareth*, London, 1968.
Brown, R. E., *New Testament Essays*. London, 1965.
Brown, S., *Apostasy and Perseverence in the Theology of Luke*. Rome, 1969.
Bruce, F. F., *The Acts of the Apostles*. London, 1952.
Bultmann, R., 'History and Eschatology in the New Testament' (*NTS* 1, 1954–5), pp. 15ff.
— *Theology of the New Testament*. London, 1955.
— *History and Eschatology*. Edinburgh, 1957.
Cadbury, H. J., 'The Titles of Jesus in Acts' in *The Beginnings of Christianity*, Part 1, Vol. 5 (London, 1933), pp. 366ff.
— *The Making of Luke-Acts*. London, 1950.
Caird, G. B., *Saint Luke* (Pelican Gospel Commentaries). London, 1963.
Clements, R. E., *Prophecy and Covenant*, London, 1965.
— *God and Temple*. Oxford, 1965.
Cole, A., *The New Temple*. London, 1950.
Conzelmann, H., *The Theology of St. Luke*, London, 1960. (= *Theology*)
— *Die Apostelgeschichte*. Tübingen, 1963.
— 'Luke's Place in the Development of Early Christianity' in *SLA*, pp. 298ff.
Cranfield, C. E. B., 'The Parable of the Unjust Judge and the Eschatology of Luke–Acts' (*SJT* 16, 1963), pp. 297ff.
Creed, J. M., *The Gospel According to St. Luke*. London, 1950. (= *Luke*)

Cullmann, O., *The Christology of the New Testament*. London, 1959. (= *Christology*)

— *Salvation in History*. London, 1967.

— 'The Significance of the Qumran Texts for Research into the Beginnings of Christianity' in *The Scrolls and the New Testament*, ed. K. Stendahl (London, 1957), pp. 18ff.

Dahl, N. A., 'The Story of Abraham in Luke–Acts' in *SLA*, pp. 139ff.

— 'A People for His Name' (*NTS* 4, 1957–8), pp. 319ff.

Davies, J. G., *He Ascended into Heaven*. London, 1958. (= *Ascended*)

— 'Pentecost and Glossolalia' (*JTS* n.s. 3, 1952), pp. 228ff.

Dibelius, M., *Studies in the Acts of the Apostles*. London, 1956. (= *Studies*)

— *From Tradition to Gospel*. London, 1932.

Dodd, C. H., *More New Testament Studies*. Manchester, 1968.

— *According to the Scriptures*. London, 1952.

— *The Apostolic Preaching and Its Developments*. London, 1950.

Downing, F. G., *The Church and Jesus*. London, 1968.

Dunn, J. D. G., *Baptism in the Holy Spirit*. London, 1950.

Dupont, J., '*Laos ex ethnōn*' (*NTS* 3, 1956–7), pp. 323ff.

— '*Le salut des Gentils et le livre des Actes*' (*NTS* 6, 1959–60), pp. 132ff. (= 'Salut des Gentils')

Easton, B. S., *The Purpose of Acts*. London, 1936.

Ellis, E. E., *Eschatology in Luke*. Philadelphia, 1972.

— *The Gospel of Luke*. London, 1966. (= *Luke*)

Evans, C. F., 'The Central Section of St. Luke's Gospel' in *SG*, pp. 37ff. (= 'Central Section')

— *Resurrection and the New Testament*. London, 1970. (= *Resurrection*)

Filson, F. F., *The Gospel according to St. Matthew*. London, 1960.

Flender, H., *St. Luke, Theologian of Redemptive History*. London, 1967. (= *St. Luke*)

Foerster, W., 'Kyrios' (*TDNT* iii, London, 1970).

Franklin, E., 'The Ascension and the Eschatology of Luke–Acts' (*SJT* 23, 1970), pp. 191ff.

Gärtner, B., *The Areopagus Speech and Natural Revelation*. Uppsala, 1955.

Grässer, E., *Das Problem der Parusieverzögerung in den synoptischen Evangelien und in der Apostelgeschichte*. Berlin, 1957.

Hahn, F., *Mission in the New Testament*. London, 1965. (= *Mission*)

— *The Titles of Jesus in Christology*. London, 1969. (= *Titles*)

Haenchen, E., 'The Book of Acts as Source Material for the History of Early Christianity' in *SLA*, pp. 258ff.

— *The Acts of the Apostles*. Oxford, 1971. (= *Acts*)

— Judentum und Christentum in der Apostelgeschichte' (*ZNW* 54, 1963), pp. 155ff.

Hanson, R. P. C., *The Acts*. Oxford, 1962.

Harnack, A. von, *Luke the Physician*. London, 1907.

Hiers, R. H., 'The Problem of the Delay of the Parousia in Luke–Acts' (*NTS*, 1974–5), pp. 145ff.

Higgins, A. J. B., *The Lord's Supper in the New Testament*. London, 1952.

— 'The Preface to Luke and the Kerygma in Acts' in *Apostolic History and the Gospel*, ed. W. W. Gasque and R. P. Martin (London, 1970).

Hill, D., *The Gospel of Matthew*. London, 1972.

Hooker, M. D., *Jesus and the Servant*. London, 1959.

Hull, J. H. E., *The Holy Spirit in the Acts of the Apostles*. London, 1960.

Jeremias, J., *The Prayers of Jesus*. London, 1967.

— *New Testament Theology*, Vol. 1. London, 1971.

— *The Parables of Jesus*. London, 1954. (= *Parables*)

Jervell, J., '*Das Gespaltene Israel und die Heidenwöller*' (*ST* 19, 1965), pp. 68ff.

—'*Paulus—der Lehrer Isaels*' (*NT* 10, 1968), pp. 164ff.

— 'The Law in Luke–Acts' (*HTR* 1971), pp. 21ff.

Jones, C. P. M., 'The Epistle to the Hebrews and the Lucan Writings' in *SG*, pp. 113ff.

Jones, D. R., 'The Background and Character of the Lucan Psalms' (*JTS* n.s. xix, 1968), pp. 19ff.

Kaestli, J. D., *L'Eschatologie dans L'œuvre de Luc*, Geneva, 1969.

Käsemann, E., *New Testament Questions of Today*. London, 1969.

— *Essays on New Testament Themes*. London, 1964.

Kilpatrick, G. D., 'A Theme of the Lucan Passion Story and Luke 23.47' (*JTS* xliii, 1942), pp. 34ff.

— 'Acts 7.52, Eleusis' (*JTS* xlvi, 1945), pp. 136ff.

— *Jesus in the Gospels and the Early Church*. Drawbridge Memorial Lecture, 1971.

King, N. Q., 'The "Universalism" of the Third Gospel' (*SE*, 1959), pp. 199ff.

Klijn, A. J. F., 'Stephen's Speech' (*NTS* 4, 1957–8), pp. 25ff.

Knox, J., *Chapters in a Life of Paul*, London, 1954.

Knox, W. L., *The Acts of the Apostles*. Cambridge, 1945.

Kümmel, W. G., *Introduction to the New Testament*. London, 1966. (= *Introduction*)

— *Promise and Fulfilment*. London, 1957. (= *Promise*)

Ladd, G. E., *Jesus and the Kingdom*. London, 1966.

Lampe, G. W. H., *St. Luke and the Church of Jerusalem*. London, 1969. (= *Jerusalem*)

— *Reconciliation in Christ*. London, 1956.

— 'The Reasonableness of Typology' in *Essays on Typology*. London, 1957.

— 'Luke' in *Peake's Commentary*. rev. edn, London, 1962. (= Luke)

— 'Acts' in *Peake's Commentary*, Rev. edn, London, 1962. (= Acts)

Leaney, A. R. C., *The Gospel According to St. Luke*, London, 1958. (= *Luke*)

Lightfoot, R. H., *The Gospel Message of Mark*. Oxford, 1950.

Longenecker, R. N., *The Christology of Early Jewish Christianity*. London, 1970.

McKelvey, R. S., *The New Temple*. Oxford, 1969.

Manson, W., *The Gospel of Luke*, London, 1930.

Marshall, I. H., 'The Resurrection in the Acts of the Apostles' in *Apostolic History and the Gospel*, ed. W. W. Gasque and R. P. Martin, London, 1970.

— *Luke, Historian and Theologian*. London, 1970. (= *Luke*)

Martin-Achard, R., *A Light to the Nations*. Edinburgh, 1962.

Menoud, P., *'Remarques sur les textes de l'ascension dans Luc–Actes'* (*BZNW* 21, 1954), pp. 148ff.

Minear, P., 'Luke's Use of the Birth Stories' in *SLA*, pp. 111ff.

Moore, A. L., *The Parousia in the New Testament*. Leiden, 1966.

Moule, C. F. D., *The Phenomenon of the New Testament*. London, 1967.

— 'The Christology of Acts' in *SLA*, pp. 159ff. (= Christology)

Mowinckel, S., *The Psalms in Israel's Worship*. Oxford, 1962.

Munck, J., *Paul and the Salvation of Mankind*. London, 1959.

Nineham, D. E., *Saint Mark* (Pelican Gospel Commentaries) London, 1963.

Oliver, H. H., 'The Lucan Birth Stories' (*NTS* 10, 1963–4), pp. 202ff.

O'Neill, J. C., 'The Six Amen Sayings in Luke' (*JTS* n.s. x, 1959), pp. 1ff.

— 'The Use of Kyrios in the Book of Acts' (*SJT* 8, 1955), pp. 155ff.

— *The Theology of Acts*, 2nd edn London, 1970. (= *Theology*)

Perrin, N., *Rediscovering the Teaching of Jesus*. London, 1967. (= *Rediscovering*)

Rad, G. von, *Old Testament Theology*. Edinburgh, 1962.

Ramsey, A. M., 'What was the Ascension?' in *Historicity and Chronology in the New Testament*, ed. D. E. Nineham (London, 1965).

Reicke, B., *The Gospel of Luke*. London, 1965. (= *Gospel*)

— 'Instruction and Discussion in the Travel Narrative' (*SE* 1959), pp. 206ff.

Rengstorf, K. H., 'The Election of Matthias' in *Current Issues in New Testament Interpretation*, ed. W. Klassen and G. F. Snyder (London, 1962), pp. 178ff.

Rese, M., *Alttestamentliche Motive in der Christologie des Lukas*. Bonn, 1965.

Ringgren, H., *The Faith of the Psalmists*. London, 1963.

Robinson, J. A. T., 'Elijah, John, and Jesus' in *Twelve New Testament Studies* (London, 1962), pp. 28ff.

— 'The Most Primitive Christology of All?' in *Twelve New Testament Studies* (London, 1962), pp. 139ff.

— *Jesus and His Coming.* London, 1957. (= *Coming*)

Robinson, J. M., *The Problem of History in Mark.* London, 1957.

Robinson, W. C., *Der Weg des Herrn.* Hamburg, 1964.

Rohde, J., *Rediscovering the Teaching of the Evangelists.* London, 1968. (= *Rediscovering*)

Russell, D. S., *The Method and Message of Jewish Apocalyptic.* London, 1966.

Schmithals, W., *Paul and James.* London, 1965.

Schoeps, H. J., *Paul.* London, 1961.

Schubert, P., 'The Structure and Significance of Luke 24' in *Neutestamentliche Studien für R. Bultmann* (Berlin, 1957).

Schweizer, E., *Jesus.* London, 1971.

— *Church Order in the New Testament.* London, 1961. (= *Church Order*)

Selwyn, E. G., *The First Epistle of St. Peter.* London, 1952.

Sherwin-White, A. N., *Roman Society and Roman Law in the New Testament.* Oxford, 1963.

Simon, M., *St. Stephen and the Hellenists,* London, 1958.

— '*Retour du Christ et Reconstruction du Temple*' in *Recherches d'Histoire* (Paris, 1962.)

— 'Saint Stephen and the Jerusalem Temple' (*JEH* 11, 1951), pp. 127ff.

Sparks, H. F. D., 'The Semitisms of St. Luke's Gospel' (*JTS* xliv, 1943), pp. 129ff.

— 'The Semitisms of Acts' (*JTS* n.s. 1, 1950), pp. 16ff.

Stempvoort, P. A. van, 'The Interpretation of the Ascension in Luke and Acts' (*NTS* 5, 1958–9), pp. 30ff.

Stendahl, K., 'Matthew' in *Peake's Commentary*, rev. edn. London, 1962.

Tatum, W. B., 'The Epoch of Israel: Luke I–II and the Theological Plan of Luke–Acts' (*NTS* 13, 1966–7), pp. 184ff.

Taylor, V., *Behind the Third Gospel.* London, 1926.

Thompson, G. H. P., *The Gospel according to Luke.* Oxford, 1972.

Tödt, H. E., *The Son of Man in the Synoptic Tradition.* London, 1965.

Unnik, W. C. van, 'Luke–Acts, a Storm Center in Contemporary Scholarship' in *SLA*, pp. 15ff.

— 'The "Book of Acts" the Confirmation of the Gospel' (*NT* iv, 1960), pp. 22ff. (= *Confirmation*)

Vielhauer, P., 'On the "Paulinism" of Acts' in *SLA*, pp. 33ff.

Vööbus, A., 'A New Approach to the Problem of the Shorter and Longer Text in Luke' (*NTS* 15, 1968–9), pp. 457ff.

Wainwright, A. W., *The Trinity in the New Testament.* London, 1962.

Wainwright, G., *Eucharist and Eschatology.* London, 1971.

Weiser, A., *The Psalms*. London, 1962.

Weiss, J., *Jesus' Proclamation of the Kingdom of God*. London, 1971.

Wilckens, U., 'Interpreting Luke–Acts in a Period of Existentialist Theology' in *SLA*, pp. 6off.

— *Die Missionsreden der Apostelgeschichte*. Neukirchen, 1961. (= *Missionsreden*)

— 'The Understanding of Revelation within Primitive Christianity' in *Revelation as History*, ed. W. Pannenberg (London, 1969). (= Revelation)

Wilcox, M., *The Semitisms of Acts*. Oxford, 1965.

Wilder, A. N., 'Variant Traditions of the Resurrection in Acts' (*JBL* 62, 1943), pp. 307ff.

Williams, C. S. C., *The Acts of the Apostles*. London, 1957.

Williams, R. R., *The Acts of the Apostles*. London, 1953.

— 'Church History in Acts: is it Reliable?' in *History and Chronology in the New Testament*, ed. D. E. Nineham (London, 1965).

Wilson, S. G., 'Lucan Eschatology' (*NTS* 15, 1970–1), pp. 330ff. (= Eschatology)

— *The Gentiles and the Gentile Mission in Luke–Acts*. Cambridge, 1973. (= *Gentiles*)

— 'The Ascension: a Critique and an Interpretation' (*ZNW* 59, 1968). (= Ascension)

Index of Modern Authors

Index of Modern Authors

Index of Scripture References

Index of Scripture References